EXISTENTIALISM,
RELIGION,
AND DEATH:
Thirteen Essays

OTHER BOOKS BY WALTER KAUFMANN

Nietzsche: Philosopher, Psychologist, Antichrist
Critique of Religion and Philosophy
From Shakespeare to Existentialism
The Faith of a Heretic
Cain and Other Poems
Hegel: Reinterpretation, Texts, and Commentary
Tragedy and Philosophy
Without Guilt and Justice: From Decidophobia to Autonomy
Religion in Four Dimensions
The Future of the Humanities

TRANSLATED

Judaism and Christianity: Essays by Leo Baeck
Goethe's Faust: A Verse Translation
Martin Buber's I and Thou
Twenty-five German Poets
Also *Thus Spoke Zarathustra* and ten other books by Nietzsche

EDITED

Existentialism from Dostoevsky to Sartre
Philosophic Classics, 2 volumes
Religion from Tolstoy to Camus
Hegel's Political Philosophy

EXISTENTIALISM, RELIGION, AND DEATH:
Thirteen Essays

by
Walter Kaufmann

A MERIDIAN BOOK
NEW AMERICAN LIBRARY
TIMES MIRROR
NEW YORK AND SCARBOROUGH, ONTARIO
THE NEW ENGLISH LIBRARY LIMITED, LONDON

SOURCES AND ACKNOWLEDGMENTS

"A Preface to Kierkegaard." Copyright © 1962 by Walter Kaufmann. From Søren Kierkegaard, *The Present Age* and *Of the Difference Between a Genius and an Apostle*, translated by Alexander Dru. Introduction by Walter Kaufmann, Harper Torchbooks, 1962, pp. 9–29. Reprinted by permission of Harper and Row.

"Tolstoy versus Doestoevsky." Copyright © 1961 by Walter Kaufmann. From Walter Kaufmann, *Religion from Tolstoy to Camus*, Harper & Brothers, 1961, pp. 2–12. Reprinted by permission of Harper and Row.

"Nietzsche and Existentialism." Copyright © 1974 by Syracuse University Press. From *Symposium: A Quarterly Journal in Modern Foreign Literatures*, XXVIII.1 (Spring 1974), pp. 7–16. Reprinted by permission of Syracuse University Press.

"Buber's Religious Significance." Copyright © 1967 by The Library of Living Philosophers, Inc. From *The Philosophy of Martin Buber*, ed., P. A. Schilpp and Maurice Friedman, Open Court & London, Cambridge University Press, 1967, pp. 665–85. Reprinted by permission of Paul A. Schilpp.

"Buber's *I and Thou*." Copyright © 1970 by Walter Kaufmann. From Martin Buber, *I and Thou*, A New Translation With a Prologue "I and You" and Notes by Walter Kaufmann, Charles Scribner's Sons & Edinburgh, T. & T. Clark, 1970, pp. 9–48. Reprinted by permission of Charles Scribner's Sons.

"The Reception of Existentialism in the United States." Copyright © 1968 by Walter Kaufmann. From *Midway*, IX.1 ·(Summer 1968), pp. 97–126. Reprinted by permission of *Midway*.

"Beyond Black and White." Copyright © 1970 by Walter Kaufmann. From *Midway*, X.3 (Winter 1970), pp, 49–79. Also *Survey* No. 73 (Autumn 1969), pp. 22–46. Reprinted by permission of Walter Kaufmann.

"The Faith of a Heretic." Copyright © 1959 by *Harper's Magazine*. From *Harper's Magazine*, February 1959, pp. 33–39. Reprinted by permission of Walter Kaufmann.

"The Future of Jewish Identity." Copyright © 1970 by Walter Kaufmann. From *The Jerusalem Post Magazine*, August 1, 1969, pp. 6–7. Reprinted in *Congressional Bi-Weekly*, April 3, 1970; in *Conservative Judaism*, Summer 1970; and in *New Theology* No. 9, 1972, pp. 41–58. Reprinted by permission of Walter Kaufmann.

"The Future of the Jews in the Diaspora." Copyright © 1976 by Walter Kaufmann. Published here for the first time by permission of Walter Kaufmann.

"Existentialism and Death." Adapted from the original essay which first appeared in *Chicago Review*, 1959. Copyright © 1959 by Walter Kaufmann. Adapted by permission of *Chicago Review*. Conclusion first appeared in *The Faith of a Heretic* by Walter Kaufmann, published by Doubleday and Company, 1961, whose kind permission is acknowledged gratefully. Copyright © by Walter Kaufmann.

"On Death and Lying." Copyright © 1976 by Yale University Press. From *Psychiatry and the Humanities*, Vol. 1, ed. Joseph Smith, Yale University Press, 1976. Reprinted by permission of The Forum on Psychiatry and the Humanities, Washington School of Psychiatry.

"Death Without Dread." Copyright © 1976 by Walter Kaufmann. Published here for the first time by permission of Walter Kaufmann.

SIGNET, SIGNET CLASSICS, MENTOR, PLUME and MERIDIAN BOOKS
are published *in the United States* by The New American Library, Inc.,
1301 Avenue of the Americas, New York, New York 10019,
in Canada by The New American Library of Canada Limited,
81 Mack Avenue, Scarborough, 704, Ontario
in the United Kingdom by The New English Library Limited,
Barnard's Inn, Holborn, London, E.C. 1, England

First Meridian Printing, October, 1976

1   2   3   4   5   6   7   8   9

PRINTED IN THE UNITED STATES OF AMERICA

CONTENTS

INTRODUCTION

I

These essays raise some vitally important questions. This volume should advance their discussion.

Some of these essays were originally written for books, and most of the rest have long been reprinted in books by others. Some have also appeared in other languages. Thus the point of collecting these essays is not simply to preserve in a book what might otherwise pass into oblivion like old newspapers and magazines. Rather, these pieces are like fragments. Few of those who have chanced across a couple of them could have inferred the whole design from them. Here they are assembled, and the new context adds to their meaning—perhaps also to their force.

My first collection of essays, *From Shakespeare to Existentialism* (1959), consisted of twenty historical studies. Most had appeared before but had been conceived all along as parts of a larger project, and I revised them extensively before reprinting them in their proper historical sequence. A year later, a revised edition appeared in paperback; in the mid-seventies the book is still in print, and the time has come for another, smaller collection.

It is smaller because since that first collection appeared, I have written few essays and articles while concentrating my energies on books. This time, only half the pieces are historical, and even in these the concern with nonhistorical, "existential" issues is plain. Revisions of the original texts have been kept down to a minimum; in some cases to zero.

My interest in existentialism, religion, and death was evident even in the fifties and has not abated. As I am critical of existentialism and religion, this calls for an explanation.

Religion deals with faith, morals, and art. I am much less interested in metaphysics and theology than in what religions do to people—how they affect human existence. In that sense, my own ultimate concern is existential.

Much of what the major religions have done to people I find quite outrageous, nor can I accept most of the views of the so-called existentialists. It is my concern with problems we share that leads me to deal with existentialism and religion again and again.

The essays are not presented in the order in which they were written, for the point is not to document the author's development. They are offered in their "logical" sequence.

In the first half of the book this sequence is historical, beginning with Kierkegaard and ending with "The Reception of Existentialism in America." One might suppose that this part deals with existentialism while the second half deals with religion and death. Yet four of the first six chapters deal with religion as much as with existentialism; and death has also been a central motif in existentialism. In sum, the essays collected here belong together in a multitude of ways. Themes sounded in one are often developed in the others.

The discussion of Buber's *I and Thou*, for example, supplements the chapters on his religious significance and on the reception of existentialism; it also develops some of the practical implications of "Beyond Black and White"; it articulates the crux of my attitude toward Kierkegaard, which is to confront him as a You, as a voice addressing us, and not merely aesthetically, as an object; and it could easily be related to some of the other chapters as well. Not all of the essays are as central as that one, but as good a case could be made out at least for "Beyond Black and White" and "The Faith of a Heretic."

While these essays belong together, the form of presentation was often influenced by the occasion. At the beginning of each chapter a footnote specifies date and occasion, but in some cases a little more information may prove helpful. I shall proceed in the order in which the pieces are reprinted here.

II

"A Preface to Kierkegaard" is not merely a preface to Kierkegaard's *The Present Age*, which was written well over a hundred years ago; it is also a comment on the *present* age, on our time, on the way people read and are taught to read. It therefore seems a fitting beginning.

While the essay transcends its occasion, it bears the marks of its original context. In February 1962 a publisher wrote me that a paperback reprint of *The Present Age* would appear shortly, and asked me for "the favor of a few laudatory sentences about the book that could be used on the back of our jacket and in our advertising. A statement from you would be a great boost to our edition, and we'd appreciate any help you can give us."

This was flattering, but Kierkegaard was hardly in need of a few words of praise from me. The very idea seemed rather grotesque. Moreover, my attitude toward him was too complex to make the task of formulating "a few laudatory sentences" inviting. *From Shakespeare to Existentialism* included an essay that spelled out my criticisms and my admiration. It contained a long "Preliminary Expectoration" (Kierkegaard's phrase) by Brother Brash and a retort by Brother Brief, "Kierkegaard's Significance." Using two pseudonyms, it approximated Kierkegaard's own manner rather than the style of most of his interpreters. Still, I was willing to have another try and offered to write a short preface from which something might be quoted on the jacket or in advertising. As for myself, I felt that I needed a larger context. I also inquired about some errors in the editorial matter of the original Anglo-American edition of *The Present Age*.

By return mail I was urged to go ahead. The translator's introduction was considered disappointing but could not very well be dropped; perhaps I could stress some of the points that he had failed to make. His introduction was enclosed "so that you can see what he fails to cover."

His introduction was typical of much comment on Kierkegaard, and my preface virtually wrote itself. What Kierkegaard needed and still needs is not a few laudatory words but an attempt to draw a line between him and most of his commentators. It would be easy at this point to paraphrase his own comments on Genesis in *Fear and Trembling*, saying: The writer of these pages is no Kierkegaard scholar and not at home in the corpus in the original Danish; if he were, he might deal with his subject as a good philologist and do what others have done.

This way of putting it, however, is too Manichaean—as if Kierkegaard had been as good as his interpreters are bad. Actually, the way Kierkegaard dealt with Genesis was anything but exemplary. He used an incident in the Abraham stories for his own purposes without making any sustained effort to hear the distinctive voice of the book. But it is that kind of effort that a good reader should make.

A famous German ballad ends: *Deines Geistes / hab' ich einen Hauch verspürt* (Of your spirit I have felt a breath). For most studies of Kierkegaard this would be a suitable epigraph, adding only one letter: *Deines Geistes hab' ich keinen Hauch verspürt* (Of your spirit I have felt no breath). In most of the literature one looks in vain for "that individual"—though this was the epitaph Kierkegaard designed for himself.

To my immense surprise, the publisher was enthusiastic about my preface. Five years earlier, when I had submitted to him the manuscript of *Critique of Religion and Philosophy*, he had sent it out to rather a lot of readers (which took a lot of time in those pre-Xerox days), in search of laudatory sentences that might make it less risky to publish a book that was so heretical. Later he was proud of having dared to publish it. But there was never any question about publishing the Kierkegaard preface.

Predictably, the translator was unhappy. Eventually it was decided that *The Present Age* should appear in the United Kingdom with his introduction, in the United States with mine, and nowhere with both. The only change made in my essay was that it was entitled "Introduction." The content makes clear why it needs to be called a preface.

III

"Tolstoy versus Dostoevsky" comes from the long Introduction to *Religion from Tolstoy to Camus* (1961) and has also appeared separately in Japanese. When I taught Social Philosophy at Princeton from the late forties to the mid-fifties, I generally began by having the students read, first, the "Grand Inquisitor" and then large parts of Tolstoy's "My Religion." Sometimes I assigned T. S. Eliot's *The Idea of a Christian Society* the third week. The contrast of Tolstoy and Dostoevsky made a marvelous beginning, and in *Religion from Tolstoy to Camus* I included over a hundred pages by Tolstoy and Dostoevsky. But what I emphasized in the Introduction, as far as Tolstoy was concerned, was less his social philosophy than his concern with a central existentialist motif: self-deception. Tolstoy's rank as a novelist is secure. But his thought still needs discussion, and that is why I reprint these pages here.

"Nietzsche and Existentialism" and "Buber's Religious Significance" are nowhere near as close to my heart as "A Preface to Kierkegaard," but I hope they are useful. They bring together a good deal of information and offer interpretations that should stimulate thought. The Nietzsche piece was originally a lecture that opened an interdisciplinary conference on "Nietzsche's Impact on Western Thought." Nietzsche scholars from many different fields, including music, literature, and political theory, came together at Syracuse University in 1972 for a very intensive program of talks and discussions. Nothing remotely like this had ever been attempted in the United States before, and many people must have come away from the conference with an unexpected awareness of Nietzsche's range.

I spoke on the basis of an outline; the talk was taped and transcribed; and then I had a chance to edit it before it appeared in a journal along with most of the other contributions. This chapter is no more than an attempt to open up a highly complex subject. We still need detailed studies and comparisons. With "Jaspers' Relation to Nietzsche" I have dealt at length in *From Shakespeare to Existentialism*, and with Nietzsche's immense influence on Sartre's *Flies* in section 51 of *Tragedy and Philosophy*. But there is much more to be said about Nietzsche's impact on Sartre and Camus, and above all on the methodological scandal of Heidegger's voluminous interpretations of Nietzsche.

The essay on Buber's significance offers an overall interpretation that gives some attention to the different aspects of his work. It draws not only on his books but also on some personal acquaintance with the man; and after the article was written, I saw much more of him than before. In the Acknowledgments in my translation of Buber's *I and Thou*, I have recounted how his son Rafael asked me to do a new translation and I eventually agreed. The request was prompted in part by Buber's appreciation of my article and our good relationship. But my reservations about *I and Thou* posed a problem.

In her long introduction to the first volume of Buber's correspondence, which appeared in German in 1972. Grete Schaeder has discussed our relationship very sensitively. "He has never been Buber's 'pupil,' but at times he seems like his 'wrathful' son." Grete Schaeder's three pages about me are as moving to my mind as most book reviews are boring.

I could not very well write a perfunctory introduction to *I and Thou*. I could neither gloss over our differences nor use the prologue to what he himself had considered his masterpiece as the occasion for a sharp critique. Yet the issues cried out for a forceful treatment.

I and Thou has become far more popular in the United States than it ever was in the original German. Its enormous success is due in part to its central defect. Buber associated the genuine relationship between an I and a You with rare moments of almost ecstatic intensity from which we are bound to lapse again and again into states in which others become for us mere objects of use or experience. This dualism of the I-Thou (or I-You) and the I-It, with its Manichaean overtones, and Buber's claim that our age is sick, provide his readers with an easy alibi for their own failings.

I have analyzed this syndrome at some length in the chapter "The Need for Alienation" in *Without Guilt and Justice*. Alienation is needful, but treating others as mere objects of use or experience is not. Ecstatic intimacy cannot be maintained; a genuine I-You relationship can be.

IV

"The Reception of Existentialism in the United States" was commissioned for a volume on the contributions made by refugees from central Europe. But it appeared not in the volume for which it was written but in two magazines and in another book, *The Legacy of the German Refugee Intellectuals*. I hope this is a useful summing up that raises some interesting questions, but I should not rank it with the chapter that precedes it or the two that follow it.

It is arguable that the omission of Herbert Marcuse from this essay on the reception of existentialism was a fault. Of course, Marcuse is associated by most people with Marx and, after that, with Freud, and few people realize that he dedicated his first book to Heidegger. But Marcuse's appeal, like Paul Tillich's a few years earlier, was based in some measure on the blend of Marx and Freud with existentialism, and his Manichaeism had roots in Heidegger's eminently superficial contrast of authenticity and inauthenticity.

"Beyond Black and White" represents an attempt to show what is wrong with Manicheaism and deals at some length with Marcuse.

But the point is not so much to criticize one writer as it is to analyze one of the most widespread and perennial tendencies of human thought.

This essay has been reprinted in several places, and it has also appeared in Italian. But it needs to be seen in the context of my own thought as an effort to lay the foundations for ethics—or at least for the ethic I developed in *Without Guilt and Justice*.

In this chapter the focus is shifted clearly from history to crucial issues. But the chapters on Kierkegaard and above all on the I-You and I-It relationships are also issue-oriented. And these chapters are meant to reinforce each other.

In the essays on *I and Thou* and Black and White I develop a view of my own, and this is even more obvious in "The Faith of a Heretic." This essay antedates my book with the same title. I have never reprinted it, although it has been included in many textbooks in different fields, ranging from freshman composition to religion and intellectual history. The book *The Faith of a Heretic* deals with the same issues as well as with many others at far greater length, but when I wrote this article I had no plans as yet for the book.

The first footnote in this chapter is clearly dated and might well have been removed, but it seemed better not to change a word in a piece that has been reprinted so often; and this footnote tells a great deal about the climate of opinion in 1958. Late in May of that year, shortly after the publication of *Critique of Religion and Philosophy*, I got a letter from Robert Silvers, who later became co-founder of *The New York Review of Books*. He was then an editor at *Harper's Magazine*.

The magazine was planning to publish a series of articles by laymen about their religious beliefs. "At present we are working with Jewish, Protestant, and Catholic authors to develop pieces which will appear under some such title as 'What I believe,' or 'Why I am a Jew' . . . We would like to include in this series an article by someone whose approach to religion is critical, rationalist, noncommitted, who would examine current religious beliefs critically, but who would also be willing to make a statement in favor of some kind of principles or attitude whether it was called humanism or the Socratic attitude of inquiry, or something else. We are hoping that there will be a strong personal element in these essays—that they will show something of how the writer arrived at his attitudes and beliefs. The length we are trying for is about 4000–4500 words."

For many reasons it would have been wiser to decline. My mother summed them up in six words—in German, though we usually conversed in English: *Das hast du doch nicht nötig.* That means, though the tone is just a little different: Surely, you don't need that!

Ten years earlier, Walter Stace, a professor in my department, had lost the remnants of his Christian faith upon reading Sartre's "Existentialism is a Humanism" and had published an article called "Man Against Darkness" in *The Atlantic Monthly*. He had been denounced from almost every pulpit in Princeton, and the article had created a great deal of embarrassment for the university. A flood of letters had demanded that he be fired. He was not fired, but it seemed only decent to me to make clear in a footnote how my own views functioned in the university to keep irate alumni from withdrawing their support.

My article did not subject the university to a torrent of mail. Most of the letters were addressed to me. My favorite began: "Dear neighbor and slave of Satan!" Many were enthusiastic, and what astonished me was not that there should have been some resentment but rather the absence of anti-Semitism. What there was of denunciations in the letters and in print was easy to take. But my mother had been right: the article impeded my career. I had never questioned that it might do that any more than that it would cost me some friendships. I felt that I would not mind losing friends who would bear me a grudge on account of this essay. But one could not very well object to the tiresome trinity of "Protestant, Catholic, and Jew" and then decline when one was offered equal space to present another point of view.

What was needful was to make the most of this rare opportunity and to write a piece that would not merely grace one issue of a magazine but survive its immediate occasion. I attempted a very succinct summary of some of my views and was delighted when the editors accepted it without suggesting changes. There *was* some discussion back and forth about the title, and "The Faith of a Heretic" was my idea and one of the rare instances when I have been entirely satisfied with one of my titles. But some readers got hung up on it and protested either that, being a heretic, I could not have any faith or that, being a decent sort, I could not be a heretic.

V

"The Future of Jewish Identity" deals with religion, not with existentialism. Yet the emphasis on choice, the refusal to bank on predictions, and the insistence that the crucial question is one of decision develop existentialist motifs. These motifs in turn come from the Hebrew prophets, if not from Moses.

This piece was commissioned for a Dialogue in Haifa in which roughly half the speakers came from the United States, the other half from Israel. There was not as much dialogue as one might have hoped, and I was attacked for what somebody thought I was going to say before I had presented my paper—which, as it happened, took an altogether different line. In a discussion it is grotesque to pigeonhole a participant like that instead of listening to him first, but readers do this very often. Instead of approaching a text with an open mind and a readiness to be addressed by it, many people have strong preconceptions and believe they know before they read a word what the author has to say.

"The Future of Jewish Identity" was picked up by *The Jerusalem Post Magazine* and subsequently appeared in a German translation, without my knowledge. It was reprinted in the *Congressional Bi-Weekly* of the American Jewish Congress, which had sponsored the Dialogue; in *Conservative Judaism*, and in a Protestant anthology, *New Theology* No. 9. If it had not been for all that, I am not sure that I should have reprinted the essay here. But as long as it has met with so much interest, I feel I should.

The next chapter is a sequel to "The Future of Jewish Identity." The World Jewish Congress invited me to develop the same themes further in a talk on "The Future of the Jews in the Diaspora." This piece has not appeared in print before.

VI

In the 1970s it has come to be said again and again that before the 1970s death had been a taboo subject. This strange cliché shows at a glance how thoughtless many current discussions of death are. They are ruled by fashion rather than respect for facts.

I sometimes wonder what sorts of books people who repeat such falsehoods have read. After all, some of us were still brought up on the _Iliad_ and Greek tragedies, on Shakespeare and Tolstoy. Many should recall the unprecedented success of Arthur Miller's play, _Death of a Salesman_ (1949). And no play of our time or any age has ever even approximated the immediate success of Rolf Hochhuth's _The Deputy_ (1963; English version, 1964)—which, to be sure, was subjected to a great deal of criticism, but not for breaching the alleged taboo of death.

In 1959 Herman Feifel published an anthology, _The Meaning of Death_, and included my "Existentialism and Death," which also appeared that summer in _Chicago Review_. He obviously did not violate any taboo; his book was well received. This shows at a glance how deep the gulf is that divides what "everybody knows" from truth. I aim to show in the last three essays how other widely held dogmas about death illustrate the same point.

A humanistic education ought to be designed to give us the perspective—or rather the perspectives—to see what is ridiculous in current fads and fashions. A humanist ought to take pride in not being a follower of fashion.

In the last essay in this volume I was responding to an invitation to contribute the final paper to a symposium on "Human Values and Aging: New Challenges for Research in the Humanities." Here, in 1975, people did proceed as if death were unmentionable, and while I was asked to speak of death, the printed program gave the title of the final session as "Old Age and the Cosmos" and divided it into "Society's View," "Self View," and—my assignment—"Reality." These euphemisms seemed odd, but I took seriously the call for new challenges for research in the humanities.

I take some pride in having tried to get people interested in Nietzsche and in Hegel, in the merits of Buddhism vis-à-vis Christianity, and in religious experience as opposed to theology when all of this was distinctly unfashionable. It was a pleasure to buck a strong current and try to turn the tide. Death, however, is not a case in point. It was never a taboo for either my own generation or my parents'. The scores of millions who died in the two world wars as well as those who lived through one or both of them were not only aware of death but knew it in their bones and did not hesitate to speak of it.

In German existentialism death was central from the start, and

Jaspers and Heidegger—quite unlike Kierkegaard and Nietzsche—were never untimely. They were always timely to a fault. They wrote about the things about which "one"—to use two Heideggerian terms—was "chattering." Heidegger's famous thesis that everybody is afraid of death and that it takes courage to admit that one is afraid was one of the clichés of the First World War and still current during the twenties when he wrote *Being and Time*.

In religion, moreover, the subject of death has always been central, especially in Christianity. Thus death is not, as it were, the third subject taken up in this book after existentialism and religion. All the essays offered here belong together and articulate a single point of view. And my reason for writing was always to change people's minds.

To be more precise, there are other reasons for writing. Creativity is its own reward, and writing can be an adventurous voyage of discovery, a way of clearing one's own mind and finding out what one should believe oneself. But speaking out in public, quite especially in print, is pointless if one has no wish to affect others.

It is arguable that a collection of essays is worthwhile if it contains a few good pieces. But the first chapter of this book calls into question this excessively aesthetic approach, and the book as a whole calls into question ever so much else. What is true of the pieces on death seems to me to apply to the whole: I raise questions that require attention, I should like to make the reader more thoughtful, and I aim to advance discussion of vital issues. My ultimate concern can be summed up in one word: humanity.

—W.K.

Princeton
January 1976

EXISTENTIALISM, RELIGION, AND DEATH:
Thirteen Essays

A PREFACE
TO KIERKEGAARD*

It is one of the characteristics of the present age that books of the previous century are reissued with more or less—usually less—learned prefaces. The point is partly that the new edition should have something new in it; partly that the reader should be told what a great classic will confront him when he is done with the preface. The reader wants to be reassured that he is not going to waste his time. And he is also supposed to be anxious to know what he should think of the book—which is another way of saying that he is supposed to be afraid of having to think for himself, though this is after all the only kind of thinking there is. In Kierkegaard's words, in *The Present Age*, the reader must be reassured that "something is going to happen," for "ours is the age of advertisement and publicity." Indeed, the preface is expected to say *what* is going to happen—or, more precisely, which parts of what is about to happen may be safely forgotten, which points are memorable, and what observations about them should be remembered for use in conversation.

The fact that a man wrote books to attack these and other features of the present age and that he strained to be offensive, especially to parsons and professors, provides no protection whatsoever. For it is also one of the features of the present age not to take offense, if only the author's reputation is above question and one can be sure that reading him is not a waste of time. If the dust has not yet settled on his books, of course, it is quite safe to say he is offensive, or his works are in bad taste or, better yet, completely "unsound" (as Freud's writings were said to be early in the twentieth century)—and therefore not to read them. But once a writer has arrived and reached the stage where other men write prefaces for posthumous editions of his books, it would hardly be sophisticated to consider him offensive. Voltaire has to be placed in his historic context,

* 1962. The origin of this essay is discussed in the Introduction, pp. x–xii.

Mephistopheles "works" in the play or in the poet's gradual development, and Nietzsche stimulated this or that development. To be offended by them would be quite as prudish as taking offense at Aristophanes or Joyce. Why, they are classics!

One of the most important functions of a preface is to forestall any possibility that after all some wayward reader, here or there, should be offended. Dates must remind such readers that the author is long dead and that the book is old. Names must assure him that the author's thoughts were influenced by other writers and thus links in a development—not really, as one might think on reading them, deliberately nasty. And, of course, there should be many references to "anticipations," lest the reader take some statement as a provocation instead of considering it as the grandfather of someone else's proposition, which may be quite dull, and even a great-grandfather, if only the later author is respectable when the preface is written.

How Kierkegaard might have enjoyed this comedy! Yet his laughter would hardly have been free of bitterness. His laughter rarely was. And in this case, there is abundant reason for sorrow. His name is now a name to conjure with, bandied about with great abandon both at cocktail parties and in books and articles that are as nourishing as cocktail party fare; but his central aspirations are almost invariably ignored, and even those who notice them often give reasons why the things that mattered most to him may be dismissed as really of no account.

That he is so often presented as a saturnine thinker, as sedate as the German existentialists, might have amused him, and he might have written a neat parody of prefaces in which there is no glimpse of his own sense of humor—not even a hint that something funny is ahead. But could he have smiled at the ever-growing literature that reassures us that he was, even if he did not know it, really a humanist?

Since Jaspers first dismissed Kierkegaard's "forced Christianity" as well as Nietzsche's "forced anti-Christianity" as relatively unimportant, lesser commentators have ornamented this notion with appalling metaphors: "Kierkegaard satisfied this need [for metaphysics] within the withered bosom of Christian dogmatics—a satisfaction which ultimately harmed rather than enhanced the genius of his thought. But by Nietzsche's time this bosom was dry, and Nietzsche gratified his penchant for a well-rounded . . ." There is no need to continue. In this interpretation Kierkegaard winds up as a man who painfully groped his way "toward a point of view which is largely identical with the insights of orthodox Hinduism, of primitive Indian Buddhism, and of . . . Zen," but who also was a humanist.

Actually, of course, Kierkegaard's religious existence culminated in a grand *Attack on Christendom* and the refusal to accept the sacraments from any ordained minister. He wanted the last sacraments from a layman but, denied this wish, died without them, hoping soon "to sit upon the clouds and sing: Hallelujah, hallelujah, hallelujah!" He did not doubt the divine grace but felt that his church had betrayed Christ by not sufficiently insisting on his authority and the fundamental offense—what Paul had called the *skandalon* and what Kierkegaard often called the absurdity—of Christian teaching. Would he have been amused by the rarely questioned notion that one can have one's Kierkegaard and go to church, too—and that Kierkegaard must naturally be assimilated to such other revolutionary spirits as Marx, Freud, and Nietzsche?

Those who consider him a humanist and those who think that the commitment called for in his writings is in essence the commitment to be either Protestant, Catholic, or Jew, and to support the church, or possibly the temple, of your choice, turn Kierkegaard into the very thing he most consistently opposed: an apostle of reassurance. These disciples, who often resent all criticism of the master and make much of their great admiration for him, really betray him with a kiss.

Indeed, the present age is the age of Judas. Who would stand up against Christ and be counted His opponent? Who openly rejects the claims of the New Testament? Who lets his Yea be yea, "Nay, nay: for whatsoever is more than these cometh of evil"? Certainly not the apologists who simply ignore what gives offense or, when this is not feasible, offer "interpretations" instead of saying Nay. To be sure, it is not literally with a kiss that Christ is betrayed in the present age: today one betrays with an interpretation. The interpretation may be bold, extremely bold, as long as it is offered as an interpretation and the reader is reassured that the original text is profound and beautiful.

This, of course, is not a pleasant way of saying something that could easily be put a little more politely. Why speak of betrayal and, worse yet, of Judas? Because Kierkegaard himself remarked in *The Sickness unto Death* that "he who first invented the notion of defending Christianity in Christendom is *de facto* Judas No. 2; he also betrays with a kiss" (218).

But surely, good sir, you must see that it is quite a different proposition in the mouth of Kierkegaard, more than a century ago, than in a preface written in the present age! Besides, he spoke of Danes while you—you are offensive. You attack men whom you should applaud: fine, decent men who do their best to make the gospel inoffensive, reading into it an ethic that you ought to welcome.

Some men who think thus have no hesitation about putting Kierkegaard's name on their banners, along with many other fashionable names, certain that positions other than their own deserve not only criticism but strong language; but their own views, well, are different and plainly should be privileged. And anyone who fails to see that simply is not nice. It is easy to see this point—at least after one has been requested to behold it from a hundred angles: every time it is the speaker, or the writer, whose outlook is clearly an exception. Against A and B and C and D one might have used far stronger language if one only had admitted that, of course, X is superior to all criticism. Next time it is Y or Z or A or B. The idea is always the same: criticism is a splendid thing, as long as we are spared. And fashionable writers, such as Kierkegaard, were marvelous—oh, simply marvelous—when they made fun of Hegel (as who did not?) or of all kinds of Danish theologians (of whom, but for him, we should not even know the names) or of "the public" (which plainly means the others and not us); but if anyone made remarks at our expense, he either was badly mistaken and may therefore be ignored, if not abhorred, or, now that his fame has passed the point where that was feasible, he either did not mean it or that aspect of his thought was marginal and clearly should be disregarded.

Kierkegaard is fine, says the present age, provided only he is cut and dried a little, milked of his unpleasant venom, and—in one word—bowdlerized. But in the present age one no longer literally changes texts; instead, to say it once more, one betrays with interpretations. It may seem that this procedure is not new: some liberals consider Paul a pioneer of this insidious method; others, yet more radical, regard the Gospels as examples. However that may be, what *is* new is the scholarly approach or rather the display of dubious scholarship: the invocation of a multitude of names of little relevance, the desiccated prose that in its deathly pallor leans on pointless footnotes, and the striking fact that the perversion is accomplished without passion. Life and death are utterly out of the picture as is any question of a mission: we breathe classroom air or, yet more often, the dust of the journal shelves.

But, good sir! the present age replies; you cannot hope to excuse your bad manners by appealing to Kierkegaard; or do you really fancy that he could have approved of a preface that makes fun of prefaces? After all, he was a great human being—witness the large literature about him, which surely proves this, even if we have not read it—and it stands to reason that he would not have been guilty of lack of respect for fellow scholars. Classroom air and dusty journal shelves! Assuredly he'd never have gone that far.

Sancta simplicitas! The present-day Judases no longer *know* what they betray, any more than they know what they like: what they know is only the preface written by another hand, the lecture given by a parson or professor, the interpretation of the well-known critic. Of course, one is sure of one's likes and dislikes—much surer than one might be if one really knew the texts. One knows that Kierkegaard was a precursor of this and that, but not his mordant humor, nor the fantastic comedy he played out with his pseudonyms who attacked each other, keeping literary Denmark guessing whether these books with their tangled prefaces and postscripts by pseudonyms and editors were written by one, two, or more writers. Could he have endured a preface to a posthumous edition of *The Present Age* that did *not* ridicule prefaces and the whole stuffy establishment that he attacked, not only in *The Present Age?* He abhorred the modern apotheosis of good taste.

What makes *The Present Age* and *The Difference Between a Genius and an Apostle* important is not so much that the former essay anticipates Heidegger and the latter, Barth: it would be more accurate to say that Heidegger's originality is widely overestimated, and that many things he says at great length in his highly obscure German were said earlier by various writers who had made the same points much more elegantly, and that some of these writers, including Kierkegaard, were known to Heidegger. Why should Kierkegaard's significance depend on someone else's, quite especially when many points that others copied from him may be wrong? And are his observations about "the public," which remind the modern German reader of long-winded "philosophical" discussions of *das Man*, and American readers of even more long-winded, but also more intelligible, discussions of "other-directedness," really very important?

Surely, they are witty in a rather innocuous way: like statistics about Protestant, Catholic, and Jew, they allow us to smile and feel superior. Gratitude repays this favor by calling the author a remarkable psychologist who anticipated twentieth-century insights.

Much of what Kierkegaard is too often praised for is not really very profound or beautiful but rather entertaining and amusing. And few writers protested more than he did against submerging challenges to our faith and morals in effusive talk about what is profound and beautiful. Sometimes he used these very words; at other times he juxtaposed what he called an aesthetic orientation with an ethico-religious outlook. One of his best-known and best books, *Fear and Trembling*, is directed in large measure against those who read the Bible from an "aesthetic" point of view, admiring Abraham along with the beautiful story which tells of his readiness to sacrifice his son, although the readers would abhor as a religious fanatic any contemporary who resolved to act like Abraham. Kierkegaard may have misread the story, but it is perfectly clear that he was nauseated by prolonged talk about the profound and beautiful when the one question needful was how we should live.

He once wrote an essay with the title: *Has a Man the Right to let himself be put to Death for the Truth?* Walter Lowrie's translation of it was published in the same volume with the original English edition of *The Present Age*, but is omitted in the paperback reprint. The essay is exceedingly prolix and takes its time to conclude that "a *man* (unlike God) has not the right to let himself be put to death for the truth"; for he should be "lovingly *concerned for others*, for those who, if one is put to death, must become guilty of putting one to death." In the long reflections that lead up to this conclusion, there is a passage that sums up succinctly (for Kierkegaard) a point also found in *Fear and Trembling* and, for that matter, throughout his works:

"The parson (collectively understood) does indeed preach about those glorious ones who sacrificed their lives for the truth. As a rule the parson is justified in assuming that there is no one present in the church who could entertain the notion of venturing upon such a thing. When he is sufficiently assured of this by reason of the private knowledge he has of the congregation as its pastor, he preaches glibly, declaims vigorously, and wipes away the sweat. If on the following day one of those strong and silent men . . . were to visit the parson at his house announcing himself as one whom the parson had carried away by his eloquence, so that he had now resolved to sacrifice his life for the truth—what would the parson say? He would address him thus: 'Why, merciful Father in heaven! How did such an idea ever occur to you? Travel, divert yourself, take a laxative' . . ."

A writer who so persistently distinguished between what he called an aesthetic approach and what we might call an existential approach should not be approached and discussed on the aesthetic plane, as he usually is. All talk not only of profundity and beauty but also of influences and anticipations remains on the aesthetic plain. And it is more in Kierkegaard's spirit to take offense and to disagree than to defend him and betray him with a kiss.

Walter Lowrie had much more feeling for Kierkegaard than most commentators, and there is nobody from whom one can learn more about Kierkegaard. In his big book on *Kierkegaard* (293), Lowrie remarked: ". . . all the trends of his thinking find their ultimate and most adequate expression in this work [*Concluding Unscientific Post-script*], in the *Literary Review*, and in *The Book about Adler*," all of which Kierkegaard wrote in his early thirties. Later (on p. 365), Lowrie makes clear that he is referring to "the latter part of . . . *A Literary Review*, published in 1846," that is, to those pages which are known in English under the title *The Present Age*. And those who have read Lowrie's complete translation of *On Authority and Revelation: The Book on Adler* will agree that it contains passages that are quite exceptionally important for an understanding of Kierkegaard; that the book is quite exceptionally verbose even for Kierkegaard; and that he did well when, instead of publishing the whole manuscript, he polished for publication only the crucial passages, which he issued under the title *Of the Difference between a Genius and an Apostle*. In sum, the unusual significance of the two essays brought together in the present volume [the book for which this preface was originally written] is that, for better or for worse, many of the central trends of Kierkegaard's thinking find superb expression in them.

Dear reader! Kierkegaard might say; pray be so good as to look for *my* thinking in these pages—not for Nietzsche's, Barth's, or Heidegger's, de Tocqueville's, or anyone else's. And least of all, dear reader, fancy that if you should find that a few others have said, too, what I have said, that makes it true. Oh, least of all suppose that numbers can create some small presumption of the truth of an idea. What I would have you ask, dear reader, is not whether I am in good company: to be candid, I should have much preferred to stand alone, as a matter of principle; and besides I do not like the men with whom the kissing Judases insist on lumping me. Rather ask yourself if I am right. And if I am not, then for heaven's sake do not pretend that I am, emphasizing a few points that are reasonable, even if not central to my thought, while glossing over those ideas which you do not like, or which, in retrospect, are plainly wrong, although I chose to take my stand on them. Do not forget, dear reader, that I made a point of taking for my motto (in my *Philosophical Scraps*): "Better well hung than ill wed!"

Alas! he might add if he saw the *present* age; who remembers that motto? Of course, it is not easy to find. When I published my *Scraps*—or *Crumbs*, if you prefer—the motto could hardly be missed because it stared the reader in the face if he but turned the title page. But when these *Scraps* appeared in the *present* age, they had to be made respectable: they were called *Philosophical Fragments* (which is almost as dignified as *Opus postumum*) and began, naturally, with a long and solemn preface. Wedged between that and my own text, the motto was easily overlooked. And now there is even a triple-decker edition of the *Fragments* in which my lowly *Scraps* are sandwiched between two prefaces and a long commentary. My book takes up little more than one-third of that, let us hope, definitive edition: and who is likely to find the motto, now lost somewhere in the middle? Of course, it is a fine commentary, and the reader who studies it will note that I misquoted Shakespeare, to whom I attributed the motto—presumably because I had read my Shakespeare in German. A good point, surely well worth making. The commentator is a scholar and knows his job, far better than most writers of prefaces. But the pity of it is that nobody remembers that I, Søren Kierkegaard, would rather be "well hung than ill wed." Almost everybody who writes or talks about me is concerned to make me the victim of some unpleasant mésalliance, and by now I have been ill wed scores of times. What a relief it would be to be well hung!

In the present age, of course, it would be out of the question to go as far as that. We could not possibly accommodate the author's own wishes when writing a preface to one of his books. But perhaps it would not be absolutely necessary to defy his spirit *in toto*, as he might have said. Let us at least try to meet him halfway.

Suppose, by a bold flight of the imagination, that an author said in 1846 that in the present age a revolution is unthinkable. Suppose further, if you can, that in 1847 seven Catholic cantons secede in

Switzerland and are forced in a short war to return to the federation; that in 1848 a revolution in France overthrows the monarchy and establishes a republic, while revolutions also sweep Germany and Austria and Italy; Denmark annexes Schleswig-Holstein (taking advantage of the fighting in Germany), a revolt flares up in Hungary, wars sweep through Italy, Prussian and Austrian troops expel the Danes from Schleswig-Holstein, the Communists in Paris rise against the new republic and are beaten down in bloody street fights, the Emperor has to flee Vienna, more bloody revolts are fought out in Paris, the Emperor of Austria is forced to abdicate in favor of his nephew—all in 1848. And then imagine things proceeding in a kindred spirit during 1849. But our author said in 1846 that "in the present age a rebellion is, of all things, the most unthinkable." Does it tax the sense of irony too far if we imagine further that, a century after the author made his statement, interpreters pretend that he made no mistake at all and actually tell us that he "perceived the deeper trends and foresaw" not, to be sure, what was just about to happen (they don't deign to mention any of the events just recited) but— what shall we say?—the future?

Of course, one could consider extenuating circumstances. After all, he might well have perceived the deeper trends even if he did not foresee the future; and a good deal of what he said about the present age in 1846 might still be true of the second half of the twentieth century. Some historians might even argue that the revolutions of 1848 were peculiar in some ways and lacked the profundity of the French Revolution. If our author was right in spite of apparent evidence to the contrary, then it is not he that deserves to be well hung but rather his interpreters who have failed to come to grips with the evidence. And if a posthumous preface to one of his books ought to breathe a little of his spirit, it is not needful after all that it should turn against him; but it is entirely proper that it should attempt to rescue him from his friends. By all means, read his book—only read it truly, and do not assume that any preface (whether this one or another) can all but take its place.

The case is similar to that of another so-called existentialist who all but borrowed Kierkegaard's title and published a little book on "The Spiritual Situation of the Age," as volume 1,000 in a popular series. Two years later, when his book had already gone through four editions, the Nazis came to power in Germany. Many people still cite it as a penetrating essay that perceived the deeper trends, even if it did not foresee what was just about to happen. And if the author considered Freud at least as dangerous as Hitler, he at least had the consistency to reiterate in 1950, in a volume on "Reason and Anti-Reason in Our Age," that Marxism and psychoanalysis are the two great representatives of anti-reason in the present age. His book, too, *was* quite perceptive in some ways; but surely his analysis "of the Age" has its comic dimension, too, if one considers when it appeared. Yet writers on existentialism never tire of paying tribute to the supposedly marvelous manner in which Kierkegaard made fun of Hegel, while they would not dream of ridiculing existentialists.

Scores of professors have made fun of the supposedly so professorial Hegel, though they consider it exceedingly bad taste to make fun of Professor Jaspers, who wrote the two books just mentioned, of Professor Heidegger, whom Kierkegaard would surely have found funnier than Hegel, or of Kierkegaard himself. But they know not what they do. They are simply ignorant of the agonies of Hegel's life, of the gradual decline into insanity of Hegel's one-time roommate, Hölderlin; of his sister, as close to him as any human being, who lived on the verge of madness till she finally fell over the precipice; of his illegitimate premarital son who brought heartbreak into Hegel's life again and again. Hegel's supposed remoteness from life and from his own existential situation is proverbial, and he is considered fair game, however unfair the dig; but if Kierkegaard made ridiculous errors, we must look the other way and pretend nothing happened.

When *The Present Age* first appeared in English, complete with preface and footnotes, there was no mention at all of politics or actual revolutions, and the author's statement that "in the present age a rebellion is, of all things, the most unthinkable" was not glossed. All one was told of 1848 was that Kierkegaard did not really "speak in his own voice . . . until after the 'metamorphosis' [?] of 1848. But he was already aware of it." O his prophetic soul!

His *Misundelse* was translated, as it still is, as *ressentiment*. A footnote explained that this French term was "first used forty years later by Nietzsche to describe the same process," and went on to cite —not Nietzsche but a French book, *L'homme du Ressentiment* by Max Scheller. Scheler ("Scheller" was a printer's error) was, of course, a German philosopher who wrote in German (even if some of his essays were later translated into other languages), and his conception of *ressentiment* did not by any means agree completely with

Nietzsche's, who had preceded him by roughly thirty years. Above all, Nietzsche did not "describe the same process" that Kierkegaard describes in *The Present Age;* Nietzsche had found *ressentiment* in the heart of Christianity, he had found it creating the values of the New Testament. A detailed comparison of Kierkegaard, Nietzsche, and Scheler might be rewarding; but not giving us the original word at all and not rendering it literally, say, as envy (the best German translation says *Neid*, which is envy), but rather with a technical term from another man's philosophy, forestalls comparison, analysis, and needful thought. Indeed, a later essay claims that Kierkegaard, in *The Present Age*, "forestalls one of the most famous passages in Nietzsche." One way wonder how an author in 1846 could have forestalled a passage written forty years later—written and not forestalled after all—but such a claim at least forestalls doubts about Kierkegaard's prophetic powers: even if he neither foresaw nor forestalled the revolutions of 1848, he at least forestalled a passage in Nietzsche.

Kierkegaard is safely dead and therefore had the right to be as nasty as he pleased and to make fun of the professors of his day and of the foibles of his age. He can even count on the applause of those, a hundred years later, who walk in the footsteps not of Kierkegaard but of the men at whom he laughed. But to make fun of them—well, don't you see that in the present age that simply isn't done because it would be in bad taste? We must admire Kierkegaard for having done what, if anyone today presumed to do it, we should find detestable. Just so, we must admire Abraham and condemn those who imitate him. To be sure, that was the very attitude which Kierkegaard opposed throughout his literary work. But if anyone should take Kierkegaard seriously, which simply would not be genteel, instead of admiring him, which is the thing to do, he would be told: "How did such an idea ever occur to you? Travel, divert yourself, take a laxative." No, not really that: such a humorous way of putting it is much too Kierkegaardian. He would just be told that it was in horrible taste.

What, then, makes *The Present Age* worth reading, if it merely forestalled a passage in Nietzsche but not the revolutions of 1848? That kind of question, so characteristic of the present age, is here on trial. It is contested by the whole literary existence of Kierkegaard. "Worth reading" and "What should I get out of reading this?" are phrases that bring to mind Nietzsche's remark: "Another century of readers—and the spirit itself will stink."

Read for the flavor, chew the phrases, enjoy the humor, feel the offense when you are attacked, don't ignore the author's blunders, but don't fail to look for your own shortcomings as well: then the book will make you a better man than you were before. But if you should find it too strenuous to read for the joy and pain of an encounter with a human being who, exasperated with himself, his age, and you, does not—let's face it—like you, then leave the book alone and do not look for marvelous anticipations!

To be sure, *The Present Age*, which formed part of a long book review published over Kierkegaard's own name, is conclusive proof that he meant it when he said in one of his most important pseudonymous books, *Fear and Trembling*, that "What our age lacks is not reflection but passion" (53); and probably he himself also believed that "the conclusions of passion are the only reliable ones . . ." (109). Surely, the first of these statements, however understandable in the Victorian era, is ridiculously false in the *present* age; our time lacks both, but it certainly does not need any depreciation of reflection. And the second statement cannot be fully excused by the age in which it was written. *The Present Age* refutes those who would dissociate Kierkegaard from these pseudonymous utterances, and it shows *why* he thought as he did, what provoked his anger, what he fought.

There are other places in his books where the same ideas find expression. In the "Diapsalmata," for example, early in *Either/Or*, he says, though not over his own name: "Let others complain that the age is wicked; my complaint is that it is paltry; for it lacks passion. Men's thoughts are thin and flimsy . . . The thoughts of their hearts are too paltry to be sinful . . . This is the reason my soul always turns back to the Old Testament and to Shakespeare. I feel that those who speak there are at least human beings: they hate, they love, they murder their enemies . . . they sin."

Surely, one can understand Kierkegaard and sympathize with him without altogether agreeing. Perhaps the revolutions of 1848 *were* paltry compared with the French Revolution and with the upheavals of the *present* age—still it remains a fact that many thousands risked and lost their lives for their beliefs. And a hundred years later it had become rather plain that the conclusions of passion are by no means reliable, and that millions may lose their lives fighting for beliefs so utterly unfounded and inhuman that not even such a bloody sacrifice can hallow them. The reader who wants nothing but the truth should not read Kierkegaard's *The Present Age*—or other classics. But those who would know Kierkegaard, the intensely religious humorist, the irrepressibly witty critic of his age and ours, can do no better than to begin with this book.

The essay on *The Difference Between a Genius and an Apostle* also shows that the extreme authoritarianism implicit in *Fear and Trembling* represents the author's considered view, and that he really considered blasphemous any suggestion that, confronted with what purports to be God's word, we should first "see whether the content . . . is divine, in which case we will accept it. . . ." Kierkegaard revered Abraham for the unflinching authoritarianism and the ethic of utterly blind obedience that he attributed to him, however mistakenly. He admired Abraham for not looking at the content of the commandment to sacrifice his son, and for not concluding that it was not divine and could not come from God. In *Fear and Trembling*, Kierkegaard added: "If faith does not make it a holy act to be willing to murder one's son, then let the same condemnation be pronounced upon Abraham as upon every other man" (41).

In *The Difference Between a Genius and an Apostle* and in *The Present Age* we find the heart of Kierkegaard. It is not innocuous, not genteel, not comfortable. He does not invite the reader to relax and have a little laugh with him at the expense of other people or at his own foibles. Kierkegaard deliberately challenges the reader's whole existence.

Nor does he merely challenge our *existence;* he also questions some ideas that had become well entrenched in his time and that are even more characteristic of the *present* age. Kierkegaard insists, for example, that Christianity was from the start essentially authoritarian —not just that the Catholic Church was, or that Calvin was, or Luther, or, regrettably, most of the Christian churches, but that Christ was—and is. Indeed, though Kierkegaard was, and wished to be, an individual, and even said that on his tombstone he would like no other epitaph than "That Individual," his protest against his age was centered in his lament over the loss of authority.

In the present age it is fashionable to lump Jesus with the prophets and the Buddha, with Confucius, Lao-tze, and Zen, with the mystics and Spinoza—sometimes even with the French Enlightenment and Freud—as if everybody who had been at all attractive must, of course, have been a humanist, and only Hitler, Stalin, Calvin, and the Catholic Church had been authoritarian. It is axiomatic that Jesus'

teaching was the most attractive teaching ever uttered, and any suggestion that it was not is branded as vilification. Only if the content was
divine—or rather what the present age considers worthy of this epithet
—may any teaching be ascribed to Jesus. The appalling possibility
that Kierkegaard insisted we consider was that God's teaching might
not agree completely with the predilections and the conscience of
the present age.

If it were really axiomatic that God could never contravene our
conscience and our reason—if we could be sure that he must share
our moral judgments—would not God become superfluous as far as
ethics is concerned? A mere redundancy? If God is really to make a
moral difference in our lives, Kierkegaard insists, we must admit that
he might go against our reason and our conscience, and that he should
still be obeyed.

That, of course, is merely one aspect of Kierkegaard, though certainly one of the most important. But even if we come to conclude
in the end that many of his ideas are untenable, or downright horrible,
that does not mean that he was not "worth reading." The same
consideration applies to Plato and Dante; and those who do not read
the Scriptures after the manner of Judas might even agree that it
applies to the Bible, too. Indeed, it is worth asking whether this is not
a feature that is more often found than not found in the greatest
books. They do not mainly seek to add to our knowledge: they do
not disdain shocking us because what they most want to do is
change us.[1]

---

[1] For a more detailed discussion of Kierkegaard, see Walter Kaufmann, *From Shakespeare to Existentialism* (Anchor Books paperback), especially Chapter 10; but also some of the other passages listed in the Index.

2

TOLSTOY
VERSUS DOSTOEVSKY*

I

It is customary to think of Tolstoy as a very great novelist who wrote *War and Peace* and *Anna Karenina*, but who then became immersed in religion and wrote tracts. His later concerns are generally deplored, and many readers and writers wish that instead he might have written another novel of the caliber of his masterpieces. A very few of his later works are excepted: chief among these is *The Death of Ivan Ilyitch*, which is acknowledged as one of the masterpieces of world literature. And some of those who have read the less well-known fable, *How Much Land Does a Man Need?* have said that it may well be the greatest short story ever written. But these are stories. Such *direct* communications as *My Religion*, with their unmistakable and inescapable challenge, one prefers to escape by not reading them. This makes it likely that most admirers of the stories, and even of *Anna Karenina*, come nowhere near understanding these works—a point amply borne out by the disquisitions of literary critics.

Lionel Trilling, as perceptive a critic as we have, has said that "every object . . . in *Anna Karenina* exists in the medium of what we must call the author's love. But this love is so pervasive, it is so constant, and it is so equitable, that it creates the illusion of objectivity. . . . For Tolstoi everyone and everything has a saving grace. . . . It is this moral quality, this quality of affection, that accounts for the unique illusion of reality that Tolstoi creates. It is when the novelist really loves his characters that he can show them in their completeness and contradiction, in their failures as well as in their great moments, in their triviality as well as in their charm." Three

* From the Introduction to *Religion from Tolstoy to Camus* (1961; rev. ed., 1964). For some discussion, see the Introduction above.

pages later: "It is chieflly Tolstoi's moral vision that accounts for the happiness with which we respond to *Anna Karenina*."

Happiness indeed! Love, saving grace, and affection! Surely, the opposite of all this would be truer than that! After such a reading, it is not surprising that the critic has to say, near the end of his essay on *Anna Karenina* (reprinted in *The Opposing Self*): "Why is it a great novel? Only the finger of admiration can answer: because of this moment, or this, or this. . . ." The point is not that Trilling has slipped for once, but that *Anna Karenina* is generally misread— even by the best of critics.

Any reader who responds with happiness to this novel, instead of being disturbed to the depths, must, of course, find a sharp reversal in Tolstoy's later work which is so patently designed to shock us, to dislodge our way of looking at the world, and to make us see ourselves and others in a new, glaring and uncomfortable light. Even if we confine ourselves to *Anna Karenina*, I know of no other great writer in the whole nineteenth century, perhaps even in the whole of world literature, to whom I respond with less happiness and with a more profound sense that I am on trial and found wanting, unless it were Søren Kierkegaard.

Far from finding that Tolstoy's figures are bathed in his love and, without exception, have a saving grace, I find, on the contrary, that he loves almost none and that he tells us in so many words that what grace or charm they have is not enough to save them.

Instead of first characterizing an apparently repulsive character and then exhibiting his hidden virtues or, like Dostoevsky, forcing the reader to identify himself with murderers, Tolstoy generally starts with characters toward whom we are inclined to be well disposed, and then, with ruthless honesty, brings out their hidden failings and their self-deceptions and often makes them look ridiculous. "Why is it a great novel?" Not on account of this detail or that, but because Tolstoy's penetration and perception have never been excelled; because love and affection never blunt his honesty; and because in inviting us to sit in judgment, Tolstoy calls on us to judge ourselves. Finding that most of the characters deceive themselves, the reader is meant to infer that he is probably himself guilty of self-deception; that his graces, too, are far from saving; that his charm, too, does not keep him from being ridiculous—and that it will never do to resign himself to this.

The persistent preoccupation with self-deception and with an appeal to the reader to abandon his inauthenticity links *Anna*

Karenina with *The Death of Ivan Ilyitch*, whose influence on existentialism is obvious. But in *Anna Karenina* the centrality of this motif has not generally been noticed.

It is introduced ironically on the third page of the novel, in the second sentence of Chapter II: "He was incapable of deceiving himself." To trace it all the way through the novel would take a book; a few characteristic passages, chosen almost at random, will have to suffice. "He did not realize it, because it was too terrible to him to realize his actual position. . . . [He] did not want to think at all about his wife's behavior, and he actually succeeded in not thinking about it at all. . . . He did not want to see, and did not see. . . . He did not want to understand, and did not understand. . . . He did not allow himself to think about it, and he did not think about it; but all the same, though he never admitted it to himself . . . in the bottom of his heart he knew. . . ." (Modern Library ed., 238 ff.) "Kitty answered perfectly truly. She did not know the reason Anna Pavlovna had changed to her, but she guessed it. She guessed at something which she could not tell her mother, which she did not put into words to herself. It was one of those things which one knows but which one can never speak of even to oneself. . . ." (268) "She became aware that she had deceived herself. . . ." (279) "He did not acknowledge this feeling, but at the bottom of his heart. . . ." (334)

Here is a passage in which bad faith is specifically related to religion: "Though in passing through these difficult moments he had not once thought of seeking guidance in religion, yet now, when his conclusion corresponded, as it seemed to him, with the requirements of religion, this religious sanction to his decision gave him complete satisfaction, and to some extent restored his peace of mind. He was pleased to think that, even in such an important crisis in life, no one would be able to say that he had not acted in accordance with the principles of that religion whose banner he had always held aloft amid the general coolness and indifference." (335)

Later, to be sure, Anna's husband becomes religious in a deeper sense; but as soon as the reader feels that Tolstoy's cutting irony is giving way to affection and that the man "has a saving grace," Tolstoy, with unfailing honesty, probes the man's religion and makes him, if possible, more ridiculous than he had seemed before. And the same is done with Varenka: she is not presented as a hypocrite with a saving grace but as a saint—until she is looked at more closely.

Inauthenticity is not always signaled by the vocabulary of self-deception. Sometimes Tolstoy's irony works differently: "Vronsky's life was particularly happy in that he had a code of principles, which defined with unfailing certitude what he ought and what he ought not to do. . . . These principles laid down as invariable rules: that one must pay a cardsharper, but need not pay a tailor; that one must never tell a lie to a man, but one may to a woman; that one must never cheat anyone, but one may a husband; that one must never pardon an insult, but one may give one, and so on. These principles were possibly not reasonable and not good, but they were of unfailing certainty, and so long as he adhered to them, Vronsky felt that his heart was at peace and he could hold his head up." (361) Here, too, we encounter a refusal to think about uncomfortable matters. Here, too, as in the passage about religion, it is not just one character who is on trial but a civilization; and while the reader is encouraged to pass judgment, he is surely expected to realize that his judgment will apply preeminently to himself.

Such passages are not reducible, in Trilling's words, to "this moment, or this, or this." The motifs of deception of oneself and others are absolutely central in *Anna Karenina*. Exoterically, the topic is unfaithfulness, but the really fundamental theme is bad faith.

Exoterically, the novel presents a story of two marriages, one good and one bad, but what makes it such a great novel is that the author is far above any simplistic black and white, good and bad, and really deals with the ubiquity of dishonesty and inauthenticity, and with the Promethean, the Faustian, or, to be precise, the Tolstoyan struggle against them.

Exoterically, the novel contains everything: a wedding, a near death, a real death, a birth, a hunt, a horse race, legitimate and illegitimate love, and legitimate and illegitimate lack of love. Unlike lesser writers, who deal with avowedly very interesting characters but ask us in effect to take their word for it that these men are very interesting, Tolstoy immerses us compellingly in the professional experiences and interests of his characters. The sketch of Karenina working in his study, for example (Part III, Chapter XIV), is no mere virtuoso piece. It *is* a cadenza in which the author's irony is carried to dazzling heights, but it is also an acid study of inauthenticity.

When Tolstoy speaks of death—"I had forgotten—death" (413; cf. 444)—and, later, gives a detailed account of the death of Levin's brother (571–93), this is not something to which one may refer as "this moment, or this, or this," nor merely a remarkable anticipation of *The Death of Ivan Ilyitch:* it is another essential element in Tolstoy's attack on inauthenticity. What in *Anna Karenina,* a novel of about one thousand pages, is one crucial element, becomes in *The Death of Ivan Ilyitch* the device for focusing the author's central message in a short story. And confronted with this briefer treatment of the same themes, no reader is likely to miss the point and to respond with "happiness."

All the passages cited so far from *Anna Karenina* come from the first half of the book, and they could easily be multiplied without going any further. Or, turning to Part V, one could point to the many references to dread and boredom, which, in the twentieth century, are widely associated with existentialism, and which become more and more important as the novel progresses. Or one could trace overt references to self-deception through the rest of the book: "continually deceived himself with the theory . . ." (562); "this self-deception" (587); "deceived him and themselves and each other" (590); and so forth. Or one could enumerate other anticipations of existentialism, like the following brief statement which summarizes pages and pages of Jaspers on extreme situations (*Grenzsituationen*): "that grief and this joy were alike outside all the ordinary conditions of life; they were loopholes, as it were, in that ordinary life through which there came glimpses of something sublime. And in the contemplation of this sublime something the soul was exalted to inconceivable heights of which it had before had no conception, while reason lagged behind, unable to keep up with it." (831 f.) Instead, let us turn to the end of the novel.

"Now for the first time Anna turned that glaring light in which she was seeing everything on to her relations with him, which she had hitherto avoided thinking about." (887) Thus begins her final, desperate struggle for honesty. On her way to her death she thinks "that we are all created to be miserable, and that we all know it, and all invent means of deceiving each other." (892) Yet Tolstoy's irony is relentless—much more savage, cruel, and hurtful than that of Shaw, who deals with ideas or types rather than with individual human beings. Tolstoy has often been compared with Homer—by Trilling among many others—but Homer's heroes are granted a moment of truth as they die; they even see into the future. Not Anna, though numerous critics have accused the author of loving her too much—so much that it allegedly destroys the balance of the novel.

Does he really love her at all? What she sees "distinctly in the piercing light" (888) is wrong; she deceives herself until the very end and, instead of recognizing the conscience that hounds her, projects attitudes into Vronsky that in fact he does not have. Like most readers, she does not understand what drives her to death, and at the very last moment, when it is too late, "she tried to get up, to drop backwards; but something huge and merciless struck her on the head and rolled her on her back."

Did Tolstoy love her as much as Shakespeare loved Cleopatra, when he lavished all the majesty and beauty he commanded on her suicide? Anna's death quite pointedly lacks the dignity with which Shakespeare allows even Macbeth to die. She is a posthumous sister of Goethe's Gretchen, squashed by the way of some Faust or Levin, a Goethe or a Tolstoy. Her death, like Gretchen's, is infinitely pathetic; in spite of her transgression she was clearly better than the society that condemned her; but what matters ultimately is neither Gretchen nor Anna but that in a world in which such cruelty abounds Faust and Levin should persist in their "darkling aspiration."

Their aspirations, however, are different. Faust's has little to do with society or honesty; his concern is preeminently with self-realization. Any social criticism implicit in the Gretchen tragedy is incidental. Tolstoy, on the other hand, was quite determined to attack society and bad faith, and when he found that people missed the point in *Anna Karenina* he resorted to other means. But there are passages in *Anna Karenina* that yield to nothing he wrote later, even in explicitness.

Here is a passage that comes after Anna's death. It deals with Levin. "She knew what worried her husband. It was his unbelief. Although, if she had been asked whether she supposed that in the future life, if he did not believe, he would be damned, she would have had to admit that he would be damned, his unbelief did not cause her unhappiness. And she, confessing that for an unbeliever there can be no salvation, and loving her husband's soul more than anything in the world, thought with a smile of his unbelief, and told herself that he was absurd." (912)

Tolstoy's interest in indicting bad faith does not abate with Anna's death: it is extended to Kitty's religion and to Russian patriotism. But in the end Levin's unbelief is modified without any abandonment of the quest for honesty. "He briefly went through, mentally, the whole course of his ideas during the last two years, the beginning of which was the clear confronting of death at the sight of his dear brother hopelessly ill." (926) And then his outlook is changed, but not, as some critics have said, into "the effacing of the intellect in a cloud of happy mysticism" (*Encyclopaedia Britannica*, 11th ed.); far from it. The religious position intimated here is articulated with full force in the works reprinted in the present volume. Neither here nor there can I find any "effacing of the intellect" nor even what Trilling, at the end of his essay, calls "the energy of animal intelligence that marks Tolstoi as a novelist." What awes me is perhaps the highest, most comprehensive, and most penetrating human intelligence to be found in any great creative writer anywhere.

These remarks about *Anna Karenina* should suffice to relate *The Death of Ivan Ilyitch, How Much Land Does A Man Need?, My Religion*, and Tolstoy's reply to his excommunication, to his previous work. They show that he was not a great writer who suddenly abandoned art for tracts, and they may furnish what little explanation the writings reprinted here require. The world has been exceedingly kind to the author of *War and Peace*, but it has not taken kindly to the later Tolstoy. The attitude of most readers and critics to Tolstoy's later prose is well summarized by some of our quotations from *Anna Karenina*: "He did not want to see, and did not see. . . . He did not want to understand, and did not understand. . . . He did not allow himself to think about it, and he did not think about it. . . ."

What is true of most readers is not true of all. The exceptions include, above all, Mahatma Gandhi, whose gospel of nonviolence was flatly opposed to the most sacred traditions of his own religion. The Bhagavadgita, often called the New Testament of India, consists of Krishna's admonition of Aryuna, who wants to forswear war when his army is ready for battle; and Krishna, a god incarnate, insists that Aryuna should join the battle, and that every man should do his duty, with his mind on Krishna and the transitoriness of all the things of the world and not on the consequences of his actions. The soldier should soldier, realizing that, ultimately, this world is illusory and he who thinks he slays does not really slay. It would be a gross understatement to say that Gandhi owed more to Tolstoy than he did to Hinduism.

Among philosophers, Ludwig Wittgenstein, whose influence on British and American philosophy after World War II far exceeded that of any other thinker, had the profoundest admiration for Tolstoy; and when he inherited his father's fortune, he gave it away to live simply and austerely. But his philosophy and his academic influence do not reflect Tolstoy's impact.

Martin Heidegger, on the other hand, owes much of his influence to what he has done with Tolstoy. The central section of his main work, *Being and Time*, deals at length with death. It contains a footnote (original ed., 1927, p. 254): "L. N. Tolstoy, in his story, *The Death of Ivan Ilyitch*, has presented the phenomenon of the shattering and the collapse of this 'one dies.' " "One dies" refers to the attitude of those who admit that one dies, but who do not seriously confront the fact that they themselves will die. In the chapter on "Existentialism and Death," below, I have tried to show in some detail how "Heidegger on death is for the most part an unacknowledged commentary on *The Death of Ivan Ilyitch*"; also how Tolstoy's story is far superior to Heidegger's commentary.

Tolstoy's magnificent *Reply to the Synod's Edict of Excommunication* is relevant to the misleading suggestion that *Anna Karenina* is a Christian tragedy. First of all, *Anna Karenina* is not a tragedy. Not only is it a novel in *form;* it is essentially not a tragedy that ends in a catastrophe but an epic story that continues fittingly after Anna's death to end with Levin's achievement of more insight. Secondly, it is rather odd to hold up as an example of what is possible within Christianity a man formally excommunicated, a writer whose views have not been accepted by any Christian denomination—a heretic.

Tolstoy drew his inspiration in large measure from the Gospels. His intelligence and sensitivity were of the highest order. And whether we classify him as a Christian or a heretic, his late writings remain to challenge every reader who is honestly concerned with the New Testament or, generally, with religion. Other writers one can take or leave, read and forget. To ignore Tolstoy means impoverishing one's own mind; and to read and forget him is hardly possible.

II

Asked to name the two greatest novelists of all time, most writers would probably choose Tolstoy and Dostoevsky. They were contemporaries, Russian to the core, at home in English, French, and German literature, and deeply concerned with Christianity. But their interpretations of Christianity were as different as their temperaments and their artistic techniques.

Tolstoy thought the Christian message involved a radical criticism of society, and his conception of the gospel was social. Dostoevsky's novels, on the other hand, urge the individual to repent of his sins; to accept social injustice because, no matter how harshly we may be treated, in view of our sinfulness and guilt we deserve no better; and not to pin our faith on social reforms. This message is particularly central in his last and greatest novel, *The Brothers Karamazov*. Mitya, the victim of a miscarriage of justice, accepts his sentence willingly as a welcome penance. And his brother Ivan, though also legally innocent, considers himself no less guilty than the murderer.

Unlike *Anna Karenina* and *Resurrection* and most great novels, *The Brothers Karamazov* contains a sequence of two chapters which, though an integral part of the work, can also be read separately without doing an injustice either to this fragment or to the novel: the conversation between Ivan and Alyosha in which Ivan tells his story of the Grand Inquisitor. These chapters help to characterize the two brothers, and the views of the Grand Inquisitor are emphatically not the views of Dostoevsky: on the contrary, what is intended is an indictment of the Roman Catholic church—and probably also of such men as Jefferson and Mill and of the ideal of the pursuit of happiness.

When "The Grand Inquisitor" is read out of context, the immediately preceding chapter is generally ignored; but the story is more likely to be understood as it was meant to be by the author, if one includes the conversation that leads up to it. Moreover, Ivan's vivid sketches of the sufferings of children deserve attention in their own right.

What makes the story of the Grand Inquisitor one of the greatest pieces of world literature is, first of all, that outside the Bible it would be hard to find another story of equal brevity that says so much so forcefully. Moreover, the story challenges some of the most confident convictions of Western Christians.

Reading the story merely as a diatribe against the Roman Catholic church and supposing that it stands or falls with its applicability to one religion is almost as foolish as supposing that the Inquisitor speaks the author's mind. What is presented to us, backed up by powerful though not conclusive arguments, is one of the most important theories of all time, for which it would be good to have a name. I shall call it *benevolent totalitarianism*.

By totalitarianism I mean a theory which holds that the government may regulate the lives of the citizens in their totality. Whether this is feasible at the moment is not essential. For political reasons or owing to technological backwardness, a totalitarian government may not actually regulate the citizens' lives in their totality: what matters is whether the government believes that it has the right to do this whenever it seems feasible.

In this sense, the governments of Hitler and Stalin were totalitarian; and their conduct explains, but does not justify, the popular assumption that totalitarianism is necessarily malignant. Ivan Karamazov submits that a man might honestly believe that, in the hands of wise rulers, totalitarianism would make men happier than any other form of government. The point is of crucial importance: what is at stake. is the dogmatic and naïve self-righteousness of Western statesmen who simply take for granted their own good faith, benevolence, and virtue and the lack of all these qualities in statesmen from totalitarian countries.

Dostoevsky's point is not altogether new: the first book on political philosophy, written more than two thousand years ago—Plato's *Republic*—presents a lengthy defense of benevolent totalitarianism. Some writers balk at calling it totalitarianism, mainly because they associate the word with malignancy. Others, seeing clearly that the doctrine of the *Republic* is totalitarian, have charged Plato with malignancy. A reading of Dostoevsky's tale shows us at a glance where both camps have gone wrong.

Plato, moreover, develops his arguments over roughly three hundred pages, introducing a great wealth of other material, while the Grand Inquisitor takes less than twenty. This chapter, then, is one of the most important documents of social philosophy ever penned, and any partisan of civil liberties might well say, as John Stuart Mill did in his essay *On Liberty:* "If there are any persons who contest a received opinion, . . . let us thank them for it, open our minds to listen to them, and rejoice that there is some one to do for us what we otherwise ought, if we have any regard for either the certainty or the vitality of our convictions, to do with much greater labor for ourselves."

Still, it may not be at all clear how the tale, if it is aimed at the Vatican, could also be aimed at Mill and Jefferson; and how, if it does not stand or fall with its applicability to Catholicism, it is important for religion. Both points depend on Dostoevsky's repudiation of the pursuit of happiness.

The ideal of the greatest possible happiness for the greatest possible number—which, though this formulation is British, is nothing less than the American dream—seemed to Dostoevsky to justify benevolent totalitarianism. He thought we had to choose between Christ and this world, between freedom and happiness.

Dostoevsky might have echoed Luther's words: "Even if the government does injustice . . . yet God would have it obeyed. . . . We are to regard that which St. Peter bids us regard, namely, that its power, whether it do right or wrong, cannot harm the soul. . . . To suffer wrong destroys no one's soul, nay, it improves the soul."[1] Or this quotation, also from Luther: "There is to be no bondage because Christ has freed us all? What is all this? This would make Christian freedom fleshly! . . . Read St. Paul and see what he teaches about bondsmen. . . . A bondsman can be a Christian and have Christian freedom, even as a prisoner and a sick man can be Christians, even though they are not free. This claim aims to make all men equal and to make a worldly, external kingdom of the spiritual kingdom of Christ. And this is impossible. For a worldly kingdom cannot exist unless there is inequality among men, so that some are free and others captive."[2]

In his politics, Dostoevsky, like Luther, was a radical authoritarian and an opponent of social reforms. His Christianity is concerned with the individual soul and its salvation; it is metaphysical, brooding, and preoccupied with guilt; it is otherworldly and content to give unto Caesar what is Caesar's. While Tolstoy wants to prepare the kingdom of God on earth, Dostoevsky seeks the kingdom only in the hearts of men. The tale of the Grand Inquisitor is meant as an indictment of all who "would make Christian freedom fleshly."

Tolstoy staked his message on his reading of the New Testament, and his interpretations and assumptions are answered to some extent by Morton Scott Enslin, Albert Schweitzer, and other interpreters of the Gospels. Dostoevsky's bland assumption, on the other hand, that the pursuit of happiness must lead to totalitarianism, and that his Inquisitor is the nemesis of democracy, has not been discussed much and should therefore be questioned briefly at this point.

If democracy meant majority rule pure and simple, it would be compatible with totalitarianism. For democracy so understood, the

---

[1] *Treatise on Good Works* (1520), in *Werke*, Weimar ed., VI, 259; *Works*, Philadelphia ed., I, 263.
[2] Cited in Troeltsch, *Die Soziallehren der christlichen Kirchen und Gruppen* (1912), 581, note 282.

men who framed the American Constitution held no brief, any more than Mill did. They were afraid of the possible tyranny of majorities and, to guard against that, devised an intricate system of checks and balances, a Constitution, and, amending that, a Bill of Rights. The whole point of the Bill of Rights is that the government may not regulate the lives of the citizens in their totality—not even if the majority should favor this. It might be objected that the Bill of Rights could be repealed. But that could be done only if the overwhelming majority of the people, and not those in one part of the country only, should insist on it over a long period of time; and in that case, of course, no framer of a constitution could prevent a revolutionary change. Any change of that sort, however, was made as difficult as possible.

What is incompatible with totalitarianism is not majority rule but belief in the overruling importance of civil liberties or human rights. You can have majority rule without civil liberties. Indeed, no country with effective guarantees of free speech and a free press is ever likely to accord its government the kind of majority endorsement which is characteristic of countries without free speech and a free press, from Hitler's Germany to Nasser's Egypt, with their 99 percent votes for the Leader. But it may well be the case that, conversely, you cannot long protect the people's civil liberties without introducing checks and balances including popular participation.

With this in mind, two answers could be given to Dostoevsky's tale. First, human nature may be different from the Inquisitor's conception of it. Three quarters of a century after the story first appeared, the people in West Germany were happier than those in East Germany. Freedom and happiness are compatible, and loss of liberty is likely to entail a great deal of unhappiness. Suffice it here to say that this is arguable—and that there has been a disturbing lack of argument. On the whole, democrats have considered this answer to the Inquisitor to be self-evident. Reading the tale again may convince at least some readers that it is not, and that much might be gained, even internationally, by developing this answer carefully instead of merely reiterating it dogmatically.

Second, one might answer, at least partly in Dostoevsky's spirit: If a choice had to be made between freedom and happiness, we should choose freedom. But precisely for that reason I cannot agree with Dostoevsky's and Luther's authoritarian politics. I believe that freedom and happiness are compatible, but I should not base the case for freedom on this point. If a vicar of Christ or secular Caesar or drug discoverer found a way to give men happiness conjoined with imbecility and slavery, I should hold out for liberty.

Instead of saying that such an attitude "would make Christian freedom fleshly," one might argue that in the New Testament Jewish freedom is made otherworldly; and it is noteworthy that both Luther and Calvin associated any attempt to realize freedom in *this* world with Moses and Judaism.[3]

[3] The themes of the last two paragraphs are developed in *The Faith of a Heretic* and in *Without Guilt and Justice.*

3

NIETZSCHE
AND EXISTENTIALISM*

"Some ancient writings one reads to understand antiquity; but others are such that one studies antiquity in *order* to be able to read *them*. To these belongs the *Apology*," said Nietzsche in a late note.[1] Scholars have to read a great deal of material as a means to understand some things better. This might be vastly depressing if there were not some works that make it all worthwhile. I agree with Nietzsche that the *Apology* of Socrates is such a work; and I also feel that Nietzsche himself was one of the few philosophers who is endlessly rewarding. Our theme during this conference is "Nietzsche's Impact," which is unquestionably fascinating. But let no one suppose that the main thing about Nietzsche is his impact. Rather, his extraordinary impact is a fringe benefit for Nietzsche scholars. Nietzsche is a key that unlocks innumerable doors, and knowing him one gets more out of scores of other writers.

My topic is "Nietzsche and Existentialism," but Nietzsche's impact on existentialism is merely one facet of his influence. To place my topic in perspective, let me at least mention some of the other dimensions of Nietzsche's impact. In 1912, Francis Cornford, whose translations with commentaries of many Platonic dialogues are still widely used, called Nietzsche's first book, *The Birth of Tragedy*, published one hundred years ago, in 1872, "a work of profound imaginative insight, which left the scholarship of a generation toiling in the rear."[2] In my own *Tragedy and Philosophy* (1968) I have argued that Nietzsche was wrong about the birth of tragedy, even wronger about the death of tragedy, and utterly wrong about Aeschylus, Sophocles, and Euripides. Still, Cornford's estimate stands, and even Nietzsche's first book, which was really one of his lesser works, was an inspired

---

* This is a radical condensation of a lecture given November 2, 1972. The occasion is explained in the Introduction, p. xiii.
[1] *Gesammelte Werke*, Musarion ed., Vol. XVI, p. 6.
[2] *From Religion to Philosophy*, p. 111.

and brilliant essay that contains many enduring insights. I have a tremendous admiration for Nietzsche, but that does not preclude many basic disagreements. In this lecture, I shall communicate my admiration rather than my criticisms.

Let us keep in mind Nietzsche's influence on the discussion of tragedy, on the novels of Thomas Mann and Hermann Hesse, on the poetry of Rilke and Stefan George, of Christian Morgenstern and Gottfried Benn, on Oswald Spengler and Max Scheler, on Malraux and Gide, on Shaw, Yeats, and Eugene O'Neill, on Freud and Buber, Jung and Adler, and ever so many others. For it would be wrong to suppose that Nietzsche was merely a precursor of existentialism.

In the subtitle of my *Nietzsche* I called him even in 1950 "Philosopher, Psychologist, Antichrist," and then devoted an Appendix to Nietzsche as a poet. But he also was one of the greatest German prose stylists, along with Luther, Goethe, and Heine. And he was a fascinating human being—far more so than most great philosophers.

Those who want to get out of Nietzsche what is there must also expose themselves to the *du* (the *Thou* or *You*) that confronts us in his writings—the man, the human reality that addresses us and will not leave us unscathed.

Even if we concentrate on the impact of Nietzsche's philosophy, we find at least three very different types of philosophy in his work.

The first of these is "metaphysics." Thus the will to power can be interpreted as a metaphysical conception, and so can Nietzsche's doctrine of the eternal recurrence of the same events. One of the leading so-called existentialists, Martin Heidegger, has stressed this side of Nietzsche out of all proportion. Heidegger sees the history of Western philosophy, beginning with Plato, as a gigantic mistake that culminates in Nietzsche as the last great metaphysician. Heidegger sees himself as pointing a way back toward the pre-Socratics, who lived, as it were, before the fall. Heidegger sees Nietzsche as the last great—very great—representative of the old order, and he sees himself as the herald of a new order, a new beginning, for which the time, alas, is not yet as ripe as he thought it was when Hitler came to power. Actually, Heidegger's high esteem for the pre-Socratics is deeply influenced by Nietzsche's esteem for them, and the role he assigns to Nietzsche would have been utterly uncongenial to Nietzsche. It depends on Heidegger's systematic preference for non-contextual readings—for taking bits out of context and using them willfully and arbitrarily. I shall return to this point. Suffice it for the moment to say that the metaphysical element *is* present in Nietzsche's writings here and there, and in some passages he seems to present the will to power as a metaphysical conception after the manner of Schopenhauer's blind and irrational will; but such passages are more than balanced by anti-metaphysical passages, and to make of Nietzsche primarily and preeminently a metaphysician is utterly misleading and perverse.

The second type of philosophy that is to be found in Nietzsche is harder to sum up in one word. If one uses the word "metaphysics" for the first type, one might use "analysis" for the second type of philosophy. I have in mind something more or less like what is today sometimes called "analytic philosophy." This side of Nietzsche is likely to be explored much more in forthcoming publications in the United States. Many young teachers of philosophy nowadays, who are interested enough to write about him, will surely stress this side of Nietzsche.

Relevant passages abound, for example, in *Twilight of the Idols*, in the discussion of God, of "the true world," of "the good," of "the four great errors," and in the remarks about "language" and "grammar." There is a good deal of such material in Nietzsche. At one time, it was falsely claimed by ever so many people that this was just a passing phase—Nietzsche's so-called "positivism" which he supposedly left behind when he wrote *Zarathustra*. By now few people would claim that any more. It is obvious that this is an abiding element in Nietzsche, and quite prominent in his late books and notes. *Twilight*, incidentally, is one of his very last works. If we had to choose, as of course we do not, between the emphasis upon Nietzsche as a metaphysician and *this* emphasis, it would be much more in Nietzsche's spirit to emphasize analysis rather than metaphysics. If you had asked Nietzsche in his maturity, in his last years, after *Zarathustra*, what he thought of metaphysics, I have no doubt that he would have emphasized his *criticism* of metaphysics.

The third type of philosophy we might call "existentialism." If one points to three types of philosophy, summing up one, not altogether aptly, as "metaphysics," another as "analysis," and then uses "existentialism" almost as a catch-all for the rest, one might include such things as the following: (1) Literary criticism, of which there is a great deal in Nietzsche. It is not perverse to assimilate that to existentialism because Heidegger, Jaspers, and Sartre have written a great deal of literary criticism. (2) The interest in psychology is also found in most of the existentialists. (3) Nietzsche's critique of Christianity is at least in some of its aspects part of a much larger undertaking that one might call a critique of *Weltanschauungen*, a critique of "world views."[3] The world view that he writes about the most is Christianity because it has had a particularly fateful importance for the Western world. Continuous with that, we find (4) an element that is also taken up by the existentialists: the analysis of "nihilism" which we encounter in a number of places in Nietzsche, but in most concentrated form in the *Nachlass*, in notes that are still most easily available in the collection that has come to be known as *The Will to Power*. The whole first book consists of notes on nihilism. What interests Nietzsche beyond nihilism is possible attitudes that man might adopt toward an absurd world—again a theme that you find in Heidegger, Sartre, and Camus. (5) One also find in Nietzsche a critique of various modes of being, or what some people today call "life styles," as well as what Nietzsche calls in *Beyond Good and Evil*, Section 212, "a celebration of a new greatness of man." Here one may think of the contrast between "authentic" and "inauthentic" existence.

Finally, (6) one finds in Nietzsche, rounding out this preliminary account of existentialism, many literary efforts. Not only did he write poetry as well as prose, but one of the things that is so exciting about him as a writer is that almost every work represents a new stylistic experiment. In fact, that is an understatement. In many works one finds, as one does in *Twilight of the Idols*, a plethora of different stylistic experiments.

For the rest of my lecture let me speak briefly about some of the major existentialists and contrast Nietzsche with them. To do this, I shall have to be frustratingly brief about every one of them, but that should facilitate vigorous discussion.

About *Kierkegaard* we can be very brief. Few of the other existentialists will be talked about and written about over a hundred years after their death. Kierkegaard may well be the greatest of the lot. But he never read Nietzsche (he died in 1855, when Nietzsche was eleven year old); and Nietzsche never read Kierkgaard. In a letter, Georg Brandes, who admired both, and who was the first person to lecture

---

[3] Cf. Jaspers, *Psychologie der Weltanschauungen* (1919).

on Nietzsche at a university, called Nietzsche's attention to Kierke-gaard. Nietzsche said the next time he was near a library, he wanted to read Kierkegaard, but he did not get around to it. The two men have much in common. What distinguishes Kierkegaard from subse-quent existentialists is that in Nietzsche's beautiful phrase he was, like Nietzsche, "born posthumously." They did not really come into their own until long after they were dead. They were *unzeitgemäss* (un-timely). They swam against the stream, while one of the shortcomings of most of the existentialists is that they are so timely, that they are so fashionable, that they have a nose for what is fashionable. Nietzsche and Kierkegaard had a nose for things that would not become fashionable for a long time.

Karl *Jaspers*, in a chapter on "Kierkegaard and Nietzsche" in his *Reason and Existenz* (1935), reprinted in my *Existentialism from Dostoevsky to Sartre*, compares the two men and emphasizes the similarities. His comparison broke new ground and was illuminating in its time, but it is misleading because Jaspers plays down the differences. In *Zarathustra*, Part I, Third Chapter, "On the After-worldly," Nietzsche said what he might have said of Kierkegaard if he had read him: "Weariness that wants to reach the ultimate with one leap, with one fatal leap, a poor ignorant weariness that does not want to want anymore: this created all gods and afterworlds." There are many similarities between Nietzsche and Kierkegaard, but what mattered most to them was precisely what distinguishes them. Jaspers says that Kierkegaard's "forced Christianity" and Nietzsche's "forced anti-Christianity" do not matter that much. But this is a way of saying that what mattered most to them really doesn't matter, while all that does matter is what matters to Jaspers.

The influence of Nietzsche upon Jaspers, the second figure I want to discuss, is tremendous. To mention merely Jaspers' major publica-tions on Nietzsche, there is first this chapter of 1935, then a big and important book on Nietzsche published in 1936, then *Nietzsche and Christianity* published in 1938; and then Jaspers came back to Nietzsche again and again in his later works. To bring out how much Jaspers got from Nietzsche, let me quote a sentence from Section 15 of *The Birth of Tragedy*. In this book there are many existentialist motifs. In Section 15, with which the book in a way should end— Nietzsche lived to regret that he appended to it a lot of material about Richard Wagner—in Section 15, which is in a way the culmina-tion of the argument (an earlier draft of the book ended at that point), Nietzsche says: ". . . science . . . speeds irresistibly towards its limits where its optimism . . . suffers shipwreck [*scheitert* is one of Jaspers' key terms]." And Nietzsche adds: "Noble and gifted men . . . reach . . . boundary points [*Grenzpunkte*] on the periphery from which one gazes into what defies illumination [*das Unaufhellbare*]" and "suddenly the new form of insight breaks through."

That reads like an inspired summary of Jaspers' philosophy. In this sentence, written before Karl Jaspers was born, science reaches its limits, *Grenzpunkte*—Karl Jaspers speaks of *Grenzsituationen*, boundary situations or ultimate situations—and in these situations one gains illumination of existence. That may show how strong the influence of Nietzsche on Jaspers is at crucial points. There are many other points; for instance, Nietzsche's pioneering appreciation of the pre-Socratics, which Jaspers himself stressed when in his first major philosophical work, *Psychology of World Views*, he dealt at great length with the pre-Socratics: "I am doing this in part because Nietzsche was the one who described the pre-Socratics as the great timeless philosophical types."

In spite of such similarities, it is important to retain some perspective. Jaspers and Nietzsche are not really commensurable. Jaspers versus Nietzsche brings to mind weak tea compared not to the best champagne but to the ocean. In Nietzsche we find an elemental force, an abundance, cosmic dimensions, something nonlinear that cannot be reduced to one direction and makes it misleading to compare these two men as if they were of a kind.

I cannot imagine that on the hundredth anniversary of the publication of Karl Jaspers' first book scholars will be discussing Jaspers and music, Jaspers and literature, Jaspers and politics, Jaspers and this, Jaspers and that. But it is unfair to single out Jaspers to make this point. After all, this applies to most recent philosophers, including the next man that we shall consider now, Martin *Heidegger*. There is no need to repeat it here.

First of all, we encounter in Heidegger, too, an enduring preoccupation with Nietzsche. A chapter in *Holzwege* (1950) deals with Nietzsche's word 'God is dead' "; an essay of 1954 is entitled "Who is Nietzsche's Zarathustra?" and in 1961 Heidegger published a vast two-volume work on *Nietzsche*. In addition he deals with Nietzsche again and again in other books. Then there is Heidegger's preoccupation with the pre-Socratics; indeed he has dealt with them much more extensively and repeatedly than Jaspers ever did.

Nietzsche was one of the first writers in Germany to consider Hölderlin one of the greatest German poets. This was then still so unfashionable that when, as a student, Nietzsche wrote a paper on Hölderlin, his teacher gave it back to him with the remark that henceforth he should occupy himself with healthier and more German subjects. Heidegger has devoted a whole book of interpretations to Hölderlin. You also find in Heidegger the conviction that literary criticism of a sort—*his* kind of literary criticism—is continuous with philosophy. You also find in Heidegger, if you read him superficially and not in the spirit in which he wants to be read, an apparent interest in psychology, and you find the contrast of which I spoke earlier between the authentic and the inauthentic state of being. You even find in Heidegger attempts to write poetry.

But now let me stress the enormous differences, and perhaps four points will suffice, though one could mention many more. The four I am singling out here are of singular importance.

First of all, there is the beautiful line spoken by Goethe's Mephistopheles about Faust, lines quoted already by Hegel, who was a contemporary of Goethe's: *Verachte nur Vernunft und Wissenschaft*— "Have but contempt for reason and for science." This could be said of Heidegger, but not of Nietzsche. Nietzsche's attitude toward reason was complex and I cannot discuss it here, but I have dealt with it very fully in my *Nietzsche*. Suffice it to say that Nietzsche had searching things to say against the fashionable overestimation of reason. But what reveals at a glance the really profound difference between Heidegger and Nietzsche is not so much the presence of strongly rationalistic elements in Nietzsche as their diametrically opposed attitude toward science. The point does not depend on using "science" in different senses of the word. I mean their attitude toward the sciences, very much including psychology. Their attitude toward psychology and toward science in general could hardly be more different. This is true not merely of Nietzsche's so-called "middle period" in which some people think he was a positivist, but also of his last works where he expresses the hope that certain problems will be solved when psychology makes some progress; and, adding insult to injury, he even hoped that physiology might resolve many basic philosophical problems. In Heidegger we encounter a tremendous animus against science, and especially against psychology. He is appalled that some readers suppose that his main work, *Being and Time*, deals with psychology. Here I can merely touch on these important differences as topics for discussion. To explore these themes fully would require a mono-graph. This, then, is the first great difference: their attitude toward reason and science.

The second great difference is that Heidegger furnishes an arch-example of what I call exegetical thinking. I am using this phrase as a technical term. What I mean by exegetical thinking is that in one way or another one assigns authority to a text, raising the text above criticism; then one reads one's own ideas into the text; and then one gets them back endowed with authority.[4] This is what Martin Hei-degger does again and again. He himself would harly consider this characterization as insulting. He does this quite openly. He lays it down as a principle that the interpreter must use "violence," and he uses pliable texts, preferably fragments of the pre-Socratics, ignoring all the other information that we have; he builds up the pre-Socratics, discouraging any kind of criticism of them by saying that we must not think of them as a bunch of "high grade Hottentots." He means that we must not look at them as in some sense primitive. They are on a plane far above us; he treats them as authorities, and reads into them his ideas and gets them back endowed with authority. This is utterly different from Nietzsche's reading of anybody.

Nietzsche is, as Jaspers once put it censoriously, "lacking in respect for greatness." What Jaspers could not forgive Nietzsche was some of his nasty remarks about Immanuel Kant, who certainly was a very great man, but hardly for that reason above criticism. Certainly Nietzsche is, in this respect, too, the diametrically opposite type of Heidegger.

Thirdly—and this is another big subject that I can only point to here—there is their attitude toward Being. In Heidegger, beginning with *Being and Time* and even much more obviously in his later work, there is a mystique of "Being." One could quote Nietzsche on and on against this. "There is no 'being' behind doing, effecting, becoming"; or "man took the concept of being from the concept of the ego; he posited 'things' as 'being,' in his image" (these are both from late works).[5] In *Ecce Homo* he praises Heraclitus for his "radical repudia-tion of the very concept of being—all this is clearly more closely

[4] For a fuller treatment of exegetical thinking in general and Heidegger's in particular, cf. my *Without Guilt and Justice* (1973), pp. 15–18, and *From Shake-speare to Existentialism* (1960 paperback ed.), chap. 17, "Heidegger's Castle."

[5] *Genealogy of Morals*, sec. 13 of the first essay; *Twilight*, Sec. 3 of "The Four Great Errors."

related to me than anything else thought to date."[6] And in the chapter "On the Afterworldly" in *Zarathustra*, from which I quoted the passage about the leap in connection with Kierkegaard, Nietzsche says: "The belly of being does not speak to humans at all, except as a human." Heidegger has sometimes been linked with Nietzsche; he has also sometimes been linked with Hegel, as if he were a disciple of Hegel. In his attitude toward Being, and not only in this, Heidegger is actually utterly different from both.

Fourthly and finally, Heidegger regresses into secularized Christianity. Heidegger is a great reactionary, as a philosopher. I am not speaking of his politics now. That is another, even more unlovely, subject. But as a thinker he is not, compared to Nietzsche, as he himself claims, a great radical but rather a philosopher who has never overcome the Christianity on which he was brought up. He can really hardly be understood until you realize that his concept of Being is a surrogate for God, and that his preoccupation with dread and death and guilt is an attempt to secularize Christian theology. All this is remote from Nietzsche indeed.

That brings me to Sartre, who is in some ways closer to Nietzsche than are the German existentialists. The German existentialists are so heavy, so professorial, so saturnine; they are so utterly lacking in the "light feet," in that defiance of the spirit of gravity, in that spirit of the dance which Nietzsche kept celebrating.

There is in Sartre a little more lightness some of the time, though not in his turgid philosophical main works, which are closer to Heidegger. Above all, Sartre resembles Nietzsche more than the German existentialists in his attack on guilt and guilt feelings. This is a crucial point. Jaspers and Heidegger stand in a Christian tradition, assuming that guilt and guilt feelings are somehow needful and fruitful and that the road to authenticity must lead through guilt feelings. Nietzsche opposes guilt feelings, and here Sartre and also Camus side with and are influenced by Nietzsche. Sartre's great attack on guilt feelings in *The Flies* is well known, and I have shown elsewhere in detail how the ethic of *The Flies* is not so much Sartre's own (in many respects, it is not) but rather Nietzsche's. Again and again the play echoes *Zarathustra* and *Ecce Homo*.[7]

Sartre is also much less anti-rationalist than is Heidegger. Sartre's

[6] In sec. 3 of the discussion of *The Birth of Tragedy*.

[7] See my *Tragedy and Philosophy*, sec. 51, "Nietzsche's Influence on *The Flies*."

ambivalence has been concisely formulated by Iris Murdoch in an early book, which she called *Sartre: Romantic Rationalist*. That is a fine title. There is a rationalist streak in Sartre that is quite different from Heidegger and closer to Nietzsche.

Next, there is Sartre's preoccupation with self-deception, one of his favorite themes. Here, too, he follows in Nietzsche's footsteps. One only needs to compare Nietzsche on lying (in Section 55 of *The Antichrist*, and also the immediately preceding and following sections) with Sartre's "Portrait of the Anti-Semite" and Sartre's early story, "The Childhood of a Leader," to see the similarities.

Finally, consider *The Birth of Tragedy* once more. In connection with *French* existentialism, Section 7 is most relevant. This is the first great culmination of the argument; the two high points are reached in Section 7 and Section 15. In Section 7 you find the absurd and nausea.

Now, what about the differences? They are not merely superficial. There are some deep differences. First of all, for better or worse, in *Ecce Homo*, in the first chapter, Section 3, Nietzsche calls himself, "I, the last anti-political German." That may have been a limitation; he *was* anti-political. Nobody can call Jean-Paul Sartre anti-political. To him his immersion in politics is crucial.

This contrast becomes even starker when we turn to the Preface to Nietzsche's *Antichrist*, from which I quote: "One must be skilled in living on mountains, seeing the wretched ephemeral babble of politics and national self-seeking beneath oneself." That is a very un-Sartrean statement; and what Nietzsche has to say about journalism and newspapers is pretty consistent all the way through his work. For him journalism is, in one word, a "disease." If it is a disease, then certainly few philosophers, if any, have ever suffered from that disease as much as Jean-Paul Sartre. He involves himself in ephemeral things to a very high degree. I do not mean to pass judgment here; for it seems to me that hardly any other individual alive has done so much to appeal to the social conscience both of the people in his own country and of people in other countries, and to impress intellectuals and students with a need to speak out against major crimes of their governments. Sartre is highly problematic, but in many ways I greatly admire him.

Turning to Camus, finally, any sensible reading of *The Fall* would indicate that the book is a Nietzschean attack on guilt and guilt feelings, which encompasses especially the Christian doctrine of original sin and the many secularized forms of this preoccupation with guilt.

Moreover, Camus's *Notebooks* are studded with references and quotations from Nietzsche,[8] including a great many from *Twilight of the Idols*. He once jotted down as a chapter heading, "We Nietzscheans," and he was certainly very much influenced by Nietzsche. The chapter on Nietzsche in *The Rebel*, which to my mind is a bad book, gives no adequate notion of the importance of Nietzsche for Camus.

Camus wrote three good novels, which is no faint praise, but he also played around with a number of other things, including philosophy, in which he is not, I think, to be taken very seriously. He was not an important thinker, even if some people overestimate him on the basis of those three novels, *The Stranger*, *The Plague*, and *The Fall*.

It is time to conclude. Existentialism is fascinating; but perhaps we have even now, in 1972, moved beyond it and left it behind. Sartre now looks back on his own early existentialism as a matter of the past. That is one of the nice Nietzschean things about Sartre; he has this capacity for detachment from himself: he can speak very critically and even caustically of his own earlier work.

Heidegger never liked the label "existentialism." He will, no doubt, be taught in graduate seminars in philosophy for some time to come, especially in the United States; but I doubt that he will endure, except as a name.

In my view, Nietzsche is timeless, like Plato and Shakespeare. When I speak about "Nietzsche and Existentialism," I see existentialism as one of the many timely phenomena, one of the many fashions with which Nietzsche has been linked for a while. Sartre will probably still be read a hundred years from now (if there still *is* a world)—but like Voltaire, as a man in the French tradition who is not only, or even mainly, a technical philosopher.

One final remark. When I link Nietzsche with Plato and Shakespeare and express my admiration for him, this might seem to be proof of what Kierkegaard might have called an "aesthetic" attitude, a non-serious attitude. Nietzsche's writings are indeed "beautiful" and "profound," but that is not all. There are exceedingly few writers in all ages who are so inexhaustibly fruitful, who keep giving our minds new directions—and not only our minds. Nietzsche was a whole human being and affects those who read him well in their entirety.

---

[8] *Notebooks* 1935–1942, translated by Philip Thody (1963), e.g., pp. 96 and 144–46; *Notebooks* 1942–1951, translated by Justin O'Brien (1965), pp. 3, 5f., 17, 33, 49, 59, 65f., 78f., 145, 149–51, 239, 249, 253, 269.

4

BUBER'S RELIGIOUS SIGNIFICANCE*

I   A Personal Approach

Most serious authors we encounter after our basic attitudes have taken shape; but there are a few whom we meet earlier—writers who neither become grist for our mill nor evoke a sense of congeniality, but who do something to us. For me, Martin Buber is one of this small number.

It might be inappropriate to even mention this; writing about a philosopher, we generally try to be impartial, putting out of mind all personal involvement. Yet Buber differs from other philosophers. His major contribution to philosophy is *I and Thou*, in which the two relationships I-It and I-Thou are contrasted. There is something problematic in writing "about" the author of this work, treating him as an object for reflection, carving up his works into such fields as ethics and epistemology, philosophy of history and social thought, or even philosophy in general as separate from Buber's other interests. In this manner one stands to lose what is most distinctive about him. To perceive his significance, we must try to listen to his voice.

It is sometimes said that Buber is an existentialist, and the term is so vague that this statement is not false. Some of the differences between Buber and other so-called existentialists will be considered below. What Buber clearly has in common with some others influenced by Kierkegaard, and, above all, with Kierkegaard himself, is his impassioned protest against the kind of philosophy to which he and the others are being reduced today by some of their admirers. Neo-Thomists write books on Kierkegaard and Jaspers, Heidegger

* Written in the 1950s for the Buber volume in The Library of Living Philosophers, which finally appeared in 1967, several years after a German translation of the volume had been published in Stuttgart.

and Sartre, forcing their rebellions against all traditional philosophy into an almost scholastic mold. When one writes on Kierkegaard today, one must begin by breaking down the systematic walls in which a growing literature is trying to confine him, to set free the individual.

The present volume on Buber, which I myself strongly urged years ago, in 1951, presents a similar danger. To bring together many different views of Buber's work within the framework of a single volume, one simply has to carve up Buber's thought more or less systematically to avoid egregious repetition, and one must proceed as if he had a system which can be considered branch by branch. I am not objecting to this method. Neither do I feel apologetic for my own attempt to seek a different approach. Both procedures may be complementary, and my own, though of necessity it will involve some overlapping with the thoughts of others, may yet fill a crucial gap.

II   Buber's Central Question

Buber, like Kierkegaard, is at heart a religious thinker rather more than a philosopher. His primary concern is not with the elaboration of a system, with the quest for certainty or the solution of some problems in epistemology or ethics, but, if it is not too bold to formulate it in a single question: What does the religion of my fathers mean to me today?

What distinguishes Buber is not this question, which is on many lips today. His significance lies in the fact that few, if any, others have said so much of such importance in answer to this question. Not only *I and Thou, Dialogue,* and *Two Types of Faith* are relevant to his central question, but also Buber's studies of the Bible and of Hasidism, his translation of the Hebrew Scripture, and his collection of the lore of the Hasidim. Almost everything else he has written also has some bearing on this question. More than any other writer of our time, specifically including those theologians whose wide popularity is such a distinctive feature of our age, Buber has shown in great detail what religion can mean at its best.

Buber is certainly not an authoritative spokesman for Judaism. It is one of the blessings of Judaism that it does not have any authoritative spokesmen. Millions of Jews disagree with Buber about their Scriptures, about Hasidism, about Judaism, and about whatever else is interesting. But he has shown a possible meaning of religion today—which sounds like faint praise until one looks around and finds how exceedingly difficult it has become for those who are loath to part with their critical spirit to find a worthwhile meaning for religion here and now.

III   Buber versus Jaspers and Heidegger

Buber's faults are not hard to find but relatively unimportant. It has been charged against him that as a teacher of social philosophy he did not give some of his students what a less subjective teacher would have given them, and that, when he retired, they still had to acquire some fundamentals of sociology. Whether this is true or not, Buber's stature certainly does not rest on his ability to coach his students for examinations.

In a similar vein, his discussions of the thought of Nietzsche, Heidegger, and Sartre—to give only three examples—are open to objections. At important points he seems to be mistaken in his views of their views. But again this is unimportant. If he had never written about these men, his stature would be unimpaired.

Buber is not a model of impartial reading. Nietzsche once spoke of "what a man has written with his blood." Buber might be said to *read* with his blood. Or, to use a more conventional term, with his heart. He involves himself in what he reads to the point where he finds what other readers would not find. As a result, his readings are often controversial.

This is true also of Buber's Biblical interpretations and of the picture he has given us of the Hasidim. There is something intuitive, personal, partial about his readings. And this may seem to be a crucial criticism.

A comparison with Jaspers and, even more, with Heidegger seems obvious at this point. They, too, have devoted a large part of their own writings to interpretations; and their exegeses, too, are open to a vast array of critical objections.

In the case of Jaspers I have tried to show in detail in another volume in this series that his two books and his several essays on Nietzsche are founded on an unsound method and his long reply to my critique confirmed my thesis that he is at least occasionally quite unable to read even a plain text. Instead of replying to the specific criticisms which I summarized in less than two pages toward the end of my essay, Jaspers devoted five pages to a piqued attempt to saddle me with views which I had not expressed and with a philosophic outlook quite at variance with the one I do profess. Whether he deals with Schelling, Kierkegaard, or Freud, the procedure is always essentially the same: nobody is accepted as he is; everybody is remodeled to play a part assigned to him. Schelling's protean development is dismissed; Kierkegaard's "forced Christianity" and Nietzsche's "forced anti-Christianity" do not really matter; and Freud becomes, next to Marx, *the* representative of "anti-reason in our age." What matters most to a man does not necessarily matter to Jaspers: Jaspers' interpretations depend on what matters to *him*.

Jaspers himself stresses communication, which he defines as a "loving struggle," but he never really exposes himself to another point of view. He is always the judge, not a combatant—or as an admirer once put it: Jaspers has remained true to his training; he has never abandoned the psychiatrist's condescension.

Nothing of the sort could be alleged of Buber. Can anyone who has ever asked him a question imagine him replying, as Jaspers occasionally answers serious questions, "I shall deal with this point in one of my books"? Buber may occasionally seem highhanded in interpretation, but as soon as he confronts a question from another human being he insists on the achievement of communication or, as he says, dialogue. Emphatically, he is not the judge nor a psychiatrist but a fellow human being, a fellow seeker, eager to speak man to man.

Buber's dialogue is not Socratic: it quite lacks the mordant sarcasm, the frank delight in the opponent's weakness, and the air of a contest. With Buber, question and answer have a religious dimension: it is not a match of intellects he seeks but an approach between two human beings which seems connected with the Biblical injunction "love thy fellow as thyself." There is a feeling of fellowship and a vivid sense that the other human being is as myself. Listening with the heart, and not merely the intellect, means the total involvement of both participants in the dialogue: it allows heart to speak to heart and illuminates the idea of neighbor-love.

One experiences nothing like this with the other so-called existentialist. Though they begin with a protest against the academic and insist, in different ways, on staying with human existence, they soon become involved in curious modes of speech, in a conceptual machinery quite as forbidding as that of avowed academicians, and, alas, in more or less impressive monologues. Questions become scarcely possible: asked in the philosopher's own language, they answer themselves; asked in a less pretentious idiom, they are rarely answered. At best, one is offered an oral footnote to a published text.

A contrast with Heidegger proves especially illuminating. If you associate Buber above all with Judaism, and Heidegger with Hitler, the idea of comparing both will seem far-fetched. Yet there is a striking similarity between Heidegger's later writings and Buber's earlier work. The following sentences from *Ich und Du* (1923) might have been written by Heidegger thirty years later: *"Man sagt, der Mensch erfahre seine Welt. Was heisst das? Der Mensch befährt die Fläche der Dinge und erfährt sie."* (11) The preoccupation with the roots of words which is so startling in Heidegger's interpretations, the attempt to penetrate the too familiar readings which allegedly impede a genuine perception of the text, and the bold departure from ordinary language are all encountered much earlier in Buber's and Rosenzweig's German translation of the Hebrew Bible.

Nevertheless, Buber and Heidegger differ decisively. Buber and Rosenzweig dealt with texts which really had been obscured by familiarity. By recovering some degree of strangeness, they created the conditions under which it became possible to hear again. Heidegger, picking out some all but unknown hymns of the late Hölderlin and a relatively little-known poem by Rilke, could hardly explain his eccentric essays on these poems in parallel fashion. Indeed, the striking charges against his interpretations entered by Walter Muschg in the essay on "Zerschwatzte Dichtung" in his book *Die Zerstörung der deutschen Literatur* must be sustained for the most part. Heidegger does not always use the best available text; he disregards the author's intentions; he shows extraordinarily little feeling for poetry and for the personalities of the poets with whom he deals; and he regularly reads his own ideas into the poems he interprets. In his Rilke interpretation he actually finds the crucial message in a passage he interpolates where the poet left three dots. Quite generally, he concentrates on obscure poems or on fragments which facilitate his highly arbitrary procedure.

Heidegger's interpretations of some of the fragments of the pre-Socratics resemble Buber's translations of the Hebrew Scriptures in the resolve to strip away facile misinterpretations and to penetrate to the roots. But in the first place the pre-Socratics had never been as much obscured by familiarity as the Bible; they had never ceased to be mysterious. Secondly, Buber has not concentrated, like Heidegger, on a few obscure passages, to point up the inadequacy of previous translations and to remind us of their overwhelming difficulty: Buber has succeeded in giving us a really new translation of the Hebrew Bible. Finally, as a stylist Buber is above comparison with Heidegger, whose prose—not to speak of his thin volume of poetry— is gradually becoming more and more indistinguishable from the parodies published here and there.

IV   Buber as a Translator

Buber's principles of translation differ widely from those generally accepted in the English-speaking world. He developed his ideas about translation in the course of his collaboration with Rosenzweig; and in 1936 he published a volume of essays, replies to reviewers, notes, and letters—some written by Rosenzweig, some by Buber, and some jointly: *Die Schrift und ihre Verdeutschung.* This book derives its unique vitality not only from its enthusiastic concern with the Bible, which comes to life for us, too, but also from the rare intensity of Buber, Rosenzweig, and their relationship. The book, though little known, is a major contribution to our understanding of the Bible and to the fine art of translation. And Rosenzweig's ready wit, at its acid best when he rebuts the strictures of reviewers, makes one forget temporarily that he was fatally ill and long unable to speak when he resolved to join with Buber to make a really new translation of the Hebrew Bible: ". . . on some tortuous machinery he would indicate, with unsteady finger, one, two, three letters of each word; and his wife would guess it." (319)

The importance of the Buber-Rosenzweig translation and its principles is twofold. First, it represents an achievement sadly lacking in the English-speaking world: a really new translation of the Bible. Both the Revised Standard Version of the Old Testament and the Bible of the Jewish Publication Society of America represent mere revisions of the King James Bible and do not at all breathe the spirit of the original Hebrew books. Neither do they strip away the familiar veils of an idiom designed "to be read in churches"—an idiom not altogether different, in spite of its magnificence, from the holy tone by which one instantly recognizes preachers on the radio. Of the unaffected immediacy and stark power of much of the Hebrew Scriptures, few English readers have an inkling, nor is there any translation to which one can refer them. In German there are two: that of Buber and Rosenzweig and that of Harry Torczyner (now Tur-Sinai), which was begun at about the same time, but completed rapidly, owing to the collaboration of fourteen scholars, and reprinted in a single volume, revised once more by Torczyner, in 1937.

Secondly, Buber and Rosenzweig revolutionized the art of translation. This art is much more highly developed in Germany than in the English-speaking world. Voss' translation of the *Iliad* and the *Odyssey* into German dactylic hexameters comes to mind immediately as an achievement without parallel in English. Before that, Luther's translation of the Old Testament came incomparably closer to the style and sensibility of the original than the King James Bible. After Voss, there are the incredibly successful Shakespeare translations of August Wilhelm Schlegel, there are Hölderlin's versions of two of Sophocles' plays, Goethe's efforts at translation, Rückert's virtuosity, and, more recently, the translations of Buddhist scriptures by Karl Eugen Neumann and the several volumes of frequently inspired translations by Stefan George and Rilke.

In English there is no comparable tradition of responsibility and faithfulness to the original texts. There is no adequate translation yet of either Homer or the Greek tragedies.[1] The last few years have

[1] This essay was contributed in 1957, before Robert Fitzgerald's version of the *Odyssey* and the Chicago edition of *The Complete Greek Tragedies* appeared. But the translations of the tragedies are uneven, and that of *Antigone* (first published in 1954) exemplifies, like other English versions of this play, the pitfalls of not accepting Buber's methods of translation. Line 332, the beginning of the famous Chorus, is rendered: "Many the wonders but nothing walks stranger than man." Although completely different words are employed to translate the Greek *deina* and *deinoteron*, this version cames closer to Sophocles' meaning than the popular translation that finds nothing "more wonderful than man." But what has been quite generally overlooked is that the same word occurs a third time, only nine lines earlier, where the Chicago translation renders it as "terrible." Quite especially in a line as often quoted as that of the Chorus, a translator should find a word that will serve in all three places; e.g., "uncanny."

seen a rash of new translations of Greek classics; but as soon as they approach poetry they arrogate liberties which seem irresponsible compared to the best German efforts. In English it is considered a truism that every age must make its own translation, and it is considered perfectly all right for the contemporary translator of— never mind what, to recast it in the idiom of T. S. Eliot or W. H. Auden. Would those who hold these principles condone translations of Shakespeare into Rilke's idiom or Brecht's?

Another almost undoubted maxim of most English translators— and especially publishers—is that the translation must read as if the work had been written in idiomatic English. The idiom may be colloquial or it may be that of Eliot, but it must not be unprecedented; it must avoid neologisms, coinages, and anything that is strange or baffling—even if the original is notable for its striking departure from the idiom of its time, even if it abounds in unusual words, even if in places it is profoundly difficult to understand or clearly ambiguous. Where the best German translators would not rest content until they had found a way of preserving every ambiguity of the original, most English-speaking publishers will expect their translators to resolve every ambiguity, to venture an interpretation which will make things easy for the reader, and, by all means, to produce a text which is smoother than the original.

Buber and Rosenzweig went much further than any previous translators of comparable stature in flouting these hallowed maxims and in going to the opposite extreme. "With the pedantry of a genius" (323), Rosenzweig insisted on Buber's faithfulness to the original in the minutest detail; and Buber brought off this feat and created a style which is equally far from ordinary German and from the holy tone of the English Bible.

A few of the Buber-Rosenzweig principles may be enumerated explicitly. The first, which is of the utmost importance, is that every word must always be translated, as far as at all possible, by the same word—not by one word here and another one there, and a third word elsewhere. This strikes many people as strange; some even think that this amounts to renouncing true translation in favor of creating a mere "crib." It does indeed amount to that, or worse, if you simply take the first "equivalent" that comes to mind and then stick by that. Obviously, this principle obliges you to try to find a truly equivalent word, one which reproduces as many of the shades of the original word as possible. If you succeed, you enrich every single sentence containing that word by animating it with all the overtones and ambiguities, allusions, echoes, and suggestions lost by translators who make it easy for themselves.

If you translate an author who has little feeling for his language and a text that lacks style and all but the barest meaning, there is no need for all this trouble. If you deal with the Bible, on the other hand, the price you pay for taking less pains than this is that your text cannot be used as the basis of any serious discussion. Any study of the love of God, or the justice of God, on the basis of the King James Bible, which translates the same word now as "love" and then as "justice," is bound to be irrelevant to the Hebrew Scriptures.

. The second principle, closely related to the first, is that you must go back to the root of the word, seeing that, especially in Hebrew, the same root may connect—quite obviously to the reader of the original—two nouns, or, even more frequently, a noun and a verb or an adjective. And this leads to a search for the, generally sensuous, basic meaning of this root which, once found, revitalizes its derivatives and enriches the meaning of the text with scores of new associations and connections. One becomes aware—and the excitement of the volume of essays on *Die Schrift* is partly due to the fact that we see Buber and Rosenzweig becoming aware—of all sorts of things which had escaped the notice of previous translators.

The third principle—another corollary of the first—is that a rare word must be rendered by a rare word. This is connected with a characteristic device of Biblical narration which Buber and Rosenzweig, varying Wagner's word, leitmotif, called *Leitwort-Stil*. A single illustration may explain it better than any attempt at definition.

After Jacob has taken advantage of Isaac's inability to see and has obtained the blessing intended for his older brother, Isaac says that he came "with guile." Later, when Laban has taken advantage of Jacob's inability to see in the dark and brought to his bed Leah to receive the love intended for her younger sister, Jacob reproaches him: "Why have you beguiled me?" As Buber points out in *Die Schrift und ihre Verdeutschung* (p. 224), this word root "occurs only in one other place in the Pentateuch: Genesis 34.13, where it refers to Jacob's son."

Another similar device, common in the Bible, is the repetition of the same root for purposes of emphasis. And then there is the frequent use of alliteration. Buber and Rosenzweig, trying to re-create the Bible for the ear, too, felt a responsibility to the sound and rhythm which brings to life the Hebrew Scriptures, liberating them from the majestic monotony of the Authorized Version.

As an example, consider a sentence from Genesis 37. Joseph has been sold into slavery by his brothers, and they have dipped his coat in the blood of a goat and brought it to their father, saying: "This have we found: know now whether it be thy son's coat or no." The Authorized Version goes on: "And he knew it, and said, It is my son's coat; an evil beast hath devoured him; Joseph is without doubt rent in pieces." The words "It is" are scrupulously italicized to indicate their absence from the original Hebrew text; and, as often in such cases, their omission constitutes a vast improvement. The words "without doubt" do not disfigure the original either; but the passage in the King James Bible has a sublime rhythm of its own which is eminently suitable "to be read in Churches," as the title page proclaims.

The Revised Standard Version does not aspire to recapture the poetry of the original; it merely tries to correct outright errors—by changing "the coat of many colors" into "a long robe with sleeves," for example—and it tries to bring the King James Bible up to date by changing "knew it" to "recognized it," "coat" to "robe," "hath" to "has," and "rent" to "torn." But "It is" and "without doubt" are both retained. All this is better than the Moffat translation, which shows no feeling for the situation whatever: "Jacob recognized it. 'It is my son's tunic,' he said; 'some evil beast has devoured him. Joseph must have been torn to pieces.' " One feels like adding: "Elementary, my dear Watson."

Buber, in the latest edition of his version (1954), *translates* the text, instead of trying to improve on it. "He saw it and said: My son's coat! an evil beast has devoured him; torn, torn is Joseph!" This may show what it means to let the Hebrew original speak to us.

In the first edition, Buber still had the disturbing "it is"; and Torczyner preceded him in rendering Jacob's outcry faithfully. What matters is that those who know the Bible only from English translations have little idea of its elementary power: they do not know how the text cries out to communicate the immediacy of experiences.

One further example may show how much is at stake. Take a verse from Hosea—14.1 in the Hebrew Bible, 13.16 in the English:

King James

Samaria shall become desolate;
for she hath rebelled against her God:
they shall fall by the sword:
their infants shall be dashed in pieces,
and their women with child
shall be ripped up.

Revised Standard

Samaria shall bear her guilt,
      because she has rebelled against her God;
they shall fall by the sword,
      their little ones shall be dashed in pieces,
      and their pregnant women ripped open.

after Buber

Atone must Samaria the guilt
that it was obstinate to its God,
by the sword they must fall,
their toddlers are smashed.
their pregnant women slashed.

after Torczyner

Damned is Shomron
for defying her God.
They fall by the sword,
smashed are their infants,
their pregnant women slashed.

Buber's translation is not definitive, and he deserves our admiration precisely for his innumerable changes in the second edition. (My English translation of his German version does not do full justice to him.)

The Authorized Version has sacrificed the sensibility of the Hebrew Bible with its unique poetry and power to its own profoundly different conception of rhetoric. In the process the translators produced the most sumptuous monument of English prose. It has its own stylistic unity, even to the extent of boldly assimilating the books of the New Testament, too, to the same style. In the end, Jacob beholding the bloody garment of Joseph, Hosea envisaging the destruction of his people, Luke telling stories, and Paul writing a letter to the Galatians all sound like early-seventeenth-century English divines with a flair for oratory.

The Epistle to the Galatians has at last come to life in the Revised Standard Version, so we can hear Paul; but the Old Testament suffers from a half-hearted compromise between Elizabethan rhetoric and a more modern idiom. The English here does not at all approach the sublime economy of the Hebrew. In many ways, it is much easier to translate into German than it is to translate into English; but precisely the succinctness, the terse, laconic quality of much of the Hebrew text, is more readily rendered in English. In the Hosea verse, the original consists of 11 words—30 syllables in all. The King James Bible requires 33 words, 43 syllables, and the Revised Standard Version one less of each. Buber, in German, uses 23 words, 44 syllables; Torczyner, respectively, 20 and 34; and my English version of Torczyner, 20 words and 26 syllables.

This method of counting may seem pedantic, but it fixes in figures the striking difference between the resplendent rhetoric of the "Authorized" prophet who speaks "to be read in Churches" and the austere immediacy of the Hebrew prophet who cries out over what he sees—even as Jacob in Genesis cries out. In English we hear a great orator who prides himself on his imposing cadences and his rich imagery. In Hebrew we hear a voice without aesthetic ambitions; a voice that cries out because it cannot contain itself, a voice that addresses us and by the sheer force of its uninhibited directness tears the heart out of its sloth.

It is easy to hear the English Bible without listening, to be edified by it without understanding. The Hebrew Bible does not speak in some special holy tone, appropriate on the Sabbath but rather out of place on weekdays—and irrelevant and almost blasphemous after Belsen and Auschwitz. There is nothing unctuous about it. It speaks to us with a singular lack of manner. The primary significance of Buber's translation is that he has let the text speak to us again.

One of the most important things one can teach any student is to read—to read not merely after the fashion of the world but with mind, heart, and soul. Torczyner's Bible has been available in a single volume since 1937, while Buber's Bible was first published book by book, volume by volume, and then, still incomplete, collected in three imposing tomes. Only in the 1950s were these replaced by three pleasant thin-paper volumes, and the fourth and last volume appeared in 1962. So far, Torczyner's edition is far handier; and it is debatable which is preferable. But it was Buber's epic struggle with the text and with the public, first jointly with Franz Rosenzweig, and later alone, that has taught thousands of young men to read—first, the Bible, and then other books, too.

My own translations are unthinkable without Buber and Rosenzweig. When I translated four of Nietzsche's books—*Zarathustra, Twilight of the Idols, Antichrist,* and *Nietzsche contra Wagner*—as well as selections from his other works, his letters, and his notes, for a one-volume edition in The Viking Portable Library, I referred to Buber and Rosenzweig and tried to explain why it was essential to be faithful to Nietzsche's stylistic peculiarities, why his terms must be rendered consistently by the same words, and how full his works are of allusions both to his own previous works and to various classics, above all the Bible. Any failure to capture a pun, however indifferent, in translation, creates the false presumption that the author said in all seriousness what but for the pun he might never have said that way (pp. 3-6, 107-110).

Translating several of Leo Baeck's essays at the same time, I must not let Baeck sound like Nietzsche, or Nietzsche like Baeck, or either of them like myself. Baeck's peculiar and difficult style had to be re-created. And the same was true a few years later when I published *Existentialism from Dostoevsky to Sartre* and translated Nietzsche, Rilke, and Heidegger. Heidegger must not sound like Nietzsche or Rilke, or, worse, Rilke like Heidegger.

Heidegger has the ambition to teach people how to read, but in many younger men he has encouraged a lack of respect for philological correctness, a penchant for an almost comic jargon, and a flair for the obscure—even an outright contempt for the whole plane of correctness. From Buber, on the other hand, one *can* learn how to read.

Heidegger—even more than Jaspers—disregards the context and prefers pliant fragments and notes. Interpretation becomes a device for having his own say, and the text a mere means. In Heidegger's readings there is no Thou.

Buber is always alive to the context—not only the immediate context: when he considers a Biblical sentence, the whole of the Hebrew Bible is the context. He is always struggling to hear the voice of the Thou. And he teaches a deep reverence for the voice that addresses us, and the patient resolve to listen and to let oneself be addressed. Few men could possibly teach anything of equal significance.

V   Buber and Hasidism

Buber's work on the Hasidim, including his collection of their lore, is probably more impressive for those of us who have no first-hand knowledge of Hasidism than it is either for the specialist scholar or for those who know it from their childhood. Here more than anywhere else the question arises to what extent Buber has projected himself into his subject matter: is he allowing Hasidim to speak to us, or is it he himself that is speaking?

Clearly, it is not a case in which the author makes the men about whom he writes mouthpieces of his own ideas. His own ideas were changed in the course of his concern with the Hasidim, and what we hear as we read is what Buber heard. Others, before him, did not hear it just like that. But he himself had not heard it just like that either until he came to listen to the Hasidim. He tells us what he heard, not what he had to say all along.

If you compare Buber's *Die Erzählungen der Chassidim* with Chagall's *Illustrations for the Bible*, you find two different worlds. Chagall's etchings and lithographs mirror a world of fantasy, magic, and ecstasy—closer to the Greek Orthodox church than to the Protestant, almost Puritan, simplicity and moral emphasis of Buber's tales of the Hasidim.

Soon after the death of Rabbi Mosheh of Kobryn, one of his students was asked by the "old Kozker," Rabbi Mendel: "What did your teacher consider most important?" He reflected and gave his answer: "Whatever he was doing at the moment." (647)

Rabbi Mosheh Loeb related: How one should love men I have learned from a peasant. He sat in an inn with some other peasants, drinking. A long time he was silent like the rest, but when his heart was moved by the wine, he spoke to his neighbor: "Tell me: do you love me or don't you?" And he replied: "I love you very much." But the first peasant answered: "You say: I love you; and yet you do not know what hurts me. If you loved me in truth, you would know." The other man could not say a word, and the peasant who had asked the question relapsed into silence, too. But I understood: that is love of men, to sense their wants and to bear their grief. (533)

Stories like these are definitive in their simplicity. That Buber did not make them up is clear. Similar ideas can be found elsewhere in the religious literature of the world. But it is the form that makes these stories, and hundreds like them, definitive. It was Buber who cut these diamonds. The fact that he did not add anything does not mean that he gave us what he found: he achieved perfection by cutting.

Rabbi Bunam once said: "Yes, I can bring all sinners to the point of return—except liars." (751)

There is courage in setting down a dictum like that, letting it stand alone. Surely, Buber was influenced, whether consciously or not, by Nietzsche's aphoristic style. He abandoned the nonfunctional opulence of the Victorian era and dared to end a story at the right point. Such courage is rare, not only among our contemporaries but even in the sacred books of the world. Luke, for example, generally makes up stories to frame sayings which in Matthew lack any such setting.

Consider the story of the anointing at Bethany which is found in all four Gospels. The four evangelists understand it very differently, and David Daube has discussed their diverse treatments in a very illuminating section of his book on *The New Testament and Rabbinic Judaism.*

> Both Mark and John take care to point out that the burial rite of anointing was performed. For Mark, it was performed at Bethany—by virtue of a fiction—and nothing was done after Jesus' death. For John, Jesus' body was actually anointed after his death, and the action at Bethany is not represented as performance of the rite. (314)

Daube shows how Matthew follows Mark and is demonstrably much more comfortable with this solution than Mark was. But what concerns me here is a dictum for which Luke finds a place in this story—a dictum which Daube does not discuss: ". . . her sins, which are many, are forgiven, for she loved much." (7.47)

These striking words are found nowhere else in the New Testament. If we assume that Jesus actually spoke them on this occasion, that amounts to a serious indictment of the other three evangelists who have put into their master's mouth so many unlovely sayings while suppressing words like these. If we assume that Luke invented these words or—as is much more likely—that they formed part of an oral tradition but lacked any context, and that he worked these words into the present story, then we must go on to ask how effectively he did this. Unless, in other words, we assume that he told the story as it actually happened while the other three distorted the story seriously, we must admit that Luke's story represents his own particular way of blending and shaping various traditions. Among these is a gem: what does he do with it?

Looked at critically in this perspective, Luke's story will satisfy few readers. The immediately preceding reproof which is not found in the other three Gospels and the immediately following words— "but he who is forgiven little, loves little"—greatly weaken the central dictum. And the two following verses detract still further from the weight of the word of love.

This approach may seem excessively subjective; but it is a historic fact that the words "her sins, which are many, are forgiven, for she loved much," and a few others like them, have long shaken off the shackles of their context and have gone far toward creating an image of Jesus and Christianity which is quite at variance with the full text of each of the four Gospels. In *Die Erzählungen der Chassidim* Buber presents gem upon gem without mounting each in a setting of inferior quality. Buber's stories cannot be improved by cutting. That is more than one can say of the art of any of the four evangelists.

The obvious objection to Buber is that he gives us too glowing a picture of Hasidism. The opponents of the movement, the Mitnaggdim, had some reasons on their side: miracles and magic, superstitions and authoritarianism were present in Hasidism from the start. As a historian, Buber is by no means above criticism.

The reply to such criticisms is implicit in the comparison with the Gospels, which, no doubt, will strike some readers as blasphemous. What saves Buber's work is its perfection. He has given us one of the great religious books of all time, a work that invites comparison with the great Scriptures of mankind. This estimate must seem fantastic to those who have not read *The Tales of the Hasidim*. But if it should be justified, then the criticism that Buber is not an impartial historian can be accepted cheerfully without being considered very damning.

We can read the Book of Genesis and the discourses of the Buddha as reports of "how it actually happened," to cite Ranke's words, or we can read them as religious literature. The question of historical accuracy is always worth raising, and a detailed answer is both interesting and important. But the rank of these works does not depend on their positivistic accuracy but on their profundity. And that is true also of *The Tales of the Hasidim*.

Buber's collection resembles the great religious Scriptures in drawing on a living religious tradition, in selecting, in giving form. Sacred Scriptures are not so much written as they grow. Buber's collection has grown out of his own long dialogue with a tradition, and it loses none of its initial impressiveness after one has lived with it for a generation. Here the adolescent can find voices that speak to him, answer him, and help him to form his notions of the meaning of religion. A growing skepticism does not mute these voices or destroy this meaning. Here is religion that stands up to philosophic questions as the sophisticated discourses of theologians don't.

There are whole books on prayer which make less sense than these few lines:

> Rabbi Shneur Zalman once asked his son: "With what do you pray?" The son understood the meaning of the question: on what he concentrated, on what he based his prayer. He replied: "The verse: May every height bow down before thee." Then he asked his father: "And with what do you pray?" He said: "With the floor and with the bench." (418)
>
> The Kozker shouted at some of his Hasidim: "What is this chatter about praying seriously? What do they mean: praying seriously?" They did not understand him. So he said: "Is there anything that one should do without seriousness?" (791)

One may safely agree with Hermann Hesse that Buber, "like no other living author, has enriched world literature with a genuine treasure" (*Briefe*, January 1950). Although Hesse has won the Nobel Prize, his great novels are hardly known in the English-speaking world—partly for the same reasons which account for the comparative neglect of Buber's great collection of Hasidic lore: the lack of translations which equal the perfection of the originals and above all the present lack in the English-speaking world of any widespread sense for the kind of religion which has found expression in Buber's stories or in Hesse's *Siddhartha*.

In the United States, *intense* religion tends to be either revivalist or theological. The pseudo-religion of the bestsellers and the most popular magazines, which finds its place between stories of wise animals and miracle drugs, reports on the latest gadgets and cosmetics, and whatever is of human interest and wholesome for the family, need not detain us here. Serious religion that produces crisis in men's lives, converts men, and profoundly influences them is best represented in America by Reinhold Niebuhr and by Billy Graham: Graham is the poor man's Niebuhr and speaks to the hearts of those who cannot afford ten-dollar words. Niebuhr, in spite of his years as a preacher in Detroit, speaks mainly to the intellectuals and offers them a Christian version of Marx, Nietzsche, Freud, and all the latest intellectual developments.

There is no revivalism and no theology in Buber's Hasidic lore. And for the still small voice of this religion which speaks to the emotions without rhetoric and to the mind without any imposing jargon, there are few ears in the English-speaking world.

That there will ever be a very large audience to hear Buber's Hasidim with an open heart is unlikely; but, before long, these stories will, no doubt, become part of the repertoire of educated people who have now begun to read selections from the Buddha's speeches and the Upanishads, and a free version of the Bhagavadgita, in huge popular editions. And these stories will surely be remembered widely when the theologians of our time have gone the way of Harnack and Schleiermacher, not to mention lesser names that have long been forgotten by all but specialists.

VI   I and Thou

In the United States, Buber is best known for a small book that has profoundly influenced Protestant theology. In German it was *Ich und Du*, and one could read quite far without being aware that Buber was concerned with religion: indeed, the point of the book was partly to break down the division between the everyday world and religion. Eventually, God is found *in* the everyday world, in the *Du*, in a primary relation paralleled in the relation *Between Man and Man*, to cite the English title of the sequel.

Buber himself considers the English title *I and Thou* inevitable.

Partly, this is surely due to the fact that men with a German back-ground feel more at home with "thou" and "thee" and "thy" than Americans. By now the Revised Standard Version has all but purged the Bible of these words. It is also relevant that the child says "you" and not "thou." But what matters here is not a positive suggestion about a point of translation; rather, two serious pitfalls due to the translation *I and Thou*.

The first is that the phrase suggests the holy tone which just Buber has done so much to eliminate from religion. We are imme-diately put out on our guard.

The second pitfall is exactly paralleled by the reception in the English-speaking world of a book that appeared in the same year, 1923: *Das Ich und das Es* by Sigmund Freud. Surely, this should have been translated as *The I and the It*; but the translator chose *The Ego and the Id*. And *das Über-ich* became the super-ego. A jargon developed and obscured the work of Freud. And a jargon developed and obscured the thought of Buber.

People began to talk of "the I-Thou relationship" and "the I-Thou" as they talk of "original sin" and the "natural man"—as if Buber's achievement had not been in part that he had managed to bring religion to life without the dubious benefit of an abstract terminology about whose meaning one is not completely sure. Buber had taken his stand not on concepts like "revelation" and "redemption" or even "God" but had started from an elementary experience about which no skeptic need have any qualms.

Most important, Buber had not just talked *about* it. Even as Freud had developed the major body of his work with its profound originality without the benefit of any Id or Ego, and then, more or less in retrospect, inquired whether one could summarize and systematize his results in terms of a few simple vivid concepts with which his findings neither stand nor fall, so Buber, midway in his work on the Hasidim, tried to state a central theme in *Ich und Du*. What he meant is not only developed in his later writings on the dialogical principle, but also in his work on the Hasidim and his translation of the Hebrew Bible.

How Buber has taught us to read can be summarized by saying that he impressed on us that the text must not be treated as a mere It; the text must become a Thou. But any jargon tends to falsify. We must learn to listen and let the text speak to us, instead of resting content with manipulating it or carving it up as the Higher Critics did.

If one approaches *I and Thou* as a philosophic essay, trying to reconstruct an argument and testing that, it is not hard to criticize the book. But if instead of examining the book as an object, an It, we open our hearts to it to hear what it has to say to us, we are confronted with a crucial question: if God is to mean something to us, can it be anything but what Buber suggests in this little book, namely *das ewige Du* (the eternal Thou)? All superstitions *about* God, all talk about him, all theology is sacrificed to the voice that speaks to us, the *Du* to which some cry out "when," as Goethe says, "man in his agony grows mute." And not only in agony.

Any formulation is disturbing; but has there ever been a better one than "the eternal Thou" (or You)? How meaningless compared to it are the "being-itself" and even "the ground of being" of Paul Tillich! The God of Abraham, Isaac, and Israel was not "being-itself"; nor was it "the ground of being" that told Abraham to leave his father's house or that commanded men "You shall be holy; for I, the Lord your God am holy" or to whom the Psalmist and, according to two of the evangelists, Jesus, cried out, "My God, my God, why have you forsaken me?" If we do not take such a phrase as "the eternal Thou" for a concept, but rather understand what it tries to say plainly, it is probably the most illuminating suggestion about the meaning of "God" ever ventured.

VII   Summary

Buber's current success in the United States is deceptive. One is conscious of his stature, one pays tribute to him, but few have ears for what Buber is saying. One attributes to him an anthropology and a theology, an ethic and epistemology, seeks "principles" of Biblical faith from him, and is a little irritated by the lack of systematic content, of clearly formulated principles, and by his excessively personal interpretations.

The Jews are proud of him and do not give full vent to their irritation, and the Christians, almost hungry for a venerable Jewish figure to whom they can show their respect, their freedom from prejudice, and their horror of the wrongs done to his people, also suppress their exasperation. Moreover, it is not fashionable to criticize religious figures. But Buber's judgments about New Testament questions are annoying to most Jews and Christians: some Jews find him not Jewish enough, while many young Jewish intellectuals are sufficiently under the influence of modern Protestant theology to question him from a curiously Christian point of view.

Buber stands in an essentially Jewish tradition, and his religion, which is opposed alike to rationalism, mysticism, and theology, is clearly continuous with central elements in the thought of the prophets, of Akiba and Maimonides, of the Hasidim, Hermann Cohen, and Leo Baeck. He speaks for himself, but he is by no means a marginal phenomenon of Judaism.

Even during World War I, at a time when baptism was no longer rare among German Jews and assimilation accepted as a goal by most of the unbaptized, too, Buber published a periodical he called *Der Jude.* Who has the right to say of him today, as some Protestants do, that he is really not a Jew? On the other hand, if some Christians consider him "the" representative spokesman for Judaism, one can only say that his present lack of rivals is not his fault.

Any such overall estimate of a man's significance is necessarily controversial. Others are bound to see him differently—but the present attempt may help them to arrive at their own estimate. Alas, Buber may well see himself differently in many ways. If so, it may be of some interest to readers of this volume to find out not only how Buber answers specific criticisms by the other contributors to this volume but also where precisely he is displeased with this attempt at an integrated picture. Corrections of specific errors are always worthwhile—but it would also be interesting to have Buber's response to the way in which I have placed accents, light, and shade.*

Buber tells of the Hasid who, asked what impressed him most about the Zaddik, said: how he tied his shoes. One gathers that this Zaddik, like another one I have mentioned, considered most important whatever he happened to be doing. Another Hasid might have been most impressed with the way the Zaddik did some other little or big thing.

What impresses me most about Buber is the way he answers questions, the way he goes about translating the Bible, the way he has opened up to us the world of the Hasidim, fashioning one of the great religious books of all time out of their lore, and the pervasive concern not with theories but with the living *Du.*

* As it turned out, Buber liked this essay especially.

Little is gained by calling Buber an existentialist and by lumping him with men with whom he disagrees as much as he does with Kierkegaard, Jaspers, Heidegger, and Sartre. But if we find the heart of existentialism in the protest against systems, concepts, and abstractions, coupled with a resolve to remain faithful to concrete experience and above all to the challenge of human existence—should we not find in that case that Kierkegaard and Jaspers, Heidegger and Sartre had all betrayed their own central resolve? That they had all become enmeshed in sticky webs of dialectic that impede communication? that the high abstractness of their idiom and their strange addiction to outlandish concepts far surpassed the same faults in Descartes or Plato? that not one of them was able any more to listen to the challenge of another human reality as it has found expression in a text? and that their writings have, without exception, become monologues?

One might well conclude that in reality there is only one existentialist, and he is no existentialist but Martin Buber.

5

BUBER'S
*I AND THOU**

I

Man's world is manifold, and his attitudes are manifold. What is manifold is often frightening because it is not neat and simple. Men prefer to forget how many possibilities are open to them.

They like to be told that there are two worlds and two ways. This is comforting because it is so tidy. Almost always one way turns out to be common and the other one is celebrated as superior.

Those who tell of two ways and praise one are recognized as prophets or great teachers. They save men from confusion and hard choices. They offer a single choice that is easy to make because those who do not take the path that is commended to them live a wretched life.

To walk far on this path may be difficult, but the choice is easy, and to hear the celebration of this path is pleasant. Wisdom offers simple schemes, but truth is not so simple.

Not all simplicity is wise. But a wealth of possibilities breeds dread. Hence those who speak of many possibilities speak to the few and are of help to even fewer. The wise offer only two ways, of which one is good, and thus help many.

Mundus vult decipi: the world wants to be deceived. The truth is too complex and frightening; the taste for the truth is an acquired taste that few acquire.

Not all deceptions are palatable. Untruths are too easy to come by, too quickly exploded, too cheap and ephemeral to give lasting comfort. *Mundus vult decipi;* but there is a hierarchy of deceptions.

Near the bottom of the ladder is journalism: a steady stream of

---

* This essay was written to introduce my translation of *I and Thou* (1970), and its original title was "I and You: A Prologue." See the Introduction above.

irresponsible distortions that most people find refreshing although on the morning after, or at least within a week, it will be stale and flat.

On a higher level we find fictions that men eagerly believe, regardless of the evidence, because they gratify some wish.

Near the top of the ladder we encounter curious mixtures of untruth and truth that exert a lasting fascination on the intellectual community.

What cannot, on the face of it, be wholly true, although it is plain that there is some truth in it, evokes more discussion and dispute, divergent exegeses and attempts at emendations than what has been stated very carefully, without exaggeration or onesidedness. The Book of Proverbs is boring compared to the Sermon on the Mount.

The good way must be clearly good but not wholly clear. If it is quite clear, it is too easy to reject.

What is wanted is an oversimplification, a reduction of a multitude of possibilities to only two. But if the recommended path were utterly devoid of mystery, it would cease to fascinate men. Since it clearly should be chosen, nothing would remain but to proceed on it. There would be nothing left to discuss and interpret, to lecture and write about, to admire and merely think about.

The world exacts a price for calling teachers wise: it keeps discussing the paths they recommend, but few men follow them. The wise give men endless opportunities to discuss what is good.

Men's attitudes are manifold. Some live in a strange world bounded by a path from which countless ways lead inside. If there were road signs, all of them might bear the same inscription: I-I.

Those who dwell inside have no consuming interest. They are not devoted to possessions, even if they prize some; not to people, even if they like some; not to any project, even if they have some.

Things are something that they speak of; persons have the great advantage that one cannot only talk *of* them but also *to*, or rather *at* them; but the lord of every sentence is no man but I. Projects can be entertained without complete devotion, spoken of, and put on like a suit or dress before a mirror. When you speak to men of this type, they quite often do not hear you, and they never hear you as another I.

You are not an object for men like this, not a thing to be used or experienced, nor an object of interest or fascination. The point is not at all that you are found interesting or fascinating instead of being seen as a fellow I. The shock is rather that you are not found interesting or fascinating at all: you are not recognized as an object any more than as a subject. You are acepted, if at all, as one to be spoken at and spoken of; but when you are spoken of, the lord of every story will be I.

Men's attitudes are manifold. Some men take a keen interest in certain objects and in other men and actually think more about them than they think of themselves. They do not so much say I or think I as they do I.

They "take" an interest, they do not give of themselves. They may manipulate or merely study, and unlike men of the I-I type they may be good scholars; but they lack devotion.

This I-It tendency is so familiar that little need be said about it, except that it is a tendency that rarely consumes a man's whole life. Those who see a large part of humanity—their enemies, of course— as men of this type, have succumbed to demonology.

This is merely one of the varieties of man's experience and much more widespread in all ages as a tendency and much rarer as a pure type in our own time than the Manichaeans fancy.

There are men who hardly have an I at all. Nor are all of them of one kind.

Some inhabit worlds in which objects loom large. They are not merely interested in some thing or subject, but the object of their interest dominates their lives. They are apt to be great scholars of extraordinarily erudition, with no time for themselves, with no time to have a self.

They study without experiencing: they have no time for experience, which would smack of subjectivity if not frivolity. They are objective and immensely serious. They have no time for humor.

They study without any thought of use. What they study is an end in itself for them. They are devoted to their subject, and the notion of using it is a blasphemy and sacrilege that is not likely to occur to them.

For all that, their "subject" is no subject in its own right, like a person. It has no subjectivity. It does not speak to them. It is a subject one has chosen to study—one of the subjects that one may legitimately choose, and there may be others working on the same subject, possibly on a slightly different aspect of it, and one respects them insofar as they, too, have no selves and are objective.

Here we have a community of solid scholars—so solid that there is no room at the center for any core. Theirs is the world of It-It.

There are other ways of having no I. There are men who never speak a sentence of which I is lord, but nobody could call them objective. At the center of their world is We.

The contents of this We can vary greatly. But this is an orientation in which I does not exist, and You and It and He and She are only shadows.

One type of this sort could be called We-We. Theirs is a sheltered, childish world in which no individuality has yet emerged.

Another perennial attitude is summed up in the words Us-Them. Here the world is divided in two: the children of light and the children of darkness, the sheep and the goats, the elect and the damned.

Every social problem can be analyzed without much study: all one has to look for are the sheep and goats.

There is room for anger and contempt and boundless hope; for the sheep are bound to triumph.

Should a goat have the presumption to address a sheep, the sheep often do not hear it, and they never hear it as another I. For the goat is one of Them, not one of Us.

Righteousness, intelligence, integrity, humanity, and victory are the prerogatives of Us, while wickedness, stupidity, hypocrisy, brutality, and ultimate defeat belong to Them.

Those who have managed to cut through the terrible complexities of life and offer such a scheme as this have been hailed as prophets in all ages.

In these five attitudes there is no You: I-I, I-It, It-It, We-We, and Us-Them. There are many ways of living in a world without You.

There are also many worlds with the two poles I-You.

I-You sounds unfamiliar. What we are accustomed to is I-Thou. But man's attitudes are manifold, and Thou and You are not the same. Nor is Thou very similar to the German *Du*.

German lovers say *Du* to one another, and so do friends. *Du* is spontaneous and unpretentious, remote from formality, pomp, and dignity.

What lovers or friends say Thou to one another? Thou is scarcely ever said spontaneously.

Thou immediately brings to mind God; *Du* does not. And the God of whom it makes us think is not the God to whom one might cry out in gratitude, despair, or agony, not the God to whom one complains or prays spontaneously: it is the God of the pulpits, the God of the holy tone.

When men pray spontaneously or speak directly to God, without any mediator, without any intervention of formulas, when they speak as their heart tells them to speak instead of repeating what is printed, do they say Thou? How many know the verb forms Thou commands?

The world of Thou has many mansions. Thou is a preachers' word but also dear to anticlerical romantic poets. Thou is found in Shakespeare and at home in the English Bible, although recent versions of the Scriptures have tended to dispense with it. Thou can mean many things, but it has no place whatever in the language of direct, nonliterary, spontaneous human relationships.

If one could liberate I-Thou from affectation, the price for that would still involve reducing it to a mere formula, to jargon. But suppose a man wrote a book about direct relationships and tried to get away from the formulas of theologians and philosophers: a theologian would translate it and turn *Ich und Du* into *I and Thou.*

II

Men love jargon. It is so palpable, tangible, visible, audible; it makes so obvious what one has learned; it satisfies the craving for results. It is impressive for the uninitiated. It makes one feel that one belongs. Jargon divides men into Us and Them.

Two books appeared during the same year. One was called *Ich und Du,* the others *Das Ich und das Es.* Rarely have two books of such importance had such simple names.

Both books proposed three central concepts: the former also *Es,* the latter also *Über-ich.* But neither book was trinitarian in any profound sense. Both were dualistic. The wise emphasize two principles.

Freud's *Ich* was the conscious part of the soul, his *Es* the unconscious part, and his *Über-ich* a third part which he also called the *Ich-Ideal* or the conscience. But it was part of his central concern at that time to go "Beyond the Pleasure Principle" and introduce a second basic drive.

Buber could also have called his book *Das Ich und das Es*. He could also have spoken of an *Über-ich*, or perhaps an *Über-du*. But he was not speaking of parts of the soul. He singled out two relationships: that in which I recognize It as an object, especially of experience and use, and that in which I respond with my whole being to You. And the last part of his book dealt with the divine You.

Men love jargon. In English one book became *I and Thou* and the other *The Ego and the Id*. Thus even people who had not read these books could speak of ego, id, and superego, of the I-Thou and the I-It.

Actually, Freud had written his most epoch-making books before *Das Ich und das Es*, without using these terms, and his system did not depend on these words. That never deterred those who loved to speak and write about the ego and the id.

Buber wrote many later works in which he did not harp on *Ich* and *Du*. He was not a man of formulas but one who tried to meet each person, each situation, and each subject in its own way. That never deterred those who loved to speak and write about "the I-It" and "the I-Thou."

There are many modes of I-You.

Kant told men always to treat humanity, in our person as well as that of others, as an end also and never only as a means. This is one way of setting off I-You from I-It. And when he is correctly quoted and the "also" and the "only" are not omitted, as they all too often are, one may well marvel at his moral wisdom.

Innumerable are the ways in which I treat You as a means. I ask your help, I ask for information, I may buy from you or buy what you have made, and you sometimes dispel my loneliness.

Nor do I count the ways in which You treat me as a means. You ask my help, you ask me questions, you may buy what I have written, and at times I ease your loneliness.

Even when you treat me *only* as a means I do not always mind. A genuine encounter can be quite exhausting, even when it is exhilarating, and I do not always want to give myself.

Even when you treat me *only* as a means because you want some information, I may feel delighted that I have the answer and can help.

But man's attitudes are manifold, and there are many ways of treating others as ends *also*. There are many modes of I-You.

You may be polite when asking; you may show respect, affection, admiration, or one of the countless attitudes that men call love.

Or you may not ask but seek without the benefit of words. Or you may speak but not ask, possibly responding to my wordless question. We may do something together. You may write to me. You may think of writing to me. And there are other ways. There are many modes of I-You.

The total encounter in which You is spoken with one's whole being is but one mode of I-You. And it is misleading if we assimilate all the other modes of I-You to I-It.

Philosophers tend to reduce the manifold to the twofold. Some of the greatest taught that there were two worlds. Why has hardly anyone proclaimed many worlds?

We have heard of the two ways of opinion and knowledge, the two realms of appearance and reality, this world and the other, matter and mind, phenomena and noumena, representation and will, nature and spirit, means and end, It and You.

Side by side with technical philosophy similar games are played. Naïve and sentimental poets have been contrasted in a lengthy and immensely influential essay that has left its mark on subsequent discussions of the classical and the romantic. Later on the Apollinian and the Dionysian emerged as a variant. And the It and You.

The straight philosophers tend to celebrate one of the two worlds and depreciate the other. The literary tradition is less Manichaean. Friedrich Schiller tried to comprehend both kinds of poetry without disparaging either naïve or sentimental tendencies, and Nietzsche followed his example in his early contrast of the two Greek gods.

Ich und Du stands somewhere between the literary and philosophical traditions. Buber's "It" owes much to matter and appearance, to phenomena and representation, nature and means. Buber's "You" is the heir of mind, reality, spirit, and will, and his I-You sometimes has an air of Dionysian ecstasy. Even if I-It is not disparaged, nobody can fail to notice that I-You is celebrated.

The year before *Ich und Du* appeared, Leo Baeck published a major essay on *Romantische Religion* that was meant to be the first part of a larger work on "Classical and Romantic Religion." Eventually, it became the capstone of his *Judaism and Christianity*.

The theme: "We encounter two forms above all, classical and romantic religiousness, classical and romantic religion . . . Judaism and Christianity."

Baeck's apologetics is inspiring, his polemic is inspired. But after a hundred pages one is bound to ask oneself if his procedure is not unsound.

Even where the two notions played off against each other in endless variations are not black and white, one is led to wonder eventually if the play impulse has not got out of hand, if repetition has not replaced argument, and virtuosity demonstration.

Certainly, Buber's delight in language gets between him and his readers. There might as well be a screen between them on which one watches the antics of his words instead of listening to him. The words do tricks, the performance is brilliant, but much of it is very difficult to follow.

Obscurity is fascinating. One tries to puzzle out details, is stumped, and becomes increasingly concerned with meaning—unless one feels put off and gives up altogether.

Those who persevere and take the author seriously are led to ask about what he could possibly have meant, but rarely seem to wonder or discuss whether what he says is true.

Instead of asking how things are in fact, and how one could possibly find out, one wonders mostly whether one has got the author's point; and if one thinks one has, one may even feel superior to those who have not.

Speaking in Kierkegaard's terms, one might say that Buber makes it all too easy for his readers to avoid his ethical challenge by adopting an aesthetic orientation. Precisely the same might be said of Kierkegaard himself.

III

Success is no proof of virtue. In the case of a book, quick acclaim is presumptive evidence of a lack of substance and originality.

Most books are stillborn. As the birthrate rises steeply, infant mortality soars. Most books die unnoticed; fewer live for a year or two.

Those that make much noise when they see the light of day generally die in childhood. Few books live as long as fifty years. For those that do, the prognosis is good: they are likely to live much longer than their authors.

In the case of a book, longevity is presumptive evidence of virtue, although survival usually also owes a good deal to a book's vices. A lack of clarity is almost indispensable.

Books that survive their authors do not weather time like rocks. They are reborn without having quite died and have several overlapping lives. Some fall asleep in one country, come to life in another, and then wake up again.

Ich und Du was fourteen years old when it began a new life in the English-speaking world as *I and Thou*, in 1937. The next year the author left Germany for Jerusalem, and the German book seemed to be headed for death at fifteen.

In his new home Buber did not meet with the acclaim that he had won from German Jewry in the years of persecution. No longer could he write in German. He had to try his hand at Hebrew. And people joked that he did not yet know Hebrew well enough to write as obscurely as he had written in German.

I and Thou survived, mainly among Protestant theologians. That a book by a man who felt so strongly about being a Jew should have been acclaimed primarily by Protestants has struck many people as ironical. What is much more remarkable is that a sharp attack on all talk about God and all pretensions to knowledge about God—a sustained attempt to rescue the religious dimension of life from the theologians—should have been received so well by theologians. They generously acclaimed Buber as a Jewish theologian, and went right on doing what they had done. Only now their discourse was enriched with frequent references to the I-Thou and the I-It.

After World War II the book gained a far wider hearing, especially in Germany, where it was rediscovered, and in the United States. After the holocaust a widespread need was felt to love and admire a representative Jew. The competition was not keen. There was no dearth of great writers and scientists who were Jews, but what was wanted was a representative and teacher of the Jewish tradition—a contemporary heir, if that were possible, of the Hebrew prophets.

In the twentieth century neither Eastern European Jewry nor American Jewry had produced such figures, while the German Jews, whom both of these far larger communities tended to regard with some resentment, could point to several. Franz Rosenzweig, with whom Buber had undertaken a new German translation of the Hebrew Bible, had died in 1929. But even after World War II there were still Baeck and Buber.

Baeck, too, gained another hearing now. But when the war ended he was in his seventies and, having spent the last part of the war in Theresienstadt, somewhat frail. Moreover, his manner had always been exceedingly refined, and he was a rabbi. He was an immensely impressive person, and the rabbinical students who sat at his feet at Hebrew Union College, where he came to teach one semester a year, will never forget him any more than those who heard him lecture in Frankfurt a few months before his death—tall, stooped, and undaunted; over eighty; speaking without notes, as brilliantly as in his prime. Here was greatness, but it belonged to a past period of history, almost to a vanished civilization. He spoke of rebirth on that occasion and, back from Theresienstadt, youthful in old age, symbolized it. But those who learned from him did not feel that he was one of them.

Martin Buber's personal appearances in Germany and the United States were different. He was very small, not at all likely to be noticed from far away; and his bearing did not create a sense of distance. Nor was he a brilliant lecturer—at least not in this last phase. Unlike Baeck, whose eyesight was so poor that he had trained himself to get along without notes, Buber often read long papers that most of the audience could not follow. But as soon as the lecture was over and the questions started, he stood revealed as the exceptional man he was. If there was any ostentation now, it was in his insistence on establishing genuine dialogue. What was unforgettable was the attempt to triumph over distance; to bridge differences in age, cultural background, and language; to listen and communicate. And those who knew him tried to keep him from lecturing in the first place and have discussion from the start. But these discussions were not ordinary. On such occasions *I and You* became incarnate.

Never was the popularity of Buber's little masterpiece as great as it became after his death. This posthumous triumph probably owed little to his personality. It was part of a larger wave.

It took Kant and Hegel a few decades to arrive in the United States. It took the German 1920's forty years.

Kafka arrived sooner. But he was almost unknown in Germany when he died in 1924; he did not belong to the German twenties as much as did Hesse and Buber, Heidegger and Brecht.

Buber's immense posthumous popularity is not confined to him. Those who read *I and Thou* also read Hesse's *Steppenwolf* and talk of Heidegger, usually without having read him, just as students did in Germany in the twenties. This goes with a sexual revolution and an interest in drugs, a vast enthusiasm for Dostoevsky, Indian philosophy, and Buddhism. The whole syndrome has come to life again along with interest in Bertolt Brecht, whose anti-sentimental and anti-romantic protests have to be seen against the background of a time that acclaimed Hesse and Buber. His toughness has some of the swagger of adolescent rebellion. But their neo-romanticism also had, and still has, a particular appeal for adolescents. A book's survival usually owes not a little to its vices.

Our first loves leave their mark upon us. In the crucial years of adolescence I loved Hesse's novels and experienced Buddhism and Indian wisdom as a great temptation to detachment. Buber taught me that mysticism need not lead outside the world. Or if mysticism does, by definition, so much the worse for it.

It was from Buber's other writings that I learned what could also be found in *I and Thou:* the central commandment to make the secular sacred.

Ich und Du I did not read in my teens, and later the style of this little book put me off as much as its dualism. Even more than Nietzsche's *Zarathustra*, it is overwritten. We are far from the clear, crisp air of a sunny autumn morning in the mountains and the bracing wit of Nietzsche's later prose. We seem even further from the simplicity of Kafka's style, schooled on the Book of Genesis.

Yet few books of our century equal the economy of Buber's *Tales of the Hasidim*. There he reached perfection. Among his own writings, *The Way of Man According to the Teachings of Hasidism* is a work of comparable beauty that distils Buber's own teaching in less than twenty pages.[1] It is also Buber's best-translated work, but he neither recalled nor was able to find out who had translated it.

[1] It is reprinted, uncut, in my *Religion from Tolstoy to Camus.*

The style of *Ich und Du* is anything but sparse and unpretentious, lean or economical. It represents a late flowering of romanticism and tends to blur all contours in the twilight of suggestive but extremely unclear language. Most of Buber's German readers would be quite incapable of saying what any number of passages probably mean.

The obscurity of the book does not seem objectionable to them: it seems palpable proof of profundity. Sloth meets with awe in the refusal to unravel mysteries.

And the Hasidic tradition meets with the conventions of German philosophy in endowing teachers with an aura of authority. In this ambience it is not for the student to challenge or to examine critically. One tries to absorb what one can and hopes to understand more in the future.

This world may be gone, but modern art and poetry, plays and films have predisposed Buber's readers once again not to ask what every detail means. One has come to suspect reasons and analysis and feels ready for Zen, for Indian wisdom, and for Buber's book. It is not even impossible that in places Buber himself was not sure of the exact meaning of his text. One of the last things he wrote was a long reply to twenty-nine mostly friendly critics who had collaborated on a volume on his work that appeared first in German (*Martin Buber*, 1963) and then also in English (*The Philosophy of Martin Buber*, 1967). His response, printed at the end of the volume, also contains some discussion of *Ich und Du;* and here Buber says: "At that time I wrote what I wrote under the spell of an irresistible enthusiasm. And the inspirations of such enthusiasm one may not change any more, not even for the sake of exactness. For one can only estimate what one would gain, but not what would be lost."

Thus Buber endowed his own text with authority and implied that he himself could not tell its full meaning. Any attempt to clarify dark passages might eliminate pertinent associations. It should be clear where that leaves the translator!

IV

It may be doubted whether the style of the book really communicates the force of inspiration. In places the aesthetic surface of the book looks like mere *Schöngeisterei;* the style seems mannered, the plays on words at best clever, and those who hate affectation may even wonder whether this virtuosity hides a lack of content. In fact, it hides a profoundly anti-romantic message.

The content may *appear* to be as romantic as the form. Of the many possible relationships in which I encounter You as another I, Buber singles out a state that is almost ecstatic. As long as we focus on this choice, we are almost bound to see him as a romantic and to miss his import.

Buber's most significant ideas are not tied to his extraordinary language. Nor do they depend on any jargon. On the contrary, they cry out to be liberated from all jargon.

The sacred is here and now. The only God worth keeping is a God that cannot be kept. The only God worth talking about is a God that cannot be talked about. God is no object of discourse, knowledge, or even experience. He cannot be spoken of, but he can be spoken to; he cannot be seen, but he can be listened to. The only possible relationship with God is to address him and to be addressed by him, here and now—or, as Buber puts it, in the present. For him the Hebrew name of God, the tetragrammaton (YHVH), means HE IS PRESENT. *Er ist da* might be translated: He is there; but in this context it would be more nearly right to say: He is here.

Where? After Auschwitz and Nagasaki, where? We look around and do not see him. But he is not to be seen. Never. Those who have claimed to see him did not see him.

Does he really address us? Even if we wanted to, desperately, could we listen to him? Does he speak to us?

On the first page of the original edition of the book one was confronted by only two lines:

> *So hab ich endlich von dir erharrt:*
> *In allen Elementen Gottes Gegenwart.*

"Thus I have finally obtained from you by waiting / God's presence in all elements." No source was indicated, but this epigraph came from Goethe's *West-östlicher Divan*. It brings to mind Goethe's contemporary, William Blake:

> To see a World in a Grain of Sand
> And a Heaven in a Wild Flower
> Hold Infinity in the palm of your hand
> And Eternity in an Hour.

But in Buber's book the emphasis actually does not fall on all elements; and that is surely one reason why he omitted the epigraph in 1957. Asked why he had deleted it, he said: Because it could be misunderstood. And in the later editions of some early works he also changed some phrases that had a pantheistic ring. But in 1923, when *Ich und Du* appeared with the epigraph from Goethe, Buber also published a collected edition of some earlier "Lectures on Judaism" (*Reden über das Judentum*), adding a Foreword that makes clear his desire even at that time to distinguish his own position from any pantheism.

We must ask to whom the "you" (*dir*) in the epigraph had been meant to refer. In Goethe's *Divan* the lines occur in the short dialogue that concludes "The Innkeeper's Book" (*Das Schenkenbuch*), and the innkeeper is addressing the poet. This dialogue, incidentally, was added only after the original edition. But of whom could Buber have been thinking? *Ich und Du* bore no dedication; but the sequel, *Zwiesprache* (1932: Dialogue) was dedicated to Buber's wife, Paula, with a four-line verse:

An P.

Der Abgrund und das Weltenlicht,
Zeitnot und Ewigkeitsbegier,
Vision, Ereignis und Gedicht:
Zwiesprache wars und ists mit dir.

"For P. The abyss and the light of the world, / Time's need and the craving for eternity, / Vision, event, and poetry: / Was and is dialogue with you."

Thus the epigraph in *Ich und Du* may be understood as a "concealed dedication" to Paula Buber, who in 1921 had published a book in which the elements, which had been pagan in her previous work, were full of God.[2] The motto could scarcely be understood as it was meant. But rightly understood, it serves notice that the book was grounded in an actual relationship between a human I and a human You.

[2] I owe the phrase in quotes, this interpretation, and most of the information about the epigraph to Grete Schaeder, who will argue her case in her introduction to the first volume of Buber's correspondence. I don't know whether she has noticed that the two lines in the *Divan* that follow upon Buber's epigraph support her reading: *Wie du mir das so lieblich gibst! / Am lieblichsten aber dass du liebst:* "How you give this to me in such a lovely way! But what is loveliest is that you love." (She has. See Martin Buber, *Briefwechsel aus sieben Jahrzehnten*, ed. Grete Schaeder, vol. I, 1972, p. 39.)

The centrality of human relationships in this book is so plain that critics have actually noted with surprise and protested with complete incomprehension that there should be any mention at all of a tree and of a cat. The central stress falls on You—not Thou. God is present when I confront You. But if I look away from You, I ignore him. As long as I merely experience or use you, I deny God. But when I encounter You I encounter him.

For those who no longer have any use for the word "God" this may be too much; and for those who do, too little. But is it too little?

> When you come to appear before me,
>   who requires of you
>   this trampling of my courts?
> Bring no more vain offerings;
>   incense is an abomination to me.
> New moon and sabbath and the calling of assemblies—
>   I cannot endure iniquity and solemn assembly.
> Your new moon and your appointed feasts
>   my soul hates;
> they have become a burden to me,
>   I am weary of bearing them.
> When you spread forth your hands,
>   I hide my eyes from you;
> even though you make many prayers,
>   I no longer listen;
>   your hands are full of blood.
> Wash yourselves; make yourselves clean;
>   remove the evil of your doings
>   from before my eyes;
> cease to do evil,
>   learn to do good;
> seek justice,
>   correct oppression;
> defend the fatherless,
>   plead for the widow.

Is that too little?

Nor is it too much. In places it seems a bit much. Buber seems so dramatic, so insistent on what seems obvious. But there are self-refuting prophecies, and Hebrew prophecy was not meant to come true.

The Hebrew prophets foretold disasters that would come to pass unless those who heard them returned from their evil ways. Jeremiah did not gloat when Jerusalem was destroyed; he was grieved by his failure.

Jonah, of course, felt aggrieved when his prophecy forestalled its own fulfillment; but this only provides the occasion for the moral of the story. He is told, and we are told, that this sort of failure is a triumph.

If Buber places so much stress on what seems obvious to me, one has to ask in fairness whether it would seem so obvious if he had not been so insistent on it.

When a religion professor makes a great point of treating students as persons, that seems almost comical. How else? But when every student who comes to my office to speak to me, and everyone who asks a question of me during or after a lecture comes to life for me as an I addressing me and I try to speak not *about him* but *to You* —would it be that way but for the influence of Martin Buber?

I am not sure and I will never know. The loves of childhood and of adolescence cannot be subtracted from us; they have become part of us. Not a discrete part that could be severed. It is as if they had entered our bloodstream.

Nevertheless, if one has no use for the word "God" it may seem merely obscurantist to make this point in this fashion. Why not say instead that we ought to be mindful that the human beings we confront are persons?

It still seems hard not to reply: what else could they be? isn't this obvious? In any case, Buber says more than this, without saying too much.

He finds in my encounter with You what Blake finds in a grain of sand and in a wild flower: infinity and eternity—here and now.

Far better than John Dewey, who tried something similar in *A Common Faith*, Buber succeeds in endowing the social sphere with a religious dimension. Where other critics of religion tend to take away the sabbath and leave us with a life of weekdays, Buber attacks the dichotomy that condemns men to lives that are at least six-sevenths drab.

While man cannot live in a continual sabbath, he should not resign himself to a flat two-dimensional life from which he escapes on rare occasions. The place of the sacred is not a house of God, no church, synagogue, or seminary, nor one day in seven, and the span of the sacred is much shorter than twenty-four hours. The sabbath is every day, several times a day.

Still why use religious terms? Indeed, it might be better not to use them because they are always misunderstood. But what other terms are there?

We need a new language, and new poets to create it, and new ears to listen to it. ·

Meanwhile, if we shut our ears to the old prophets who still speak more or less in the old tongues, using ancient words, occasionally in new ways, we shall have very little music.

We are not so rich that we can do without tradition. Let him that has new ears listen to it in a new way.

In Buber's little book God actually does not appear much before the Third Part. But a heretic need not consider that last part embarrassing or *de trop*. On the contrary.

Those without ties to organized religion who feel that, although much of institutional religion is repulsive, not all scriptures are bare nonsense, have to ask themselves: what about God?

Those who prefer the God of Abraham, Jacob, and Job to the God of the philosophers and theologians have to ask: what about God?

Those who read the Bible and the Sacred Books of the East not merely as so much literature but as a record of experiences that are relevant to their own lives must ask: what about God?

They do not ask: what is he really like? what are his attributes? is he omniscient? can he do this or that? Nor: can his existence be proved? They do not assume that they know him and only need one additional piece of information. They do not even believe in him. What they ask about is not some supernatural He. And the theologians are of little help, if any.

If only one knew the meaning of one's own question! If only one could ask it properly or formulate it more precisely! Is it really a question? Or is it a deep concern that finds no words that do it justice?

This book responds to this concern. God as the eternal You whom men address and by whom they in turn feel—Buber would say, *are* —addressed makes sense of much literature and life. The book does not save, or seek to prop up, a tradition. Even less does it aim to save any institution. It speaks to those who no longer believe but who wonder whether life without religion is bound to lack some dimension.

V

The book is steeped in Judaism. This is often overlooked and perhaps as often denied explicitly. Jesus is mentioned, as is the Gospel according to John; but so are the Buddha and the Upanishads. The author is widely read, conversant with many traditions—a modern intellectual with deep roots in the German language. The volume abounds in coinages, but it is difficult to be quite sure in any case whether a particular word is really a coinage: so thorough was Buber's knowledge of German literature, all the way back to Luther and even Eckhart and beyond. He was far from any orthodoxy, far even from being conservative in almost any sense of that word. Of labels of that sort, even radical would fit him better.

He was possessed by the desire to get back to the roots. His handling of the language makes that plain at every turn. And when he resolved to translate the Hebrew Bible with Franz Rosenzweig, he found a fertile field for this great passion. For in Hebrew it could be argued that one did not really understand a word until one had grasped its root and considered its relations to other words with the same root.

The whole endeavor of translating the Hebrew Bible represented an attempt to get back to the roots of Judaism—back beyond the roots of Christianity. Buber sought a way back beyond the Shtetl and the Shulhan Arukh, back beyond the Talmud and the Mishnah, even beyond Ezra and Nehemiah, and in some ways his own Judaism was pre-Mosaic.

The Greeks were an eminently visual people. They gloried in the visual arts; Homer's epics abound in visual detail; and they created tragedy and comedy, adding new dimensions to visual art.

The Hebrews were not so visual and actually entertained a prohibition against the visual arts. Neither did they have tragedies or comedies. The one book of the Bible that has sometimes been called a tragedy, Job, was clearly not intended for, and actually precluded, any visual representation.

The Greeks visualized their gods and represented them in marble and in beautiful vase paintings. They also brought them on the stage.

The Hebrews did not visualize their God and expressly forbade attempts to make of him an object—a visual object, a concrete object, any object. Their God was not to be seen. He was to be heard and listened to. He was not an It but an I—or a You.

Modern Christian attempts to get back to a pre-Hellenistic primal Christianity are legion. They are also doomed.

There never was any pre-Hellenistic Christianity. The soil on which Christianity was born had soaked up Hellenism for more than three centuries. Paul wrote his epistles in Greek, and he was a Hellenistic Jew—a Jew, to be sure, and deeply beholden to Judaism, but a Hellenistic Jew and not by any stretch of the imagination a pre-Hellenistic Jew. And the four Gospels were written in Greek somewhat later than were Paul's epistles.

Christianity was born of the denial that God could not possibly be seen. Not all who considered Jesus a great teacher became Christians. Christians were those for whom he was the Lord. Christians were those who believed that God could become visible, an object of sight and experience, of knowledge and belief.

Of course, Christianity did not deny its roots in Judaism. Jesus as the Son of God who had ascended to the heavens to dwell there with God, as God, did not simply become another Heracles, the son of Zeus who had ascended to the heavens to dwell there with the gods, as a god. He did not simply become another of the legion of Greek gods and demigods and sons of Zeus. He had preached and was to be heard and listened to. His moral teachings were recorded lovingly for the instruction of the faithful.

But were they really to be listened to? Or did they, too, become objects—of admiration and perhaps discussion? Was the individual to feel addressed by them, commanded by them—was he to relate his life to them?

The new dispensation was hardly that. The New Testament keeps saying, nowhere more emphatically than in the Gospel according to John, that those who only live by Jesus' moral teaching shall not enter the kingdom of heaven; only those can be saved who are baptized, who believe, and who take the sacraments—eating, as that Gospel puts it, "of this bread."

Of course, Christian belief is not totally unlike Jewish belief. It is not devoid of trust and confidence, and in Paul's and Luther's experience of faith these Jewish elements were especially prominent. Rarely have they been wholly lacking in Christianity. Still, this Jewish faith was never considered sufficient. Christian faith was always centered in articles of faith that had to be believed, and disputes abounded about what precisely had to be believed by those who wanted to be saved.

When the Reformation did away with visual images, it was only to insist more firmly on the purity of doctrines that must be believed. And for Luther the bread and wine were no mere symbols of Christ's flesh and blood—otherwise he might have made common cause with Ulrich Zwingli and prevented the splintering of Protestantism—but the flesh and blood itself: as an object.

Buber does not say these things, and I have no wish to saddle him with my ideas. His views are developed in his *Two Types of Faith*, mine in my *Critique of Religion and Philosophy* and *The Faith of a Heretic*. Why introduce these problems here? Because the notion of so many Christians and some Jews that Buber was really closer to Christianity than he was to Judaism should not go unchallenged. In fact, *Ich und Du* is one of the great documents of Jewish faith.

One of the central concepts of the book is that of *Umkehr*. This is Buber's German rendering of the Hebrew *t'shuvah* and means "return." The noun is found in the Bible, but not in the distinctive sense which is common in Jewish literature and liturgy. The verb is frequently used in the Bible with the connotations that are relevant here: Deuteronomy 4:30 and 30:2, Isaiah 10:21 and 19:22, and Jeremiah 4:1 are among the many examples. What is meant is the return to God.

The modern reader is apt to feel that this is a churchly notion, presumably dear to preachers but without significance for those who do not greatly care for organized religion. In fact, the idea is quite unecclesiastical and it constitutes a threat to organized religion. Christianity in particular is founded on its implicit denial.

The Jewish doctrine holds that a man can at any time return and be accepted by God. That is all. The simplicity of this idea is deceptive. Let us translate it into a language closer to Christianity, while noting that Buber refrains from doing this: God can at any time forgive those who repent.

What the Hebrew tradition stresses is not the mere state of mind, the repentance, but the act of return. And on Yom Kippur, the Day of Atonement, the Book of Jonah is read in synagogues the world over. When Jonah had cried out, "Yet forty days, and Nineveh shall be overthrown," the king called on his people "to return, every man, from his evil way and from the violence on his hands. Who knows, God may return . . ." Nineveh was the capital of the Assyrians who had conquered the kingdom of Israel, laid waste Samaria, and led the ten tribes away into destruction. Could God possibly forgive them without at least demanding their conversion and some ritual observances? "When God saw what they did, how they returned from their evil way, God repented of the evil that he had said he would do to them and did it not."

This conception of return has been and is at the very heart of Judaism, and it is for the sake of this idea that Jonah is always read on the highest holiday of the year. But the theology of Paul in the New Testament is founded on the implicit denial of this doctrine, and so are the Roman Catholic and the Greek Orthodox churches, Lutheranism and Calvinism. Paul's elaborate argument concerning the impossibility of salvation under the Torah ("the Law") and for the necessity of Christ's redemptive death presuppose that God cannot simply forgive anyone who returns.

If the doctrine of the return is true, Paul's theology collapses and "Christ died in vain." Nor does any need remain for baptism and the sacrament of confession, or for the bread and the wine. Man stands in a direct relationship to God and requires no mediator.

Buber's whole book deals with such immediate relationships, and in this as well as in his central emphasis on return he speaks out of the Jewish religious tradition.

It was both a symptom and then also a cause of profound incomprehension that in the first English translation *Umkehr* became reversal. Twenty years later, in the second edition, this was changed to "turning." Meanwhile the choice of "Thou" did its share to make God remote and to lessen, if not destroy, the sense of intimacy that pervades Buber's book.

Buber's lifelong Zionism was prompted in large measure by his concern for the creation of a new way of life and a new type of community. His Zionism has been called cultural rather than political, but it was not altogether unfitting that when he finally went to Jerusalem in 1938 it was to accept an appointment to a new chair in Social Philosophy in the Hebrew University's Department of Sociology. (He was first offered the chair of Pedagogy and declined it.)

The recurrent "Thou" in the first translation mesmerized people to the point where it was widely assumed that Buber was a theologian. In fact, the book deals centrally with man's relationships to other men, and the theme of alienation (*Verfremdung*) is prominent in the Second Part.

The aim of the book is not to disseminate knowledge about God but, at least in large measure, to diagnose certain tendencies in modern society—Buber speaks of "sick ages" more than forty years before it became fashionable in the West to refer to our "sick" society —and to indicate how the quality of life might be changed radically by the development of a new sense of community.

The book will survive the death of theology, for it appeals to that religiousness which finds no home in organized religion, and it speaks to those whose primary concern is not at all with religion but rather with social change.

But there is much more to the book than this.

Among the most important things that one can learn from Buber is how to read. Was it from him that I learned it? I am not sure, and I will never know. Does it matter? *You* could learn it from this book.

Modern man is a voracious reader who has never learned to read well. Part of the trouble is that he is taught to read drivel that is hardly worth reading well. (There was a time when Jewish children learned to read by reading the Bible.)

One ends up by reading mainly newspapers and magazines— ephemeral, anonymous trash that one scans on its way to the garbage can. One has no wish to remember it for any length of time; it is written as if to make sure that one won't; and one reads it in a manner that makes doubly sure. There is no person behind what one reads; not even a committee. Somebody wrote it in the first place— if one can call that writing—and then various other people took turns changing it. For the final result no one is responsible; and it rarely merits a serious response. It cries out to be forgotten soon, like the books from which one learned to read, in school. They were usually anonymous, too; or they should have been.

In adolescence students are suddenly turned loose on books worth reading, but generally don't know how to read them. And if, un- taught, some instinct prompts them to read well, chances are that they are asked completely tone-deaf questions as soon as they have finished their assignment—either making them feel that they read badly after all or spoiling something worthwhile for the rest of their lives.

We must learn to feel addressed by a book, by the human being behind it, as if a person spoke directly to us. A good book or essay or poem is not primarily an object to be put to use, or an object of experience: it is the voice of You speaking to me, requiring a response.

How many people read Buber or Kierkegaard that way? Nietzsche or Hegel? Tolstoy or Euripides? Or the Bible? Rather, how few do? But Buber himself wants to be read that way.

VI

One can also learn from Buber how to translate. Nowhere is his teaching more radical. Nowhere is he more deeply at odds with the common sense of the English-speaking world.

Nor did anything he ever published seem as absurd to his readers in Germany as did his translation of the Bible. What was familiar seemed to have become incomprehensible.

In the beginning all this was due at least as much to Rosenzweig's uncompromising nature as to Buber, but Buber persisted even after Rosenzweig's death, and neither ridicule nor criticism ever moved him to relent. When he left Germany in 1938, the vast undertaking that had required so much effort looked like an almost total loss.

After the war, Buber was delighted when two German publishers asked him to resume his enterprise. He did, and brought it to completion shortly before his death. Gershom Scholem, a great scholar whose view of Hasidism differs from Buber's, toasted the accomplishment, adding: But who will read it?

What had seemed outrageous in the twenties and thirties was merely ahead of its time. A new generation that no longer expects all prose and poetry to be so easily accessible finds no extraordinary difficulty with the Buber Bible. It is widely read in Germany.

What can be learned from Buber as a translator before one explores devices and techniques is the basic commitment to the writer one translates. As a translator I have no right to use the text confronting me as an object with which I may take liberties. It is not there for me to play with or manipulate. I am not to use it as a point of departure, or as anything else. It is the voice of a person that needs me. I am there to help him speak.

If I would rather speak in my own voice, I am free to do that—on other occasions. To foist my thoughts, my images, my style on those whom I profess to translate is dishonest.

Mundus vult decipi. The world winks at dishonesty. The world does not call it dishonesty.

In the case of poetry it says: what is most important is that the translator should write a poem that is good in its own right. The acceptance of this absurdity by so many intellectuals helps us to understand the acceptance of so many absurd religious and political beliefs by intellectuals in other times and climes. Once a few respected men have fortified a brazen claim with their prestige, it becomes a cliché that gets repeated endlessly as if it were self-evident. Any protest is regarded as a heresy that shows how those who utter it do not belong: arguments are not met on their merits; instead one rehearses a few illustrious names and possibly deigns to contrast them with some horrible examples.

Anyone able to write a poem that is good in its own right should clearly do so, but he should not pass it off as a translation of another man's poem if the meaning or the tone of his poem are in fact quite different. Least of all should he claim that the tone or meaning is the same when it is not.

Tone is crucial and often colors meaning. If we don't know what is said seriously and what in jest, we do not know the meaning. We have to know what is said lightly and what solemnly, where a remark is prompted by a play on words, if something is ironical or a quotation, an allusion, a pastiche, a parody, a diatribe, a daring coinage, a cliché, an epigram, or possibly ambiguous.

A German translator who rendered William Faulkner into the equivalent of the King's English would serve his public ill. But if he tried hard to be faithful to his author, then his publisher might say to him—if things were as they are in the United States: "My dear fellow, that simply isn't German"; and an editor, utterly unable to write a single publishable page over his—or more often her—own name, would be asked to rewrite the translation to make it "idiomatic."

Ah, we are told, every generation needs its own translation because a book has to be done into the idiom of the day. If it is poetry, it had better sound like Eliot. Alas, no more; we need a new translation. But why should Goethe, Hölderlin, or Rilke sound like Eliot in the first place? Should Eliot, conversely, have been made to sound like Rilke—and then perhaps like Brecht—and now like someone whom a publisher or critic fancies as a modern voice?

The point of reading a poet is surely in large measure to hear *his* voice—his own, distinctive, novel voice. Poetry read in the original stands a better chance of being read well than prose. But when we deal with translations, the roles are reversed.

Again I do not want to saddle Buber with my own views. What he translated was Scripture. Perhaps I am *extending* the lessons one could learn from him—and from Rosenzweig, who also translated ninety-two hymns and poems by Yehuda Halevi, with a brilliant postscript, and dedicated the book to Martin Buber. The point is not to invoke Buber as an authority but rather to spell out some of the implications of this book.

Buber ought to be translated as he translated. The voice should be his, the thoughts and images and tone his. And if the reader should cry out, exasperated, "But that simply isn't English," one has to reply: "True, but the original text simply isn't German." It abounds in solecisms, coinages, and other oddities; and Buber was a legend in his lifetime for the way he wrote.

He makes very difficult reading. He evidently did not wish to be read quickly, once only, for information. He tried to slow the reader down, to force him to read many sentences and paragraphs again, even to read the whole book more than once.

The style is not the best part of this book, but it is a part and even an important part of it. Nobody has to chew passage upon passage more slowly than a translator who takes his work seriously and keeps revising his draft. Nobody has occasion to ask himself more often whether a play on words really adds something worthwhile. But once he starts making an effort to improve upon his text, keeping only the most brilliant plays on words while leaving out and not calling attention to inferior ones, possibly substituting his own most felicitous plays for the ones he could not capture, where is he to stop on the road to falsehood?

When adjectives are piled up in profusion and some strike him as decidedly unnecessary, should he substitute a single forceful word for a two-line enumeration? Make long and obscure sentences short and clear? Resolve all ambiguities in favor of the meaning he likes best? Gloss over or leave out what seem weaknesses to him? Perhaps insert a few good images that the author might have liked if only he had thought of them, and that perhaps would have occurred to him if he had written his book in English, and if he had shared more of the translator's background—and sensibility? Perhaps add a thought or two as well?

The book has many faults. Let him that can write a better one do so with all haste. But to meddle with a text one translates and to father one's inventions on another man is a sin against the spirit.

What one should try to do is clear. What can be done is something else again. This book is untranslatable.

It abounds in plays on words—don't call them plays if that should strike you as irreverent—that simply cannot be done into English. How can one translate the untranslatable?

By adding notes. By occasionally supplying the German words. By offering explanations.

But now the text seems much less smooth. One is stopped in one's tracks to read a note. One is led to go back to reread a paragraph. And having read the book with so many interruptions, one really has to read it a second time without interruptions.

To quote Rilke's "Song of the Idiot": How good!

Some of the key terms in this book are hard to render. Examples abound in the notes. Here it must suffice to comment on a few points.

Buber loves the prefix *Ur*, which has no exact English equivalent. An *Urgrossvater* is a great-grandfather; an *Ururgrossvater*, a great-great-grandfather. *Urwald* is forest primeval; *Ursprung*, origin. These are common words, but the prefix opens up endless possibilities for coinages. In the following pages it has been rendered by "primal."

Buber also loves the suffix *haft* (for adjectives)—and *hatftigkeit* (for nouns). This can have two altogether different connotations. It can mean "having": thus *lebhaft* means vivacious (literally: having life); *launenhaft*, moody (having moods); and *tugendhaft,* virtuous (having virtue). But it can also mean "somewhat like": *märchenhaft* means fabulous (somewhat like a fairytale). This suffix opens up endless possibilities for coinages, and occasionally it is not altogether clear which of the two meanings is intended. Usually, Buber definitely intends the second: he adds the suffix to introduce a lack of precision or, to put the matter more kindly, to stress the inadequacy of language.

One of his favorite words is *Gegenwart*, which can mean either the present, as opposed to the past and the future, or presence, as it does when he speaks of God's presence in the epigraph to the first edition. The German language does not distinguish between these two senses of the word; nor does Buber. To add to this difficulty, "present" is ambiguous in English: it can also mean "gift." In the following pages "present" is never used in that sense. Like "presence" it is used exclusively to render *Gegenwart*.

Gegen means "against" but also figures as a prefix in a great many words; and Buber uses a number of these. *Gegenstand* is the ordinary German word for "object" (literally that which stands against). *Gegenüber* means "vis-à-vis" (literally that which is over against), and this in turn can become a prefix and figures in many different constructions. In this book "confront" has been used in all such cases. *Begegnung* (noun) and *begegnen* (verb) have been translated consistently as "encounter." The list could be continued, but there is no need here to anticipate the notes.

Buber's persistent association of *Wirklichkeit* with *wirken* can be carried over into English to some extent by using "actuality" for the former (saving "reality" for the rare instances when he uses *Realität*) and "act," in a variety of ways, for the verb. And when he says that in prayer we can, incredible as it may seem, *wirken* on God, although of course we cannot *erwirken* anything from him, the translator can say that we can act on God but not exact anything from him.

One of Buber's most central terms is *Wesen*.

The word is not uncommon, and those who know a little about German philosophic terms know that it means "essence." They also know that Buber has sometimes been called an existentialist, and that some other philosophers have been called, more rarely, essentialists. But in this book *Wesen* recurs constantly. Sometimes "essence" is clearly what is meant; sometimes "nature" would be slightly more idiomatic; but quite often neither of these terms makes any sense at all.

Wesen can also mean "a being" or, when the context indicates that it is used in the plural, "beings." To complicate matters further, we sometimes encounter *Wesenheiten*, a much more unusual word that it would be easy to do without; but Buber shows a preference for rare words and coinages.

Any contrast of essence and existence is out of the picture. Deliberately so. Every being I encounter is seen to be essential. Nothing is essential but a being. Doing something with my whole being or my whole essence is the same.

The realm of essences and what is essential is not outside this world in some beyond. Essential is whatever is—here and now.

If romanticism is flight from the present, yearning for deliverance from the cross of the here and now, an escape into the past, preferably medieval, or the future, into drugs or other worlds, either night or twilight—if romanticism can face anything except the facts—then nothing could be less romantic than the central appeal of this book.

Hic Rhodos, hic salta!

"Here is Rhodes; jump here!" That is what Aesop's braggart was told when he boasted of his great jump in Rhodes.

Hegel cited this epigram in the preface to his *Philosophy of Right* by way of contrasting his approach and Plato's. He was not trying to instruct the state how it ought to be: "To comprehend *what is*, is the task of philosophy, for *what is* is reason. . . . Slightly changed, the epigram would read [seeing that *rhodon* is the Greek word for rose]:

Here is the rose, dance *here*. . . .

To recognize reason as the rose in the cross of the present and thus to delight in the present—this rational insight brings us that *reconciliation* with actuality which philosophy grants those who have once been confronted by the inner demand to *comprehend* . . ."

To link Buber with Hegel may seem strange. But in 1920 Franz Rosenzweig had published a major work, in two volumes, on "Hegel and the State," dealing at length with this preface. The differences between Buber and Hegel far outnumber their similarities. But they are at one in their opposition to any otherworldliness, in their insistence on finding in the preset whatever beauty ad redempton there may be, and in their refusal to pin their hopes on any beyond.

Ich und Du speaks to men and women who have become wary of promises and hopes: it takes its stand resolutely in the here and now. It is a sermon on the words of Hillel:

> "If I am only for myself, what am I?
> And if not now, when?"

6

THE RECEPTION OF EXISTENTIALISM IN THE UNITED STATES*

It is difficult to deal briefly with the reception of existentialism in the United States. The response to even one or two of the writers who are often lumped together as "existentialists" could easily be made the subject of a monograph, and to deal adequately with about ten writers in a single essay is impossible. Broad generalizations about "existentialism," on the other hand, are bound to be of very dubious value if it is not clear to whom precisely they apply. What is needed is a combination of generalizations with attention to the individual "existentialists."

I shall first attempt a sketch in very broad strokes of the influence of European on American philosophy before 1930. Next I shall ask what existentialism is, and offer first an ostensive, historical definition and then a more analytical answer that brings out what the so-called existentialists have in common. After that I shall briefly consider the reception of the major figures, one by one;[1] and in the end I

---

* This essay was originally written for a volume devoted to the contributions of refugees from Nazi Germany, but it first appeared in *Midway*, then in *Salmagundi*, and eventually in *The Legacy of the German Refugee Intellectuals* (1972), which was not the book for which it had been written.

[1] Comprehensive bibliographies of their writings, including English translations, are included in the following volumes: *The Philosophy of Martin Buber*, ed. Paul Arthur Schilpp and Maurice Friedman (1967); *The Philosophy of Karl Jaspers*, ed. Paul Arthur Schilpp (1957); and *Religion and Culture: Essays in Honor of Paul Tillich*, ed. Walter Leibrecht (1959). William J. Richardson, S.J., *Heidegger* (1963), lists Heidegger's lectures and seminars, 1915–58, on pp. 663–71, his writings in order of publication, 1912–62, on pp. 675–78, and in order of composition, pp. 678–80, while English translations are listed on p. 688. The bibliography in Walter Kaufmann, *Nietzsche* (4th rev. ed., 1974), includes Nietzsche's writings, collected editions, and translations, as well as studies of his thought by over one hundred writers.

In the following pages I shall not attempt any philosophical criticisms, as I have done that elsewhere. Critical essays on Kierkegaard, Jaspers, and Heidegger are included in my *From Shakespeare to Existentialism* (1959; rev. ed., 1960), and critical discussions of Tillich in my *Critique of Religion and Philosophy* (1958), secs. 50, 53, and 57 and *The Faith of a Heretic* (1961), secs. 32–34; the chapters on commitment and death also deal with Heidegger, Sartre, and Camus; and Sartre's attempt to offer an ethic is criticized in sec. 86.

shall offer some systematic conclusions about the impact of existentialism in the United States.

I

Only three or four peoples have produced more than three or four truly original philosophers whose impact has been widely felt beyond the languages in which they wrote: the Greeks, the British, the Germans, and perhaps also the French. American philosophy may turn out to be comparable to Roman philosophy: mainly derivative. There is no Washington or Lincoln in American philosophy; unlike American history, American philosophy cannot boast of figures that can hold their own against the best men anywhere.

Philosophy is altogether unlike history or literature or sculpture; it is more like tragedy. All of Western philosophy has its origin in Greek philosophy, and all Western philosophers to this day share an international European tradition. Within this tradition, the British were the first in modern times who developed a distinctive strain of their own, beginning with Bacon and Hobbes, Locke, Berkeley, and Hume. When Hume died in 1776, no other people since the Greeks could point to such a subtradition. The other giants of modern philosophy were loners: Descartes, Spinoza (whose genius was not widely recognized until the end of the eighteenth century), and Leibniz.

The French *philosophes*, of whom there were many, did not attain to the first rank, except for Voltaire and Rousseau (both died in 1778), who dwelt on the margins of philosophy in the rich border land of literature. Soon Rousseau became the second French philosopher to influence the course of European philosophy; like Spinoza, he was embraced by nascent German philosophy.

The influence of Greek and British philosophy on American philosophy does not need to be stressed. All modern European philosophy is based on that of the Greeks, and the British influence on American institutions, literature, and thought is obvious and not surprising, given a common language. But in 1781 German philosophy came into its own with the publication of Kant's *Critique of Pure Reason*, and since the early nineteenth century the German impact on American philosophy has been immense. The pattern has remained remarkably constant down to our own time.

As soon as Kant's influence in Germany had given way to Hegel's, Kantianism arrived in England; when Hegel went into eclipse in Germany, Hegelianism came to dominate British philosophy; and both times it took a little longer for German thought to cross the Atlantic Ocean. But eventually the influence on American thought was at least as great as it had ever been in England.

The reception of existentialism in the United States should be considered against this background and compared with the impact of other contemporary philosophies, such as logical positivism, phenomenology, and neo-Thomism. The spread of all four in the United States was helped by the arrival of refugees, but there is no reason for doubting that all four would have won some popularity in America even without any such assistance, allowing only for the usual time lag.

This is not to say that Nazi persecution made no difference at all to American philosophy. At the very least it changed the timetable by forcing positivism into eclipse in the thirties, while Heidegger was discredited in Germany in 1945 when the Nazi state collapsed. It might be supposed further that by expelling some philosophers who subsequently found a home in the United States, the process was speeded up, as it did not have to move by way of England. But this is more doubtful, although positivism was the last European philosophy that reached America via England.

The case of positivism was unusual in at least two ways. First, Ludwig Wittgenstein (1889–1951) left his native Austria for England long before 1930, and at Cambridge he became a teacher of exceptional intensity and passion. Thus his influence was naturally felt in England long before it reached the United States. Secondly, Wittgenstein went to Cambridge because he felt some affinity for G. E. Moore and Bertrand Russell; and the various philosophies that are sometimes collectively called positivism were in many ways congenial to the British tradition, all the way back to David Hume. Existentialism, on the other hand, was and is profoundly uncongenial to the British philosophers. That it did not come to the United States by way of England was not due to the direct migration of Central European philosophers to America. Existentialism never found a home in England. After World War II communication between the two continents was greatly speeded up, owing to technological advances; and it was only after 1945 that existentialism really impinged on the American consciousness.[2]

II

What is existentialism? The question can be answered in two ways: ostensively, by naming the writers meant, or analytically, by characterizing the movement and its tenets or characteristic tendencies. To begin with such an analysis is methodologically unsound; that way there is no guard against arbitrariness, and different analysts come up with different descriptions. Some writers who are generally identified as existentialists may turn out, in the light of such analyses, not to be existentialists at all, while someone else whom the analyst happens to fancy—or dislike—becomes the paradigm. We ought to keep in mind in all such cases that the writers come first and the label afterwards, as part of an attempt to group some men together.

Descartes, Spinoza, and Leibniz *are* "the continental rationalists," and it makes good sense to study them together, not because they shared the same philosophy but rather because Spinoza set himself the task of correcting what he considered Descartes' errors; and Leibniz, although he found fault with both, tried to integrate their valid insights. Those who wish to devote a course, anthology, or study to these three men often find it useful to have a single label—and that is the primary meaning of "continental rationalism." What the three continental rationalists have in common is a question that arises only after that.

The situation is precisely the same with British empiricism. Primarily, that means Locke, Berkeley, and Hume. But once a tradition has been identified, we can meaningfully ask whether John Stuart Mill or Bertrand Russell was a British empiricist, too. Nothing much depends on the answer: the question is one not of fact but of convenience, although it is interesting to point out what marginal figures have in common with the Big Three and to what extent they differ.

The term *Existenzphilosophie* seems to have been introduced in 1929 by Fritz Heinemann, then a Privatdozent at the University of Frankfurt, in a book entitled *Neue Wege der Philosophie: Geist/*

[2] Thus *Partisan Review* devoted its spring 1946 issue to "New French Writing" and in 1947 published William Barrett's "What is Existentialism?"

Leben/Existenz: Eine Einführung in die Philosophie der Gegenwart (New paths of philosophy: spirit/life/existence: an introduction to contemporary philosophy). The book begins with "A Postscript as a Preface" in which it is suggested that the antithesis of "spirit" and "life" is overcome by "existence"—the new principle of a number of new, existential philosophies: *das neue Prinzip einer Reihe von Philosophien, der Existenzphilosophien.*[3]

Around 1800, "the *Geistphilosophien* of European rationalism" gave way to "the principle of life in Herder, Hamann, and Jacobi," while Goethe and Humboldt championed *Existenz*. Similarly, in the nineteenth century, "the rationalism of German idealism gave way to the *Lebensphilosophie* of romanticism, and this in turn to the *Existenzphilosophie* of Marx, Feuerbach, and Kierkegaard."

Finally, these three principles succeeded each other in the development of the phenomenological school, in which Edmund Husserl, according to Heinemann, represents *Geist*, Max Scheler *Leben*, and Martin Heidegger *Existenz*.[4]

Heinemann's book does not seem to have been widely read or discussed, but the term *Existenzphilosophie* stuck, and his use of it prevailed. The notion that it is in Kierkegaard that we find "the first beginnings of an *Existenzphilosophie* that fits thinking again into the inviolable unity of man, that makes philosophizing a communication of existence,"[5] the suggestion that some earlier movements might also be called existential, and the point that the principle of existence was also championed by Karl Barth, Martin Buber, Franz Rosenzweig, and several others[6]—all this and much else, including the long appreciation of Heidegger and the passing references to Jaspers, has been repeated again and again by others after World War II, without any reference to Heinemann or any clear awareness of the time lag of which we spoke earlier.

Heinemann himself participated in the migration of the thirties, went to England, and eventually published *Existenzphilosophie Lebendig oder Tot?* (1954), as well as an expanded English version, *Existentialism and the Modern Predicament* (1958). Although both appeared in prestigious paperback series[7] and called attention to the

---

3 Heinemann, *Neue Wege*, p. xviii.
4 Ibid., p. xxi.
5 Ibid., p. 54.
6 Ibid., p. xx.
7 Urban-Bücher in Stuttgart and Harper Torchbooks in New York.

1929 book, I cannot recall ever having seen that book discussed in the mushrooming literature on existentialism. Heinemann's stress on *Existenz* was clearly derived from Heidegger's *Sein und Zeit* (1927, Being and Time), in which that term had been invested with a new significance, suggested much earlier by Søren Kierkegaard, especially in his *Concluding Unscientific Postscript* (1846). But neither Kierkegaard nor Heidegger had spoken of *Existenzphilosophie*, and Heinemann's use of that term was very casual; he did not call attention to it as a coinage. Perhaps the term had even been used orally by others before it turned up in Heinemann's book.

We find it next in Jaspers' little volume, *Die geistige Situation der Zeit* (1931), which appeared in a popular hardcover pocketbook series (Sammlung Göschen, vol. 1000) and reached a very large audience. In 1933, English, Spanish, and Japanese translations appeared, the first under the title *Man in the Modern Age*. The first French version appeared in Louvain in 1951 and in Paris in 1952; and in 1954 another Japanese translation appeared. The fifth of the six chapters was entitled "How Being Human is Comprehended Today," and was divided into two parts: "(1) Sciences of Man: Sociology — Psychology — Anthropology" and "(2) *Existenzphilosophie*." Rather oddly, the last-named section, comprising four pages, reported on *Existenzphilosophie* as if it were a well-known feature of the contemporary situation, but what Jaspers actually offered was a miniature summary of his own *Philosophie*, which appeared in three volumes the following year. Indeed, following the last page there was an announcement of this work, complete with the titles of the three volumes which coincided with the three phases of *Existenzphilosophie* as described in the summary.[8] Jaspers gave credit to Kierkegaard, Schelling, and Nietzsche but did not mention Heidegger, and in effect gave the impression that the only contemporary philosophy that contributed to the comprehension of man was his own.

In his *Philosophie* (1932), *Existenz* is a key concept, and the second volume bears the title *Existenzerhellung* (Illumination of existence); but the terms *Existenzphilosophie* occurs only a couple of times near the end of volume 3.[9] It thus seems highly likely that Jaspers picked up this label from Heinemann, although he does not mention him and may have come by the word indirectly, with-

[8] P. 145.
[9] Pp. 215, 217.

out any awareness of Heinemann. He may even have thought it was his own coinage. At any rate, he henceforth appropriated the term for *his* philosophy, without, however, looking on his own philosophy as merely one among others. There is more than a suggestion that he shared the conviction classically formulated by Hegel: "Philosophy is its age comprehended in thought."[10]

In Jaspers' three-volume *Philosophie* no other philosopher is referred to anywhere near so much as Kant and Hegel; Schelling and Kierkegaard are the runners-up, mentioned less than half as often; Nietzsche is cited a few times, Heidegger once, and no other living philosopher more than once. The footnote reference to Heidegger reads in full: "About being in the world and about *Dasein* and historicity *M. Heidegger* (*Sein und Zeit*, Halle 1927) has said things of significance."[11] In *Sein und Zeit*, Jaspers' *Psychologie der Weltanschauungen* (1919) was cited in three footnotes that were almost equally insignificant.[12] Jaspers and Heidegger have never dealt with each other's ideas in print, although it is no secret that they were friends for a while before the Nazis came to power and that they have not been on speaking terms since then.

In his "Philosophical Autobiography"[13] Jaspers discusses many minor figures and devotes a whole section to Heinrich Rickert, but one looks in vain for a single mention of Heidegger—or of Dilthey.

In 1935 Jaspers published a volume of five lectures, *Vernunft und Existenz* (Reason and existence), of which one was devoted to "The historical significance of Kierkegaard and Nietzsche."[14] The following year, he published a full-length interpretation of Nietzsche,[15] and in 1938 a book consisting of three lectures, which he called *Existenzphilosophie*.

The term "existentialism" (or *Existentialismus*) was not yet in use at that time, and *Existenzphilosophie* brought to mind Kierkegaard, Heidegger, and Jaspers. It was understood that Nietzsche

---

[10] *Philosophie des Rechts* (1821), pp. xxi–xxii.

[11] 1: 66n.

[12] In sections 49, 60, and 68.

[13] In *The Philosophy of Karl Jaspers*, ed. Paul Arthur Schilpp (1957), pp. 5–94.

[14] English translation by William Earle in *Reason and Existenz* (1955), reprinted in *Existentialism from Dostoevsky to Sartre*, ed. Walter Kaufmann (1956; rev. and expanded ed., 1975).

[15] English translation of *Nietzsche* by Charles F. Wallraff and Frederick J. Schmitz (1965).

was a precursor of twentieth-century *Existenzphilosophie*, though that label did not fit his philosophy. Not only Jaspers kept stressing Nietzsche's significance; Heidegger did, too, and eventually, after World War II, published several essays as well as a two-volume work on him.[16] By that time, Jaspers had come more and more to prefer Kierkegaard to Nietzsche, although he had published much more about Nietzsche,[17] while Heidegger openly disparaged Kierkegaard, whom he had cited with respect in *Sein und Zeit*, and proclaimed Nietzsche as a world-historical figure. (It is arguable that Heidegger owes as much to Kierkegaard as he does to Nietzsche—and that his originality is widely overestimated.)

It was further understood that *Existenzphilosophie* was not merely a name for the philosophies of Jaspers and Heidegger, which had roots in Nietzsche, Kierkegaard, and the late Schelling (Jaspers' *Schelling* appeared in 1955), but that it signified a way of thinking to which some other contemporary writers, including Martin Buber and Franz Rosenzweig, were also close.

During the war, Jaspers was not allowed by the Nazis to teach or publish, and Heidegger published nothing except his collected *Erläuterungen zu Hölderlins Dichtung* (1944, Elucidations of Hölderlin's poetry). In 1945, when the Nazi state collapsed, Heidegger was temporarily discredited while Jaspers resumed his chair at Heidelberg and began to publish again; but at that point Jean-Paul Sartre, who called his own philosophy *existentialisme*, made existentialism the most widely discussed philosophy of our time. Even in Germany it was he who redirected attention to Heidegger; and in the United States and elsewhere the sudden interest in the so-called existentialists was created largely by Sartre's works.

We are now ready to give our first answer to the question, What is existentialism? When we speak of the continental rationalists or the British empiricists, we do not imply that the men concerned welcomed, or would have welcomed, this label. If this is firmly kept in mind, we may call Kierkegaard, Jaspers, Heidegger, and Sartre the Big Four existentialists. We shall have to deal briefly with the

16 "Nietzsches Wort 'Gott ist tot'" in *Holzwege* (1950); "Wer ist Nietzsches Zarathustra?" in *Vorträge und Aufsätze* (1954), English translation by Bernd Magnus in *Lectures and Addresses* (1967); and *Nietzsche*, 2 vols. (1961).

17 In addition to the works named, most notably a short book, *Nietzsche und das Christentum* (n.d. [1946]), English translation by E. B. Ashton, *Nietzsche and Christianity* (1961).

reception of all four and of Nietzsche, before we consider some other writers who have often been lumped with the existentialists, notably Tillich and Buber. But before we consider these men one at a time, we must attempt a nonostensive, analytical answer to the question of what existentialism is.

III

"Existentialism" is not merely a label that happens to have been applied to the philosophies of several men; it represents an attempt to call attention to the fact that they have something in common. To list affinities and get involved in the crisscross of family resemblances—these two share this feature, and one of them shares that trait with those two—would serve little purpose. Let us be bold and suggest a fundamental conviction common to all: philosophy should begin neither with axioms nor with doctrines, neither with ideas nor with sense impressions, but with experiences that involve the whole individual.

In his *Psychologie der Weltanschauungen* (1919), Jaspers called them *Grenzsituationen* (border situations) and paid particular attention to four: struggle, death, accident (*Zufall*), and guilt. In his *Philosophie* (1932) he changed the sequence and substituted suffering for accident. Toward the middle of the nineteenth century, Kierkegaard had written books on dread, fear and trembling, and the sickness unto death which is despair. Heidegger, in *Sein und Zeit* (1927), dealt at length with care (*Sorge*), dread, and attitudes toward one's own death. In Sartre's literature even more than in his philosophy, the experience of one's own impending violent death is again and again central, as it is also in both *The Stranger* and *The Plague* by Camus. Camus' third and last novel, *The Fall*, like Sartre's *Flies*, deals centrally with guilt feelings and both works are very close to Nietzsche in their strong opposition to guilt feelings and in linking them with Christianity. The twentieth-century existentialists also stress our always being in situations, and Sartre, following Kierkegaard, the dread-full dizziness of freedom that typically accompanies crucial decisions. Martin Buber is most interested in genuine dialogue that involves the whole person. Buber calls this *Zwiesprache* or

Dialog, Jaspers, *Kommunikation*. Buber also wrote a book on guilt and guilt feelings (*Schuld und Schuldgefühle*, 1958), and so (in 1912) did Tillich.[18]

When we call these men existentialists we do not imply that they are all very fond of each other or that they share a common philosophy. What they have in common is a notion about how philosophers might fruitfully *begin*. This may seem little enough, especially if one keeps in mind how much these men disagree about ever so much else, but it is enough to distinguish them from the continental rationalists and the British empiricists, Kant and Hegel, Bertrand Russell and G. E. Moore, as well as positivists and analytical philosophers. Moreover, close family resemblances are never any warrant that those who look similar to outsiders are pleased to hear how much they look alike or get along well with each other. As we have seen, the continental rationalists defined their own contributions in terms of their differences, and the same is true of the British empiricists.

The notion that philosophy is, and ought to remain, closer to literature than to the sciences, and the active interest many of the existentialists have taken in literature are corollaries of their common starting point; for our "ultimate" experiences have long been a staple of great literature and especially of tragedy. The widespread assumption that the existentialists stay closer to real life and are less academic than other philosophers is belied by the scholasticism of so many existentialist tomes, but is due to their common starting point.

Sartre's passing suggestion in one of the most widely read lectures of all time that there are two kinds of existentialists, Christian and atheist, has been parroted ad nauseam, but would be unhelpful even if he had not falsely classified Jaspers as a Catholic.[19] You might as well say that there were three kinds of continental rationalists— Catholic (Descartes), Jewish (Spinoza), and Protestant (Leibniz); or two kinds—theist and atheist (or pantheist). And there were also three kinds of British empiricists: unitarian or deist (Locke), Christian or theist (Berkeley), and atheist or agnostic (Hume). And American pragmatism can be divided the same way: theist (Peirce), agnostic or believer in a finite god (James), and atheist (Dewey).

---

[18] See n. 22 below.

[19] *L'existentialisme est un humanisme* (1946). Philip Mairet's translation, originally entitled *Existentialism and Humanism*, is included, under the title *Existentialism is a Humanism*, in *Existentialism from Dostoevsky to Sartre*, ed. Walter Kaufmann.

In other words, none of these convenient labels justifies the notion that those grouped together agreed on essentials or that they would have been happy to be lumped together. The opposite was true in every case, and existentialism is not singular in this respect. What is unusual is that historical self-consciousness has become so acute that men are labeled, pigeonholed, and all but embalmed while still alive and vigorous, and hence have ample opportunity to explicitly repudiate the ways in which others would classify them.

No sooner had Sartre called his philosophy *existentialisme* and a form of *humanisme* than Heidegger and Jaspers sought to dissociate themselves both from him and from each other; and eventually even Sartre grew tired of existentialism and pronounced it a parasitic growth on the margins of Marxism, which he proclaimed the philosophy of our age.[20]

IV

Turning now to the reception of existentialism in the United States, let us consider the major writers, one at a time, before attempting some generalizations in the end. We shall begin with the two nineteenth-century thinkers.

Before World War II, Kierkegaard was not widely known in the United States, but David Swenson and Walter Lowrie had begun their translations of his books; and by 1945 most of them, including all the major works, were available in English along with two biographies by Lowrie, one long and one short. This tremendous labor—most of it undertaken by Walter Lowrie—had been independent both of the migrations prompted by the Nazis and of the sudden explosion of interest in existentialism after the war, which vastly increased the audience for this literature and in time led to new translations from the Danish as well as a large secondary literature.

For almost a hundred years, Kierkegaard's books had had to wait to be translated into English. Untimely when they were written, they were not yet timely when they were first translated. In Germany trans-

[20] *Search for a Method*, translated by Hazel E. Barnes (1963), p. 8. "*Question de méthode*" is the prefatory essay in Sartre's *Critique de la raison dialectique* (1960). The relevant passages are included in the revised edition of *Existentialism from Dostoevsky to Sartre* (1975).

lations had begun to appear before the end of the nineteenth century, but it was only after World War I that Kierkegaard became popular, as dread and despair became common concerns. Before the war one had not spoken much of such things. Now one spoke of little else, and here was a writer who had devoted whole books to these extreme experiences. Jaspers and Karl Barth discovered him before the war was over, Heidegger and the general public a little later. But in the United States widespread interest in Kierkegaard, and in existentialism generally, was aroused only after World War II, by Jean-Paul Sartre. Thus American interest in Kierkegaard owes little or nothing to the migration from Central Europe.

Nietzsche was well known but little understood in the United States since at least 1900, and unreliable translations of all of his works had appeared in England before World War I. Many writers paid tribute to him, but when George Allen Morgan, Jr., published *What Nietzsche Means* in 1941, hardly any American philosophers were as yet taking Nietzsche seriously; and Morgan, who did, promptly left academic life, went into the Department of State, and ceased publishing philosophical books or articles.

Nietzsche's reception in the United States does owe something to the expulsion of the Jews from Germany. In 1950 the first edition of my *Nietzsche: Philosopher, Psychologist, Antichrist* appeared. I had left Germany in 1939, studied at Williams College and Harvard University, and started teaching at Princeton in 1947. In 1954 I published new translations of four of Nietzsche's books, as well as selections from his other works, his notes, and his letters (*The Portable Nietzsche*), and in 1966–67 translations with commentaries of five more books (collected in one Modern Library Giant, *Basic Writings of Nietzsche*, in 1968) and also of *The Will to Power*. In 1968, a third, revised and greatly expanded, edition of my *Nietzsche* appeared, and in 1974 a fourth edition as well as my translation with commentary of *The Gay Science*. In the late forties some American academicians were still astonished that a young man should be working on a book on Nietzsche, and the incredulous remark "I thought Nietzsche was dead as a doornail" voiced a common feeling. Twenty years later the same remark would only suggest that the speaker was wholly out of touch with the American scene.

I presented Nietzsche neither as an existentialist nor in the perspective of existentialism. While Nietzsche is now often studied as a precursor of existentialism, he has been linked even more often with other movements and currents; and earlier generations associated him with Darwin and evolutionary ethics, with Freud and psychoanalysis, with Schopenhauer or Spengler, Shaw or Gide, or Mussolini and Hitler; and in the mid-sixties the "death of God" theologians drew inspiration from him while some philosophers began to claim him as a precursor of analytic philosophy. It seems safe to predict that interest in Nietzsche will outlast the fashionable concern with existentialism. To what extent the fact that large numbers of young American philosophers have begun to read Nietzsche will affect American philosophy, it is too early to say. The effect on American theologians, on the other hand, is palpable and would have distressed Nietzsche.

V

American interest in Jaspers and Heidegger is largely due to Sartre, although—indeed in part because—neither of them admires Sartre. In the United States, as elsewhere, it was not the philosophical community that discovered Sartre. *The Flies* and *No Exit, Nausea,* his short stories, and his later plays and novels won a large audience before *Being and Nothingness* appeared in English, and they are still incomparably more widely read than any of his philosophical essays. Only his lecture *Existentialism Is a Humanism* is anywhere near so well known. But from the start of his international popularity it was common knowledge that Sartre was also a philosopher and that his *Being and Nothingness* owed something to Heidegger's *Being and Time*; also that the concern with nothingness could be traced back to Heidegger, and that Heidegger and Jaspers were full-fledged professors of philosophy who taught at old universities and did not spend much of their time in cafés or on fiction. Thus one read Sartre's literary works and his famous lecture but for the most part not *Being and Nothingness*, and one talked knowingly of Heidegger, often by way of suggesting that his *Being and Time*, which one had not read either, was of course incomparably more profound than Sartre's philosophy.

Even if it was not the professional philosophers that started these rumors, they had to reckon with them; and gradually the demand for English translations of Heidegger mounted. As enough translations became available, many departments of philosophy introduced courses in which they were studied.

With the exception of Descartes, French philosophers of note have tended not to be "pure" philosophers. Few are the philosophy courses at American colleges and universities in which Montaigne, Montesquieu, or Voltaire are discussed at all, and Comte and Bergson fare little better. Rousseau and Sartre *are* studied, but not by themselves. Rousseau may be linked with other social contract theorists; Sartre is lumped with Heidegger and other "existentialists" or—the new wave of the late sixties—with phenomenology. The refugee phenomenologists had never succeeded in creating any wide interest in phenomenology, but Sartre has.

Interest in Jaspers is not at all keen among American philosophers; there is a little but not much more of it at theological seminaries. That his three-volume *Philosophie* of 1932 had not yet appeared in English thirty-five years later, any more than his *Psychologie der Weltanschauungen* (1919) and his *Von der Wahrheit* (1947, On truth), is surely due to this fact, not the other way around. All this is the more remarkable when one considers that not one avowed Heidegger disciple emigrated to the United States, while Jaspers' most famous student, Hannah Arendt, made her home in the United States and acquired considerable influence. Yet her labors on behalf of Jaspers have not won for him the recognition Heidegger enjoys even among many philosophers who feel uncomfortable about his Nazi past.

The major translators of Jaspers, Heidegger, and Sartre are not immigrants; nor have studies by refugees helped notably to acclimatize these three writers. Although many students have approached the subject by way of my own *Existentialism from Dostoevsky to Sartre* (1956; rev. and expanded ed., 1975), which includes a long introduction as well as essays by Jaspers and Heidegger that had not been done into English before, I have never published any study of Sartre, and my essays on Jaspers and Heidegger are sharply critical.

Of course, several studies of Sartre and of existentialism generally have been contributed by American scholars born in Europe, but they were published to meet an existing demand that none of them affected significantly. And *Being and Nothingness* was translated by Hazel Barnes (1956), *Being and Time* by Edward Robinson and John MacQuarrie (1962), the first two born in the United States, the last in Scotland.

In sum, the American reception of Jaspers, Heidegger, and Sartre owes surprisingly little to the migrations set in motion by the Nazis. We may add that the differences between the reactions to Jaspers and to Heidegger parallel their reception in their native land. There, too, Jaspers' many popular books reach a wider audience than any of Heidegger's volumes, while professional philosophers have manifested far more interest in Heidegger, especially in *Sein und Zeit*. Ever since that book first appeared in 1927, Heidegger has attracted a much larger following and elicited far more discussion among professors and professors-to-be than Jaspers ever did. There are several reasons for this.

The first involves the personalities of the two men. Philosophers hesitate to touch upon such points because it seems indelicate and they are taught that ad hominem arguments are fallacious, but historians cannot always avoid personalities, seeing how often influence and success depend on them. To understand the different receptions with which Jaspers' and Heidegger's philosophies have met from the start, we must discuss their personalities, if only briefly. The basis for my juxtaposition is threefold: the printed record, which includes their writings and some essays about them; conversations with scholars who studied under them; and my personal impressions during the years 1946 to 1956. The picture that emerges from these sources is remarkably consistent.

Heidegger, a short man vibrant with energy and a demonic touch, may put one in mind of Napoleon. There was something electric about him, and he generated a sense of excitement. Whether in conversation—"under four eyes," as the Germans say—or in a huge auditorium, lecturing to thousands, he created the expectation that something of the first importance was at stake and on the verge of discovery. When he entered a lecture hall, the atmosphere was charged, and though his large audience soon got lost and many people went literally to sleep, he always managed to regain their attention before he concluded with some intimation that, although everything was dark now, next time a great revelation was to be expected. And most of the audience always blamed itself for its failure to understand what he had said, and came back. Some professors who were his students before 1933 and felt appalled by his quick embrace of Nazism—Herbert Marcuse and Hannah Arendt, for example—still felt a quarter of a century later that he was the greatest teacher they had ever had, especially in seminars.

Jaspers, very tall and pale, tried to keep students and colleagues at a distance; having a hole in one lung, he had to guard against catching cold. His life was spent largely at his desk, writing, not in seminars or in discussion. His aristocratic reserve appealed to many who like to listen to one or two lecture courses in philosophy, not to many professors-to-be.

Jaspers' second handicap was much less important but still deserves mention. Between 1923 and 1931 he published nothing, and his major philosophic work, his three-volume *Philosophie*, appeared less than a year before the Nazis came to power. Had this effort appeared five years earlier, the year *Sein und Zeit* was published, it would obviously have had more time to gain a hearing before World War II. But this point was not crucial.

The third point was much more decisive. Jaspers was more interested in *philosophieren*, philosophizing—or as one now says, in *doing* philosophy—than he was in offering doctrines; but unlike Wittgenstein, of whom the same could be said, Jaspers neither taught nor even seemed to teach a method. He was not primarily a teacher, he did not *desire* disciples, and he did not offer what professional students of philosophy, hoping to become professors, were looking for. His books do not lend themselves as well to endless discussions in seminars as does *Sein und Zeit*. Jaspers' works have the hortatory quality of Kierkegaard's and Nietzsche's, but without their literary grace, passion, and wit.

Heidegger's fame depends almost entirely on *Sein und Zeit*, which, though long-winded and repetitious, is much less so than Jaspers' three-volume magnum opus, not to speak of *Von der Wahrheit* (1947; xxiii plus 1,103 pages). A hostile critic might say that Heidegger's forbidding jargon strikes many philosophers as an uncomfortable challenge and that, having figured out how many pages that at first reading made little sense could be interpreted, one can then teach a seminar. But there is more to it than that, and it is noteworthy that Sartre, who never had the least liking for Nazism, discovered Heidegger after 1933 and was fascinated by his thought, while Jaspers, from whom Sartre also accepted important ideas, never appealed much to him, although Jaspers, devoted to his Jewish wife, never became a Nazi.

Sartre lacks the professorial bearing of both men and plainly does not desire disciples. Though he owes much to both, he is in many ways

closer to Kierkegaard and Nietzsche. His versatility, his restless bril-
liance, and his literary gifts exert a fascination that few writers can
match. Both the popular image of, and the wide interest in, existentialism are inseparable from these qualities. The spell Sartre has cast
over generations of American students, beginning right after the war,
has created an almost unique interest that courses in philosophy, religion, literature departments, and humanities have been designed to
satisfy or to exploit. Jaspers and Heidegger have been among the
major beneficiaries. But this is not merely an American phenomenon.

Even in Germany it was the French who permitted Heidegger to
teach again at Freiburg, after he had first been retired in 1945. And
the Germans, having little to boast of at that time, even culturally,
were persuaded by Sartre that at least they had a great philosopher of
international repute. Jaspers' decision in 1948 to leave Heidelberg,
where he had resumed teaching in 1945, to accept a call to Basel certainly did not increase his influence in postwar Germany; nor did he
acquire any influence in Switzerland.

That Sartre's impact in the United States has been so much greater
than either Jaspers' or Heidegger's is less a function of his philosophy
than of his literature. His lecture *Existentialism Is a Humanism*
(1946) along with his two plays, *No Exit* and *The Flies*, and some
awareness of his major philosophic work, *Being and Nothingness*—
all three published during the war in occupied Paris—hit the American consciousness and much of the rest of the world all at once; and
while *Being and Nothingness* alone might not have attracted very
much more attention than the tomes of the German existentialists,
the knowledge that there was a philosophy behind the plays, the
novels, and the short stories unquestionably added a great deal to
their attraction. That existentialism elicits greater interest in the
United States than any previous philosophic movement is almost
entirely due to Jean-Paul Sartre.

VI

Several other writers have often been called existentialists. Dostoevsky and Tolstoy, Rilke and Kafka, though dead before anyone had
ever heard of "existentialism" or *Existenzphilosophie*, profoundly

influenced Jaspers, Heidegger, and Sartre;[21] but judicious writers are agreed that these four men, like Nietzsche, ought not to be called existentialists.

Given our account of existentialism, we can readily see why this should be so. These men, being novelists or poets, were not especially concerned with the proper starting point for philosophy. They were profoundly concerned with extreme situations, but so were Shakespeare and the Greek tragic poets, Heinrich von Kleist and Georg Büchner, the Buddha and the prophets. These experiences have always been close to the heart of religion and of tragic literature, and to call dozens of poets and religious figures of all ages existentialists would be exceedingly unhelpful.

In any case, these four writers do not owe their richly deserved fame in the English-speaking world to refugees. Dostoevsky's and Tolstoy's works had been translated and their reputations were secure long before 1930. Rilke was the greatest German poet since Goethe's death. And Kafka was one of the most original novelists of all time.

Kafka was a Jew, and it might be supposed that his vast reputation and influence in the United States did owe something to the exodus of Jews from Germany. He died in 1924, and his unfinished novel *Der Prozess* (*The Trial*) was published by his friend Max Brod the following year, although Kafka had asked him to destroy the manuscript. In 1926 Brod published *Das Schloss* (*The Castle*), and in 1927 *Amerika*, both also against the author's express desire and unfinished. When the Nazis came to power, Brod, long a Zionist, went to Palestine. His editorial labors on his friend's behalf continued, and he also wrote a biography of Kafka. Other refugees did their share, but it does not appear that the expulsion of so many intellectuals from Central Europe made any decisive difference to Kafka's reception abroad. Willa and Edwin Muir, who were not refugees, translated *The Castle*

---

21 Kafka may not have influenced Jaspers and Heidegger; his influence on Camus was formative.

The central section on death in *Sein und Zeit* is plainly inspired by Tolstoy's *The Death of Ivan Ilyitch* (1886). For Tolstoy's concern with self-deception, one of the major themes of Sartre's philosophy and fiction, see chap. 2 above.

Dostoevsky, like Nietzsche, exerted a decisive influence on the whole climate of thought, especially after World War I.

Of Rilke's *Aufzeichnungen des Malte Laurids Brigge* (1910, The Notes of M.L.B.) one feels reminded especially by Sartre's *La Nausée* (1938, Nausea). See also Heidegger's essay on Rilke in *Holzwege* (1952). In 1975 I learned from Hans-Georg Gadamer that he had introduced Heidegger to *Malte Laurids Brigge* in 1923, long before the publication of *Sein und Zeit*.

in 1930, *The Trial* in 1937, and *Amerika* in 1938; and as Kafka's visions turned into reality, his fame spread.

The most important way in which the Nazi regime promoted existentialism and the literature associated with it was not by compelling many people to emigrate but rather by killing so many more. As fear and trembling, dread and despair, and the vivid anticipation of one's own death ceased to be primarily literary experiences and, like the absurd visions of Kafka, turned into the stuff of everyday life, the originally untimely Kafka and Kierkegaard became popular along with Jaspers and Heidegger, Sartre and Camus, who were fashionable from the first; and Dostoevsky, Tolstoy, and Nietzsche, whose fame was long established, suddenly appeared in a new light.

The case of Camus may seem different because for a while he was Sartre's friend, before their political differences estranged them; and, like Sartre, he tried to write philosophy as well as plays, novels, short stories, and journalism. But his philosophical efforts were so feeble that it makes more sense to see him as a literary figure whose reputation depends on his three novels and, to a lesser extent, on his plays and short stories. His *Myth of Sisyphus* and *The Rebel* have been highly successful with American undergraduates but have been almost wholly ignored by philosophers. For good measure, Camus disdained the label of existentialism (this in itself would not be decisive); and his American reception owes nothing to the mid-century migrations.

VII

It might be argued that Paul Tillich and Martin Buber, who were above all religious writers, should be left out of account here; but we shall consider both. Tillich's case is relevant and instructive because in 1933 he left Germany for the United States; because after the war he often called himself an existentialist; and because he saw himself, and others came to see him, as a philosopher-theologian who to some extent transformed both disciplines by infusing existentialist ideas into them.

While Sartre moved from existentialism to Marxism, Tillich traveled in the opposite direction, from Marxism to existentialism. He had been a Christian socialist in Germany in the 1920's and, far from trying to recant his Marxist past when the Nazis came to power, accepted an invitation to teach at Union Theological Seminary in New York although he was unable as yet to speak English. He had the vitality to begin a new life at the age of forty-six, soon lectured in English, then began to write in English, and eventually, after World War II, became incomparably more influential in the New World than he had ever been in the Old. As existentialism became popular, Tillich, by now in his sixties, identified with it—he liked to say that he was an existentialist when he asked questions and a theologian when he gave answers—and he quickly became the most widely acclaimed Protestant theologian in the United States, far outstripping his only rival, Reinhold Niebuhr. (The competition in this field is not as keen as in nuclear physics.)

An admirer might say that quality gains recognition, even if it takes time, while a cynic might suggest that Tillich offered the latest intellectual fashions and Christianity, too. There is a good deal of truth in both points. Most theologians pour new wine into old skins, and that Tillich's impact became so much greater than that of the others was due partly to the quality of what he had to offer, though it also owed something to the unusual vigor and charm of his personality.

His frequent use in the 1950's of the term "existentialism" was unquestionably opportune and shrewd, but Tillich's ideas were not improvised to meet a new demand. His dissertations had been on Schelling;[22] Nietzsche's influence on Tillich had been formative; and Tillich's interest in Freud long antedated Sartre's. He was a contemporary of Jaspers and Heidegger, between them in age, shaped by similar reading and experiences—an authentic exemplar of that German philosophical tradition to which a new generation was suddenly seeking an indirect approach by way of Sartre. Unlike all the others, Tillich was in the United States, writing and teaching and preaching in English, and available for lectures and symposia.

Even so, his popularity also exemplified the time lag of which we have spoken. For Tillich's thought always remained closer in essen-

[22] *Die religionsgeschichtliche Konstruktion in Schellings positiver Philosophie* (The construction of the history of religion in Schelling's positive philosophy) . . .: *Inaugural-Dissertation zur Erlangung der philosophischen Doktorwürde* . . . *Breslau* (1910) and *Mystik und Schuldbewusstsein in Schellings philosophischer Entwicklung* (Mysticism and the consciousness of guilt in Schelling's philosophical development): *Inaugural-Dissertation zur Erlangung der Lizentiatenwürde der hochwürdigen theologischen Fakultät Halle-Wittenberg*, in *Beiträge zur Förderung christlicher Theologie*, 16:1 (1912).

tials to Schelling than to Sartre, and what he brought to Union Theological Seminary and then, after his retirement, even more obviously to Harvard, and eventually, during his last years, to the University of Chicago, was not so much a new wave as the final ripple of German idealism and romanticism.

At the University of Berlin, the old Schelling had replaced Hegel in 1841, ten years after Hegel's death. The king of Prussia had called him there expressly to root out "the dragon seed of the Hegelian pantheism."[23] Schelling in his last years characterized Hegel's philosophy along with his own early efforts as merely negative philosophy and demanded a new positive philosophy. Hegel was, first according to Schelling and then also in the writings of Kierkegaard, who heard the old Schelling lecture in Berlin, a mere conceptmonger, while what truly mattered was genuine existence and eternal happiness. In the later nineteenth century, Protestant theology became more modest. While Hegelianism lost its hold on German philosophy it found a new home not only in British and American philosophy but also in German Protestant theology. What had struck King Frederick William IV as "pantheism" now passed for liberalism. And the revival of philosophical interest in Hegel was spearheaded by the fine new editions of his *Encyclopädie* (1905) and *Phänomenologie* (1907) that were produced by Georg Lasson, a Protestant pastor whose father, Adolf Lasson (originally, Ahron Lazarussohn), had championed Hegel's philosophy at the University of Berlin. The revival of Hegel in Germany also owed a great deal to Wilhelm Dilthey's study of the young Hegel (1906); and Dilthey's own "philosophy of life" and his concern with *Weltanschauungen* left their mark on German existentialism.[24]

While in many ways close to the old Schelling, Tillich was far from merely trying to bring back a system that was a hundred years old, and even further from Schelling's pathetic resentment against his erstwhile friend Hegel, whose fame had long exceeded his own; nor was Tillich up in arms against the dragon seed of pantheism. He had himself come out of that liberal Protestantism which was permeated

[23] See Kaufmann, *Hegel* (1965), secs. 68 and 70.
[24] See, e.g., Jaspers, *Psychologie der Weltanschauungen*; Heidegger, *Sein und Zeit*, pp. 46–47, 205n., 209–10, 249n., 376–77, 385n., and 397–404; and Buber's occasional references to Dilthey as "my teacher" (once even as "my master")—but see also Buber's protest in *The Philosophy of Martin Buber*, ed. Paul Schilpp and Maurice Friedman (1967), p. 702.

by Hegelianism; he had been a student when Dilthey's *Jugend-geschichte Hegels* appeared in 1906, followed the next year by the first publication of *Hegels theologische Jugendschriften*—his early, really rather antitheological, fragments on Christianity, written during the last decade of the eighteenth century. And Tillich liked to say that Marx, Nietzsche, and Freud had been the greatest Protestants of the past hundred years.

Philosophical idealism in America had had a definitely Protestant tinge, and the many theologians and the few philosophers who still looked back nostalgically to Josiah Royce and idealism were not ready to take the leap to Barth or Kierkegaard. Tillich met their needs perfectly. He did not propose a renaissance of idealism; he combined Schelling and Hegel with the most modern movements, spoke approvingly of everything that was avant garde, and, while acclaimed as an existentialist like Kierkegaard, excelled in the art of obviating any either-or.

Only a few years earlier, being *au courant* with Kierkegaard had meant being neo-orthodox, contemptuous of liberalism, and exposed to the charge of fundamentalism. Tillich was liberalism incarnate.

It seems safe to predict that his influence will be confined to theology. His *Systematic Theology* has little competition. No other American theologian of comparable *niveau* has written a systematic theology in this century. Hence Tillich's may well continue to be studied in seminaries. And some of his many short and relatively popular books will, no doubt, continue to find readers. As far as new directions in Protestant theology are concerned, the much publicized death-of-God theology may be seen as an attempt to push beyond Tillich. While he unquestionably paved the way for it, he is obviously not responsible for the fact that it is more notable for the headlines it has produced than it is for thoughtful or substantial writings.

In sum, Tillich took existentialism away from Barth and the neo-orthodox and used its popular appeal to liberalize American Protestantism and to animate it with more interest in German philosophy—including Nietzsche—as well as doubts about God. Incidentally he proved that all this can command the widest popular interest and even, as long as it is fused with homage to Christ, the covers of the slickest news magazines. This lesson was not lost.

VIII

Martin Buber left Germany for Jerusalem in 1938. His *Ich und Du* (1923) appeared in English in 1937 and in French the following year. *I and Thou* was translated by Ronald Gregor Smith and published in Edinburgh. With the exception of *Jewish Mysticism and the Legends of the Baal-Shem*, which appeared in London and Toronto in 1931, it was until 1945 the only one of Buber's many books available in English. Considering the migration of so many Jews from Central Europe, this is a remarkable fact; for among the German-speaking Jews who fled from the Nazi terror Buber's prestige was immense. But when the war ended, interest in his ideas was still largely confined to Christian theologians who considered *I and Thou* a seminal work.

Buber had long been a Zionist, and it was thus no mere accident that he went to the Hebrew University; and he would never have wished to teach at a theological seminary. But if he had taught in the United States, beginning in 1933 or 1938, and learned to write and publish in English—as he did learn to write and publish in Hebrew— his impact would surely have been far greater than it has been in fact. Whether this would have made any very great differences to long-range currents of thought is another question. By the time he died in 1965—the same year Tillich died—most of his books were available in American paperbacks.

Tillich is the only influential American writer who is regularly classified as, and who frequently labeled himself, an existentialist; and Buber's belated arrival in the United States coincided with the arrival of existentialism, and was understood in this context. Tillich is the only so-called existentialist whose reception was facilitated by his immigration, and it is instructive to juxtapose Tillich and Buber.

Buber's acceptance was also facilitated by his many visits to the United States after World War II; but these cannot be accounted part of the large-scale migrations from Central Europe. Rudolph Bultmann weathered the war in Germany, as a Protestant theologian, and also visited the United States after the war, although, lacking Buber's charisma, his personal appearances had relatively little to do with the spread of interest in his program of demythologizing the New Testament. But if he had taught here for a quarter century, or if Karl Barth, who went to Basel after the Nazis came to power, had done so, there would unquestionably be large numbers of American preachers and professors now who could be classified as their disciples. It is different with Buber.

In spite of his charisma, Buber did not develop disciples any more than he developed doctrines. If one accepted the notion that existentialism, unlike other philosophies, sticks to experience instead of becoming preoccupied with concepts and doctrines—that the existentialists deal with existence, while other philosophers deal with essences—then the men we have discussed are not really existentialists, excepting only Buber.

This may be a reduction to the absurd of the popular notion of existentialism, and it shows that our earlier suggestion that it is only the common starting point in our extreme experiences that sets off the existentialists is more judicious. Yet our account of the reception of existentialism would be grossly misleading if we ignored one of the most crucial facts. The insistence that philosophy is, or ought to be, closer to literature than to science and that we must begin with our most intense experiences has been the bait that has led thousands to swallow some new scholasticism that differs from one fisher of men to another. Not only do the concepts and the doctrines furnish meat for seminars and the backbone of solid respectability, the jargon is part of the bait. The neophyte knows that once he has mastered that, he is "in," he belongs, and he has a spiritual home. This is the central irony of existentialism: *the jargon of anguish, solitude, and authenticity allays anguish, liberates from solitude, and facilitates inauthenticity.* One sneers at the anonymous "one," chatters about mere "chatter," is curious about the latest diatribes against "curiosity," and feels superior.

Buber never fitted into this pattern. He did not only begin with experience, he stayed with it. His greatest achievements were literary—notably his collection of *Tales of the Hasidim*,[25] his translation of the Hebrew Bible into German,[26] and his novel[27]—and his own prose always remained literary and never degenerated into jargon. His rhapsodic *Ich und Du* is no exception, although English-speaking theolo-

---

[25] 2 vols., translated by Olga Marx, 1947–48. *Die Erzählungen der Chassidim* (1950), Manesse-Bibliothek der Weltliteratur, is the definitive edition of the original.
[26] Definitive edition in 4 vols., *Die Schrift*, 1954, 1955, 1958, 1962. The enterprise was undertaken jointly with Franz Rosenzweig, in the 1920's, and the books of the Bible appeared one at a time.
[27] *Gog and Magog* (1949); English translation by Ludwig Lewisohn, *For the Sake of Heaven* (1945).

gians soon derived from it "a Thou," "a Thou-relationship," and a few other phrases one could juggle somewhat like Sartre's *en-soi* and *pour-soi*. Buber's stance did not only forestall disciples, it also went so much against the grain of organized religion in America, and of the universities as well, that, his prestige notwithstanding, his approach was little understood or appreciated. What he offered was neither theology nor philosophy, and least of all fundamentalism or revivalism. It was a highly literate and somewhat literary experience of religion as a dialogue.

The single person who did the most to popularize Buber in America was Maurice Friedman, born in Oklahoma, who wrote a book and innumerable articles on Buber while also translating him tirelessly. The migration from Central Europe affected Buber's reception scarcely at all, and when he died his personal prestige was ever so much greater than his actual influence. No doubt, he has begun to reach single individuals here and there; but whether his books will give either American Judaism or American philosophy new directions remains to be seen.

IX

Existentialism developed in at least three stages: Danish, German, and French. The first stage was represented by a single writer who rightly saw himself as an exception. He bucked the currents of the early Victorian era and projected his own extraordinary sensibility in a highly original and eccentric series of books. He deliberately remained outside every establishment—church, state, and university—countered a favorable notice in the press by declaring his contempt for the journal in which it had appeared, and added that in that publication he would prefer to be pilloried—which he promptly was.

The second stage is represented by two German professors. Both began to publish over half a century after Kierkegaard's death, rose to the top of their profession, and attracted some notice, but no more than several of their colleagues who did philosophy in a different key; for example, Edmund Husserl, Max Scheler, Nicolai Hartmann, Ernst Cassirer, and Rudolf Carnap.

Then Jean-Paul Sartre captured the imagination of the Western world with *his* version of existentialism. His plays and fiction were unusually philosophical, his academic philosophic volumes were enlivened by a wealth of vivid unacademic examples, his political and critical journalism was tireless, and his autobiography a masterpiece. He did not only get himself read all over the world; he also created international interest in German existentialism; and he led large numbers to study Kierkegaard and Nietzsche as forerunners of existentialism, and Camus, Buber, and Tillich as existentialists. Initially, it was fashionable to see him as a mere journalist without genuine depth or genius. What a few saw soon was so plain twenty years after the end of the war that he was named winner of the Nobel Prize for literature although he had let it be known that he would not accept the prize—a gesture that shows how much closer he is in some ways to Kierkegaard than to the German existentialists. He wears the mantle of Voltaire and Rousseau, and the subtitle of Iris Murdoch's *Sartre* (1953) may show how he does have ties to both: *Romantic Rationalist.*

Indeed, we may speak of a fourth stage in the development of existentialism. After the arrival of Sartre, a number of other writers who had not called themselves existentialists or been so labeled before 1945 became identified with this label and triumphed *in hoc signo.*

We can also distinguish four levels in the *reception* of existentialism. The first is the stage of fashion, chatter, and journalism. This phase is not over yet, either in the United States or in Europe, although in France and Germany anthropology and sociology have begun to replace existentialism, also at the second level, which is that of research, seminars, and scholasticism. In the United States, the second phase, unlike the first, has not yet reached its high point, although it is well along its way. By the time it reaches its climax, existentialism will probably be in eclipse in the countries of its origin.

The third phase eludes easy observation and remains a subject for conjecture, but in the case of existentialism we must also ask to what extent the writers mentioned have had the impact they explicitly desired, changing the quality of men's lives. This level cannot be inferred from the first two. On the contrary, insofar as the journalistic and the scholastic reception permit any inference about it, they give the impression that there has been very little of this and that both the popular and the academic approach have, each in its own way, pulled the fangs of existentialism and made it innocuous. This, of course, does not preclude that here and there an individual's life may have been changed by reading one or another of these writers. I have no doubt even so that on this level the impact of Jaspers and Heidegger, Sartre, Tillich, and Buber is not remotely comparable to that of Tolstoy, Nietzsche, and Kafka.

This may seem no more than a surmise, but an examination of the fourth and final level bears it out. What has been the impact of the writers whom we have considered on those individuals who have in turn become influential writers? Nietzsche's influence on all the writers we have been considering, excepting only the three who belonged to an earlier generation, is as obvious as his impact on Thomas Mann and Hermann Hesse, André Gide and André Malraux, Shaw, Yeats, and O'Neill, Freud, Adler, and Jung, Stefan George, Rilke, and Gottfried Benn, Max Scheler and Nicolai Hartmann, and any number of others. That this became evident only after his death is irrelevant, considering that he died early. His impact on these men was plain as soon as they had read him, and he had left a decisive mark on world literature and philosophy well before he would have been eighty. When we ask about the impact of existentialism in the United States in *this* sense, we find that as yet there is no evidence that the writers here discussed have changed the quality of American philosophy or poetry, drama or fiction, or our intellectual life. Nor are there signs as yet that many American philosophers have been persuaded that our extreme experiences furnish a fruitful starting point for philosophical reflection. Insofar as such experiences are mentioned at all, the question discussed is usually what Heidegger may have meant when he said this or that. In our philosophical community, existentialism is acquiring some respectability only in its scholastic form.

There is one exception. One idea that is widely associated with existentialism is making some headway among professional philosophers: *engagement*. In the civil rights movement and the protests against the Vietnam war, many professors of philosophy have followed Sartre's lead in committing themselves publicly. Unlike Sartre, however, they do this, as it were, after hours, without claiming any close connection between such activities and their philosophies. Moreover, it might be questioned whether *engagement* is really a part of existentialism or merely a notion that Sartre, with his experience of the resistance during World War II, has championed all along. To be sure, *engagement* was never that central in Heidegger's philosophy, and his brief flirtation with political commitment is humiliating to recall.[28] But not only has the later Jaspers written several books in which he adopts stands on questions of the day, but Sartre's message and the popular image of existentialism were from the beginning associated with *engagement*. Here, if anywhere, the impact of existentialism on American intellectuals is striking. Or is this a case of *post hoc ergo propter hoc?* Is there after all no causal link?

I cannot prove here that there is a link, but I believe there is. In support of this surmise one might adduce these points. The impetus for commitment has come largely from students and younger faculty, as well as some of the younger clergy—the generation that grew up reading Sartre. Then, Sartre's protests against the Algerian war have left a deep impression on American intellectuals and persuaded many that an intellectual minority can have an influence on stopping what is felt to be an unjust and immoral war. Finally, Sartre's protests against the Vietnam war have helped to rouse the conscience of large numbers of Americans. But this impact of existentialism on the American conscience owes little to the migration of intellectuals during the Nazi period, even though some refugees have greatly welcomed this development.

X

The most surprising result of our study is surely that the migration of so many Central European intellectuals to the United States has had so little impact on the spread of existentialism in America. Almost all of the major translations were done by native English speakers, and few refugees published pioneering studies of the so-called existentialists. Only Nietzsche's influence was decisively advanced by an immigrant, but then Nietzsche was not really an existentialist. Sartre and Camus, Kierkegaard, Buber and Heidegger, owe little or nothing to the migration; and although Jaspers' favorite student has gained some influence in her own right, few American philosophers are particularly interested in him.

Only Tillich's impact on the American scene is almost wholly due to the migrations set in motion by the Nazis. Had he stayed in the

28 See above all Heidegger's *Die Selbstbehauptung der deutschen Universität* (1933).

Old World, writing his later works in German, Swedish, or Hebrew, Americans would hardly speak of "ultimate concern" and "being-itself." Clearly, intellectual fashions would be different. And had Karl Barth come here instead of Tillich, it is even possible that the history of Protestant theology in the United States would have proceeded differently. American theology is even more derivative than is American philosophy.

The main reason why existentialism has not had more effect on American philosophy is that some other Central European philosophers have been so much more influential: to some extent, Rudolf Carnap, Herbert Feigl, and C. G. Hempel; to an even far greater extent Ludwig Wittgenstein. For this there are many reasons.

The first three came to the United States and taught and wrote in English. Their ideas were highly teachable and discussable, admirably precise, and congenial to students brought up on a high regard for the exact sciences. Teaching at different universities, they all attracted excellent students who then became teachers and attracted students of their own. Wittgenstein also taught in English and showed his students a highly contagious way of doing philosophy that, while not so scientific, did fit in with contemporary tendencies not only at his own Cambridge but also at Oxford.

Since World War I, competence in foreign languages has been a rarity among American graduate students in philosophy, and many of the most promising young philosophers have had difficulty in satisfying such requirements as showing the ability to translate one printed page of German philosophy in an hour, with a dictionary. Few indeed knew German well enough to be able to read untranslated books by Hegel, Dilthey, Heidegger, or Jaspers. The best students and young professors, given a chance to spend a year abroad on some fellowship, have for the most part gone to England, both because there are more bright philosophers at Oxford than at any other European university and because they did not have sufficient competence in any foreign language. As a result, ties between British and American philosophy have been very greatly strengthened, and most of the best British philosophers have also been invited to American universities—once, twice, three times, or permanently—while few continental European philosophers have taught at American institutions.

It would be an egregious error to think of contemporary American philosophy as merely an offshoot of British philosophy. Besides the Central Europeans mentioned above, there is also Sir Karl Popper, born in Vienna, who turns out disciples at the London School of Economics. But it would be entirely fair to say that philosophy nowadays is wholly tied to our universities, that professors are trained in graduate schools, and that our graduate programs are built around the general examinations which, at least in most of the best departments, stress logic, theory of knowledge, the philosophy of science, meta-ethics, and the way philosophy is done in our journals, à la Oxford. Those who have no stomach for all this tend to go into other fields, such as literature or religion. The Nazis kept Heidegger and drove out the positivists; but in the United States "The stone which the builders rejected has become the chief cornerstone."

7

BEYOND BLACK AND WHITE
A Plea for Thinking in Color*

I

It is time to move beyond black and white and to start thinking in color. Dualism is as colorblind in ethics as it is in aesthetics. Those who approach the riches of the moral life with the traditional dichotomies of good and evil or just and unjust are like aestheticians who know only two terms, *beautiful* and *ugly*, and possibly pride themselves on their progressiveness because they actually recognize degrees of beauty and ugliness.

The radicals of the New Left, who see the world in black and white, lend this issue intense urgency. Were it not for them, the problem might seem merely philosophical.

Radicalism facilitates progress by pushing old errors to the extremes of absurdity, making plain what is wrong with ideas that had seemed quite tolerable as long as they were taken none too seriously. Traditional morality had become reasonably comfortable by means of endless compromises, and it had come to be taken less and less seriously. Our new radicals remind us that millions have long found security in world views that reduce an inexhaustible variety to black and white, and many will not even suffer shades of gray.

It is by no means clear that this is an inveterate and ineradicable habit of the human race that only rare sophisticates have managed to escape. Those interested in a pluralistic reconstruction of morality should try to see this Manichaeism in historical perspective.

Men cannot stand the staggering diversity of life. Threatened by

* The project to which this essay belongs was supported in part by the National Endowment for the Humanities. The essay appeared in England in 1969, in *Survey: A Journal of Soviet and East European Studies*, and in the U.S. in 1970, in *Midway*. Subsequently it has also appeared elsewhere and been translated into Italian.

a chaos of sounds, colors, and nameless impressions, and by a frightening whirl of possibilities and options, they seek order and stability. Yet the early Greeks and Indians were pluralists. Not blessed with any major prophets, their religions picked up gods and goddesses from neighbor tribes and conquered populations, and they wound up with many sun gods and with a jumble of divine genealogies. They did not count their deities or draw clear lines between the gods and men but were content in practice that it was sufficient to pay heed to relatively few. The greatest powers in the world were frequently in conflict with each other, but none was always right or always wrong.

Let us consider the Greeks first and then ancient India before we turn to Zarathustra and the Manichean heritage that our student radicals are—let us thank them for it!—leading to the absurd. Good riddance!

II

The Greeks' power to organize the chaos has rarely been equaled. During the century bounded by Winckelmann's pioneering studies of Greek art and Matthew Arnold's effusion about "sweetness and light" this Apollinian genius was so widely and so fervently admired that those other aspects of Greek culture which Nietzsche lumped together as "the Dionysian" were largely ignored.

In keeping with a German tradition that had played off against each other classical and romantic, naive and sentimental poetry (Schiller), and representation and will (Schopenhauer), Nietzsche sought to understand the Greeks in terms of the Apollinian and the Dionysian. Following the precedents that had inspired his contrast, he did not paint his two principles black and white, more nearly blue and red.

My view of the Greeks differs decisively from Nietzsche's.[1] It would be hazardous, and there is no need, to offer sweeping generalizations about ancient Greece. But we do know the *Iliad* as well as fourteen of Aeschylus' and Sophocles' tragedies, and these poems are outstanding in the craftsmanship of their design. From Homer to Aeschylus and Sophocles we witness a crescendo of economy. Conflict

[1] See my *Tragedy and Philosophy* (1968), on which the following account of the Greeks is based.

is at the very core of all these works, but never are the adversaries colored black and white. The immensity of this achievement ought to give us pause.

In the *Iliad* we do not encounter any great concern with moral problems. Homer built the *Iliad* around contests, stressing the humanity of both sides. The gods participate, but some on this side and some on that, and like the heroes they are neither wholly good nor altogether evil. One might feel tempted to call the *Iliad* premoral, but it is merely premoralistic: the poet does not moralize, but his insistence on the humanity of Hector no less than Achilles, of Sarpedon no less than Patroclus, and of the Trojans no less than the Achaeans, is anything but premoral or amoral—it puts to shame the morality of later ages.

This Homeric attitude left its mark upon Greek tragedy. In Aeschylus' *Libation Bearers* Orestes actually says: "Right clashes with right" (line 461). Hegel's notion that it is of the essence of tragedy to represent a collision in which both sides are justified was based squarely on Greek tragedy, although Hegel overshot the mark when he occasionally insisted that both sides were *equally* justified.

In Greek tragic poetry, from the *Iliad* to the *Bacchae*, it was recognized that nobility and even divinity did not imply that all right was on one side and all wrong on the side of those who opposed Apollo, Dionysus, or even Zeus.

Greek philosophy, too, was nourished by the spirit of Homer. Plato did not cast his philosophy in the straight didactic or homiletic mode but preferred to vie with the tragic poets, having been one himself before he met Socrates. And although some figures in Plato's dialogues say little but "Yes" and "Obviously," "That necessarily follows," "True," "Certainly," and "I think so," the ethos communicated by most of the dialogues of Plato is that of a common quest for knowledge in which even the most intelligent men make mistakes and must go back and try again. Here Socrates' influence pointed in the same direction as Sophocles', for Socrates had insisted that he did not know the answers to the most important questions and that if he was wiser than other men it was solely because they thought they knew what they didn't know.

The great Greeks from Homer to Socrates were not fanatics, and bequeathed to us a spirit that is anything but Manichaean.

III

Reading the Vedas, which belong to the period before 1000 B.C., and looking at the temples built in India during the Middle Ages, one may feel that here is a world in which the Dionysian was never subdued by the Apollinian. It has been claimed that the Hindus have literally millions of gods; yet only a totally untrained eye will mistake this colorful world of abundance for chaos. However remote the sculptured facades of India's temples are from Greek simplicity, they are structured with extreme care, and the rigors of self-discipline were extolled in India far more than they ever were in Greece or China.

It was because the Greeks were so prone to the temptations of excess that they revered the adage "Nothing in excess," and the Indians developed elaborate systems of austerities because they felt that they needed them. Yet Hinduism absolutized neither the inexhaustible multiplicity of the world nor the means by which holy men might try to exorcise the chaos. There were always many means, many ways, many yogas; and the sages of the Upanishads taught that the multifarious world of appearance was illusion and ultimate reality One.

Dualistic metaphysical systems made their appearance during the age of the Upanishads—in Jainism, for example—but classical Hinduism, or proto-Hinduism, rejected them. Even in the moral realm it preferred something less simplistic and more pluralistic, while insisting that in the last analysis all moral distinctions were illusory and man must eventually rise above good and bad to enter the undifferentiated unity of Brahma.

Any conception of Hinduism that is based only on the Upanishads, supplemented by the Bhagavad-Gita, is as wide of the mark as any picture of Christianity based exclusively on the New Testament. Such readings would not prepare anyone for the realities of India or the "Christian" world. One Hindu scripture that helps at least a little to bridge the gap to historical reality is *The Laws of Manu*. In its present metrical form it may be barely older than the New Testament, but its substance goes back to the age of the Upanishads. In these laws we find the caste system as well as detailed provisions for the outcastes. Many of the rules and the whole ethos that they implement are paradigms of what almost all modern students of religion would consider social injustice; hence they are generally omitted from modern anthologies. For these collections of scriptures are generally designed to create highly favorable rather than truly representative images of religions.

Manu's caste system differentiates three twice-born castes, which correspond to the three classes in Plato's *Republic*. At the top are the Brahmins, a caste of priests and sages; then come the Kshatriya, the warrior caste; and next the Vaishya. The distinctions between them cut deep and are hereditary and inviolable. Even more profound, however, is the gulf that separates the twice-born from the fourth caste, the Shudras, the slaves.

Few, if any, transgressions were considered more outrageous than for a Shudra to beget children with a Brahmin woman, and the offspring of such unions were Chandalas, outcastes, living abominations, not fit to be treated like human beings. They were not the only outcastes; there were other kinds, traced to different types of miscegenation (chap. 10). Outcastes, of course, did not carry their certified pedigrees with them: rather were they presumed to be the products of sin, however remote in the past, and hence it was proper to despise them.

The belief in transmigration of souls reinforced this cruel attitude and served as another form of rationalization. If men are reborn in accordance with their deserts, then the soul that is reborn as an outcaste, or as a Shudra, deserves to be treated as such men and women are treated traditionally. And the Shudras are assured explicitly that if they are good slaves in this life they may hope to be reborn as members of a higher caste (9.334f.).

The differences between the three upper castes were also rooted in color; *Varna*, the Indian term for caste, literally means color. The Brahmins were light-skinned and largely managed to remain that way down to the twentieth century (Nehru was a Brahmin), while the Shudras were dark-skinned, a conquered population reduced to servitude. The Indian way always remained very different from the dualism of the American South, and in time the pluralism of Manu developed into an incomparably more complex system of innumerable castes and subcastes. There even are some black Brahmins.

Those who see the world in black and white, with pluralistic India colored white and the dualistic West colored black, are not only involved in a logical absurdity but also out of touch with the facts.

Hinduism *is* probably the most pluralistic of the world's major religions, and its metaphysical tolerance is as admirable as its caste system is outrageous. But the religious tolerance of Hinduism has often been exaggerated. The Buddha, who based his teaching on argument and refused to read his ideas into the Vedas, as the sages of the Upanishads did in his time, was considered a great heretic for denying the authority of the Vedas: Buddhism survived only in Ceylon, in Southeast Asia, and in the Far East, and as to the Hindu attitude toward Islam, the less we say the better. The Muslims, to be sure, divided mankind into believers and infidels, but both Buddhism and Islam transcended distinctions of caste and color. The point here is not to give marks but rather to counteract any inclination to see some of the great religions as good and others as wicked.

IV

Ancient Greece and India refused to see the world in black and white. Halfway between the two countries, Persia in Zoroastrianism, taught that there were two great cosmic forces, that of light and good and that of darkness and evil, Ohrmazd and Ahriman. It called on man to help the former vanquish the latter. We do not know when Zarathustra lived, but most scholars now consider him a contemporary of Jeremiah and believe that it was in part his message that electrified his people and set them to conquering the Babylonian Empire, thus bringing to an end the Babylonian exile of the Jews.

No sooner did the new religion come to the attention of the Jews than the Second Isaiah countered its dualism: "I am the Lord and none else, that forms light and creates darkness, makes peace and creates evil. I am the Lord that does all this" (45:6–7).

Some Zoroastrian ideas gained entrance into Judaism without achieving any great prominence in Old Testament times, notably the notions of the resurrection of the dead and the last judgment. But the concept of the Lord of Darkness made no headway in the light of Isaiah's impassioned pronouncements. In the Book of Job, Satan could acuse Job before the Almighty, but neither Job nor his friends, neither Satan nor God, even considered the possibility that God was not responsible for the sufferings of the blameless Job. Nor can we discount the possibility that the folktale of Satan and God antedated Zarathustra, and that Zoroastrianism raised a relatively minor figure to a status almost equal to that of the Lord of Light.

The *morality* of the ancient Hebrews was not free of dualism. Toward the end of the Law of Moses we find this summing up: "See, I have set before you this day life and good, death and evil. If you obey the commandments of the Lord your God which I command you this day, by loving the Lord your God, by walking in his ways, and by keeping his commandments and his statutes and his ordinances, then you shall live and multiply. . . . But if your heart turns away, and you will not hear, but are drawn away to worship other gods and serve them, I declare to you this day, that you shall perish. . . . I call heaven and earth to witness against you this day, that I have set before you life and death, blessing and curse; therefore choose life. . . ." (Deuteronomy 30:15–19).

Monotheism is here accompanied by a morality of good and evil. There is only one way to be good—at least for those addressed here—and that is to love the Lord and obey his laws. All other ways and any worship of other gods are evil. In a later age, humane rabbis allowed for the just among the Gentiles. The distinction between the moral core of the law and the statutes and ordinances made it possible to recognize that men could be moral without worshiping the Lord. But there were not two moral laws but one, and those who followed it were considered good, and those who did not were not good.

In many ways the Gospels are more dualistic and come much closer to a black and white view than the Law of Moses. This may have been due in part to Zarathustra's influence: Moses and most of the prophets had come before Zarathustra, and the religion of the Old Testament had gained its distinctive character before it came into contact with Persian and Hellenistic ideas, while the New Testament is a product of the Roman Empire and was written in Greek in a period in which some Persian and Greek notions had become common coin.

Moses and the prophets had been concerned largely with a way of life, and a large portion of the Pentateuch was given over to minute legislation. The central concern of the Gospels is with salvation and the terrifying question of what one must do to be saved, or (to put the point negatively) to escape eternal damnation. There are the sheep and the goats, and according to both Matthew (12:30) and Luke (11:23), Jesus said: "He who is not with me is against me."

The Devil became a far more powerful figure in Christianity than Satan had been in the Old Testament; he became the Evil One, the Lord of Hell; and mankind was divided into two camps, those headed for heaven and those headed for hell.

V

Even so, Christianity did not follow Zarathustra all the way. In the third century another Persian prophet, Mani, arose in southern Babylonia and preached what might be called a more Zoroastrian version of Christianity. He was martyred at the instigation of Magian priests but was survived by the doctrine that still bears his name, Manichaeism. For a while its impact in the Roman Empire rivaled that of Christianity, and Augustine came under its spell. Eventually the church condemned the Manichaean heresy, and as a religion it died. The details of this form of Gnosticism are now known only to a few historians of religion; yet Manichaeism is far from dead, if we use the name inclusively to label that view in which history is a contest between the forces of light and darkness, and men are divided into two camps, with all right on one side.

Metaphysically, the great advantage of Manichaeism over Christianity is its ability to solve the so-called problem of evil. If God is omnipotent as well as unsurpassable in goodness, love of man, and justice, then the suffering that we actually find in the world cannot be accounted for, and the innumerable attempts of Christian theologians and philosophers to solve this problem represent a vast "expense of spirit in a waste of shame." Indeed, the position of the Christian is even worse than most Christian writers on this subject realize: there is yet the doctrine of hell and eternal damnation. Historically approached, the problem becomes clear: you can no more endow God with the virtues of Ohrmazd while denying the existence of Ahriman, and square this conception with the Persian notions of the last judgment and eternal damnation, or with the suffering in this world, than you can square the circle.

The Second Isaiah had voiced the spirit of the Hebrew Scriptures: the one Lord and none else forms light and darkness, "makes peace and creates evil." This had been the view of Jeremiah mourning the fall of Jerusalem: "Is it not from the mouth of the Most High that good and evil come?" (Lamentations 3:38). And in the eighth century Amos had asked: "Is a trumpet blown in a city, and the people are not afraid? Does evil befall a city, and the Lord has not done it?" (3:6). This was how the ancient Hebrews met the problem of innocent suffering.

The friends of Job, like generations of Christian theologians, insist that God is good and just beyond compare and conclude that Job's suffering proves that he is guilty and deserves punishment, although the Bible insists that Job was in fact blameless. Job never questions God's power, but he does question his justice; and in the end the Lord reproaches Job's friends, saying twice: "You have not spoken of me what is right, as my servant Job has." But most readers have felt so certain that God's moral perfection is above question that they have refused to recognize what the Book of Job actually says, and when Christian theologians and philosophers have tried seriously to offer arguments to solve the problem of evil they have almost invariably sided with the friends of Job and have moreover implied without saying so outright that God is not altogether omnipotent.

It is understandable how in the context of this problem some of the philosophers of the French Enlightenment became interested in Manichaeism. And a modern Bayle scholar has said: "Perhaps, after the catastrophes of the twentieth century have shaken our Pelagian confidence to its roots, and the strength of theological and metaphysical monism has been further eroded, a new Bayle will appear to show how *really* plausible Manichaeanism is in the context of recent human history.[2]

Yet anyone who reads up on Manichaeism can scarcely find this late product of gnostic syncretism "*really* plausible." Anyone with a developed critical spirit must find this system of beliefs utterly incredible. The mere fact that Mani was not confronted by an insoluble problem of evil does not establish any strong presumption for his message. After all, that is also true of most other religions, including biblical Judaism as well as Hinduism, Buddhism and Jainism, Taoism and Confucianism, Homer's religion and Plato's; and for the non-religious the problem of squaring God's goodness and omnipotence with the facts of life does not arise.

The perennial appeal of Manichaeism is not due to the fact that if

[2] Richard H. Popkin, "Manichaeanism in the Enlightment" in *The Critical Spirit: Essays in Honor of Herbert Marcuse*, ed. Kurt H. Wolff and Barrington Moore, Jr. (1967), p. 54 (the last sentence of the essay).

we postulate an evil deity, a traditional problem of Christian theology dissolves: that much Mani's doctrine has in common with most religious and nonreligious world views. The Manichaean heresy will not die because it invites men to see themselves as the children of light and their foes as the forces of darkness. This dualism was not invented by Mani: "the children of light" are encountered earlier in the New Testament[3] and in the Dead Sea Scrolls, and the moral dualism can be traced back at least to Zarathustra.

In the last chapter of his *Ecce Homo* (sec. 3), Nietzsche remarked two years after the publication of *Beyond Good and Evil* that "Zarathustra was the first to consider the fight of good and evil the very wheel in the machinery of things: the transposition of morality into the metaphysical realm, as a force, cause, and end in itself, is *his* work." Thus the historical Zarathustra was "just the opposite of" Nietzsche's Zarathustra: "Zarathustra created this most calamitous error, morality; consequently, he must also be the first to recognize it."

Here the idea is dramatized so much that one is apt to miss it: morality as a "calamitous error" sounds so shrill that Nietzsche's point is not heard. And "beyond good and evil" is such a brilliant phrase that generations of readers have been blinded by it and did not absorb the plain declaration in the second section of that book that it was intended as an attack on "The fundamental faith of metaphysicians [which] is *the faith in opposite values.*"

Let us speak of Mani and Manichaeism rather than Zarathustra and Zoroastrianism because "Zoroastrianism" would suggest an ancient religion, and "Zarathustra" would invite confusion with Nietzsche's mouthpiece, while "Manichaean" is a term *often* used figuratively. In the following pages, "Mani" is not a third-century martyr but a symbol for that outlook which reduces the world and moral collisions to black and white.

VI

The virus of Mani has taken a fearful toll in Christianity, but in our time the churches are going far toward ridding themselves of this disease—or the plague is leaving the sinking ship of Christianity to smite our ideologues. When Manichaeism struck the Right in the

[3] Luke 16:8, John 12:36, Eph. 5:8, 1 Thess. 5:5.

nineteenth century, it was apparent that the infection had come from the church. In the Dreyfus affair the clerical background of anti-Semitism met the eye, and even in the Nazis' leading anti-Semitic journal, *Der Stürmer*, no text was quoted more often than Jesus' dictum in the Fourth Gospel that the Devil was the father of the Jews. Joe McCarthy and the John Birch Society left anti-Semitism behind and cast the Communists in the role of the forces of darkness, while still trying to explain all social evils in terms of conspiracies; but the Nazis had destroyed the intellectual respectability of the far Right, and few have taken McCarthy or the Birchers seriously on an intellectual level. Their attempts to explain events in Manichaean terms have not been dignified with the name of philosophy.

When the New Left appeared, the dreadful silence, apathy, and despair of the McCarthy period gave way to a new ferment in the intellectual community. Students and young faculty formed the vanguard, and the fusion of intellectual and moral concerns roused premature hopes. But almost at birth the New Left succumbed to the virus of Mani.

Why? However unfortunate it is that the New Left swallowed the basic scheme of the Old Right, merely reversing the value signs, the case is anything but exceptional. When the tables are turned, the tables themselves are not subjected to critical scrutiny.

It may seem as if the Old Right could not have had that much influence. But precisely its Manichaeism triumphed internationally, and the young radicals of the New Left grew up during the period of the cold war. For those whose memories extend back of World War II, McCarthyism was a shameful interlude that is either forgotten or recalled only as a brief and wretched excess. For those who entered colleges and universities in the 1960s, it was neither brief nor an interlude nor an excess. Nazism and Pearl Harbor happened before their time. The student radicals were born under the aegis of Hiroshima and Nagasaki, their childhood was dominated by the cold war and, if they are Americans, by McCarthyism, and their adolescence by the civil rights struggle. It is all too understandable that democracy seems much sicker to them than it does to their parents who lived through World War II.

To understand the New Manichaeans, who reduce the most complex issues to black and white, one must further consider the color problem. Like the cold war, it is international; but one must begin somewhere, and we shall focus on the United States first.

American blacks are visually a heterogeneous group and look much less alike than do the whites, but they have been treated and continue to be treated without any regard for the actual color of their skin. Whether that is black, dark brown, light brown, or white, they have been classified as Negroes and made to see the world in black and white, whether they liked it or not; and until the middle of the twentieth century few of them did.

At the same time, black and white were by no means neutral terms. In Horace's *Satires* "he that backbites an absent friend" is called black, *niger* (1.4.85), and Horace also speaks of "the whitest souls earth ever bore" (1.5.41). In his *Genealogy of Morals* Nietzsche surmised that the Latin *malus* (bad) was probably related to Greek *melas* (black), and that such words reflect the ancient contempt of blond conquerors for the black-haired native population. Perhaps there is some truth in this hypothesis; but the notion that darkness is uncanny, dangerous, and the enemy, while the light dispels threats and is friendly, a savior, and the force of good is probably far older.

Clearly, "black" hearts, "black" days, "blackmail," "blacken," and the connotations of "dark" were not invented by American whites to make the Negro feel inferior. Nevertheless, the value judgments embedded in the language did undermine the self-esteem of American blacks. To regain that, it would not do to suggest a more pluralistic perspective and insist that men do not fall into one of two categories, that there are an indefinite number of shadings, and that it is arbitrary to lump the almost white with the truly black. While that approach would have come closer to the Latin American way, it would have left intact the vicious notion that black is bad. There was nothing for it but to insist that "black is beautiful."

Why should millions of people model themselves on an alien ideal of beauty, admire light skin and straight hair, despise their own looks, and either try to change them by straightening their hair or feel ugly and hopeless? Taken out of its historical context, "black is beautiful" is as silly as the insistence that white is beautiful. In its context, it was a long overdue cry of humanity. Nor is it any wonder that it was often accompanied by the charge that white is wicked and that white men are devils. This turning of the tables by some of the radicals is one source of the Manichaeism of the New Left, but it is not the major source, not even in the United States.

One might discount these facts altogether because the virus of Mani has struck the New Left in Europe, too, where no comparable color problem exists; but this would be a mistake. The white man's oppression of the nonwhites furnishes the prime example of the kind of conflict that lends itself to a black and white diagram. White radicals could agree with black rebels that the way white America had treated the blacks for centuries was indeed wicked and inexcusable. And then the question arose whether the A-bombs dropped on Hiroshima and Nagasaki were not of a piece with this wickedness: were not the Japanese also colored people? The Algerian war could be seen in the same perspective: nonwhite people fighting successfully against their white oppressors. And the Vietnam war fell into place.

Intellectuals did not suppose that all whites were devils or that all nonwhites were beautiful or virtuous. But many did come to see the world divided into two camps: white oppressors who did not shrink from using atom bombs, napalm, and torture against the oppressed, mostly nonwhite, who were fighting for their freedom. Given this model, one could readily cut through the complexities of Latin American politics and the Palestinian situation. One need hardly wonder at the popularity of a world view that makes so many crucial and exasperating problems so simple, that makes it so easy to choose sides, and that provides the assurance that, having done that, one is wholly in the right and in the company of the vast majority of struggling humanity.

VII

Anyone grounded in Greek tragedy and philosophy, in history or literature, must respond to such simplicity with a conditioned reflex of mistrust. And the more he knows about the issues, the more will suspicion give way to stunned surprise that anyone who claims to be devoted to the life of the intellect should actually believe in such a Manichaean view.

In the summer of 1963 I attended some religious services in a Zen monastery in Kyoto. They always began at 7:00 A.M. and lasted an hour. The first twenty minutes were marvelous: chants accompanied on drums by the master's sons. During the next twenty minutes I became conscious of my legs, squatting on the floor, listening to recorded music that I could also have heard at home. But the last twenty minutes truly tried my patience: every morning we listened to a tape of a voice with an unmistakable New York accent, reading us passages from the writings of D. T. Suzuki that I had read before—contrasting East and West and explaining how Westerners are aggressive and feel impelled to dominate, while the Japanese are totally unaggressive and have no desire to dominate but seek harmony with nature.

Anyone who had lived through the invasion of Manchuria and the rape of Nanking, through the tide of Japanese aggression and World War II could scarcely swallow this; but the students who started "digging" Zen in the sixties had no memories of any of these events. Their impressions of Zen were wholly bookish and yet utterly unhistorical. They were apt to come to Suzuki by way of Erich Fromm and his arch-Manichaean contrast of authoritarian and humanistic religions, in which Zen is adduced as a prime example of humanistic religion.

In fact, Zen does not acknowledge the authority of either the Buddha or the ancient scriptures that transmit his teaching: what matters is the experience of enlightenment, which can be acquired without such intermediaries—by going to a Zen monastery and submitting entirely to the authority of the master. It was thus by means of Zen that the originally pacifistic message of the Buddha was transformed into the religion of the Samurai, for whom war was a way of life.

One can and should grasp the profundity of Zen, delight in its whimsical charm (the Chinese contribution, the injection of Taoism into Buddhism), and still comprehend its historical and sociological function. Similarly, the Bhagavad-Gita is one of the great religious scriptures, but it does sanctify the caste system. Conversely, one can and should criticize the dropping of the two atomic bombs on Hiroshima and Nagasaki without seeing the Japanese in 1945 as a peace-loving and innocuous Asian people who suddenly became the innocent victims of American brutality. The bombing of Nagasaki was even more inexcusable than that of Hiroshima, but it is by no means clear that the fact that the Japanese are Asian or nonwhite influenced these two decisions. The fire-bombing of Dresden was also inexcusable, and there was far less reason, if any, to suppose that it would greatly shorten the war.

The world is full of outrages, and it is easy to sympathize with the indignation of those who paint them black. It is less easy to follow such rhetoric when it goes on to paint the other side white. As a rule, wrong clashes with greater wrong.

VIII

All this is so plain that it seems difficult to understand how large numbers of students in many different countries can fail to see it. But even when the world was less complex, many people found peace of mind in simplistic world views. Now that the world situation and the societies into which youth finds itself thrown are of truly frightening complexity, the hunger for Manichaeism is greater than ever. As social and international problems become more involved and unmanageable, the prospect of finding security in a world view that reduces everything to black and white becomes more attractive.

One despairs of finding solutions through study; one does not feel up to it; the outcome it too uncertain. The Manichaean need not despair: he knows the solution before immersing himself in the problems; he studies to find corroboration; and he has the faith that his side will win, even if he does not happen to know how and when.

But isn't Manichaeism too simple to be intellectually respectable? It would certainly be of inestimable advantage if a philosopher could be found who, without spoiling the simplicity of this ancient scheme, had brought it up to date with suitable references to Marx and Freud, adding enough jargon and obscurity to make everything seem very academic and profound. It is easy to imagine the joy of the European students when they discovered such a philosopher. Carried away by their understandable delight, they proclaimed their prophet the third member of a rather unlikely trinity—so unlikely, in fact, that the slogan was picked up by the mass media and spread to the four corners of the globe (the world of Mani could hardly be round): "Marx, Mao, Marcuse." As long as a sense of proportion was considered irrelevant anyway, a slightly different trio would have been more illuminating: Mani, Marx, Marcuse.

Herbert Marcuse's books had never attracted one-tenth of the attention lavished on Jeau-Paul Sartre's. An immensely likable professor at the University of California in San Diego, he was approaching seventy when lightning struck. And suddenly he was cast in the role for which Sartre had prepared himself for twenty years. Even in France the students did not hail Sartre as their prophet. Yet Sartre had tried much more conspicuously to make philosophy "relevant" and to bring together Marxism and existentialism. And in ever so many ways, Sartre was incomparably less bourgeois and more outside "the establishment." Why, then, did the students prefer Marcuse?

Sartre's complexity is not of the surface only but of the very essence of his work. He is subtle to a fault. *Les mains sales* is a fine example of his mistrust of all simple answers. He does not offer any security; he calls into question every perspective by exploring two more. In one of his first attempts to deal with social questions he attacked anti-Semitism—for reasons and in words that are no less applicable to many student radicals:

> The rational man seeks the truth gropingly, he knows that his reasoning is only probable, that other considerations will arise to make it doubtful. . . . But there are people who are attracted by the durability of stone. They want to be massive and impenetrable. . . . They want to exist all at once and right away. They do not want acquired opinions, they want them to be innate; since they are afraid of reasoning, they want to adopt a mode of life in which reasoning and research play but a subordinate role, in which one never seeks but that which one has already found. . . . If you insist too much they close up, they point out with one superb word that the time to argue has passed.[4]

Sartre went on to point out that this type of man is afraid of solitude and that "If he has become an anti-Semite, it is because one cannot be anti-Semitic alone."

Sartre has never ceased to exemplify the archindividualism of an intellectuals' intellectual who has a profound mistrust of mass movements and those who join them. In the 1960s, to be sure, he came to hail Marxism as the philosophy of our age, while disparaging existentialism as merely "a parasitical phenomenon on the margins of knowledge."[5] But it was also during the sixties that he refused to accept the Nobel Prize, giving as one of his reasons that he must stand alone and that even the tag "Prix Nobel" after his name would compromise him. Clearly, he was objecting not only to the establishment that wanted to confer the prize on him but to any bond to an organiza-

[4] "Portrait of the Anti-Semite" (*Réflexions sur la question juive*, 1946), tr. Mary Guggenheim, in *Existentialism from Dostoevsky to Sartre*, ed. Walter Kaufmann (1956; rev. ed., 1975), pp. 333f.

[5] *La question de la méthode* (1960); English *ibid.*, p. 370.

tion. And his depreciation of existentialism has to be seen as a repudiation of his following. His tributes to Marxism did not balance these negations: his version of Marxism is so eccentrically individual and at the same time so longwinded, tortuous, and forbidding that *Critique de la raison dialectique* could scarcely have become a rallying point for the New Left.

Marcuse's earlier books on Hegel and Marx (*Reason and Revolution*), on Freud (*Eros and Civilization*), and on *Soviet Marxism* had not made any great splash. Nor was *One Dimensional Man: Studies in the Ideology of Advanced Industrial Society* (1964) reviewed very widely or prominently. But after a delay of two years *One Dimensional Man* came to the notice of thousands of radical students, probably in large measure because during that interval Marcuse published an extraordinary essay on "Repressive Tolerance"[6] and gave some lectures in Europe in a similar vein. In the summer of 1966 he was still hoping for fame and recognition in his lifetime; by the following summer he was one of the most famous of living philosophers, but had passed the peak of his popularity with the students because in May 1967 he said that in the universities there was probably more freedom than anywhere else in our society and that he did not approve of the disruptions.

What concerns us here is not Marcuse's philosophy but the light his international acclaim by the radical students throws on *them*. We shall therefore concentrate on "Repressive Tolerance." This essay of thirty-odd small pages is fascinating because it would be hard to find a more Manichaean tract by a philosopher of any standing; and that is the secret of Marcuse's popularity.

IX

Marcuse attacks "the active, official tolerance granted to the Right as well as to the Left, to movements of aggression as well as to movements of peace, to the party of hate as well as that of humanity" (p. 85). This tolerance he calls " 'pure' inasmuch as it refrains from taking sides" (p. 85).

[6] *A Critique of Pure Tolerance* [three essays] by Robert Paul Wolff, Barrington Moore, Jr., and Herbert Marcuse (1965).

Clearly, if there were really two parties, "the party of hate as well as that of humanity," it would be unpardonable not to take sides. The implication seems to be that the former party is "the Right" and for aggression while the forces of light are "the Left" and for peace.

The critique of "pure" tolerance proceeds to charge that "the stupid opinion is treated with the same respect as the intelligent one, the misinformed may talk as long as the informed" (p. 94). Again, the case is easy if the intelligent are also informed and, of course, for peace and humanity, while the stupid are also uninformed and for aggression and hate. But suppose this Manichaean scheme did not hold. After all, some people are intelligent but misinformed; and some are intelligent or informed—either one or both—but for aggression. And there is a lot of hate on the Left and among the blacks. The moment Mani's perspective breaks down, Marcuse's argument against pure tolerance does too.

He advocates "the withdrawal of toleration of speech and assembly from groups and movements which promote aggressive policies, armament, chauvinism, discrimination on the grounds of race and religion, or which oppose the extension of public services, social security, medical care, etc." (p. 100). And he goes on to say that "the distinction between liberating and repressive, human and inhuman teachings and practices . . . is not a matter of value-preference but of rational criteria" (p. 101). Three pages later this becomes the "distinction between true and false, progressive and regressive (for in this sphere, these pairs are equivalent)." The suggestion that all criticism of the extension of social security, medical care, etc., must be suppressed depends entirely on the claim that such criticism is linked indissolubly with ignorance, stupidity, hate, inhumanity, aggression, and whatever else is evil.

If the crucial distinction—the singular here is significant: there is no need for many subtle distinctions; all we need is the power to tell darkness from light—"is not a matter of value preference but of rational criteria," who can be trusted to handle these criteria correctly? "Everyone 'in the maturity of his faculties' as a human being, everyone who has learned to think rationally and autonomously" (p. 106). The emphasis on maturity and on having *learned* to think rationally and autonomously makes it odd that the students should ever have invoked Marcuse in their battles at the universities; but then adults, too, rarely *know* what they like.

Three pages later we are told that "liberating tolerance, then, would mean *intolerance against movements from the Right, and toleration of movements from the Left*" (p. 109, italics supplied). Here Marcuse's Manichaeism stands revealed full-blown—and this is what accounts more than anything else for his immense, though short-lived, popularity.

Marcuse's criticism of our society contains little that is new. The same complaints stud the books of such fellow refugees from Germany as Hannah Arendt and Erich Kahler, Paul Tillich and Erich Fromm; Marcuse explicitly relies on Vance Packard; and his critique of analytic philosophy, which today dominates the Anglo-American scene, adds little to what others have pointed out earlier. What distinguishes Marcuse's stance is his threefold claim that all the ills of which he makes so much are closely connected; that they are all due to one evil force; and that there is a chance of redemption if we resolutely fight this force, alias the Right. Instead of complaining or viewing with alarm, Marcuse has the contagious vitality of a vigorous fighter who issues a call to battle. It is an ancient battle: the war of the children of light against the children of darkness.

X

What humanity needs is hardly "a new Bayle" who will show "how *really* plausible Manichaeanism is." Nor do we need more theologians like Tillich or ideologues like Marcuse who mix the new wines of Marx, Freud, and existentialism and then pour this heady brew into the dry skins of some ancient scheme. Our need is rather to question traditional schemes and to reconsider the dualistic tables we have inherited. Insofar as a "revaluation of all values" means calling good what has been called evil, and vice versa, we have had more than enough of that during the Nazi period and now from the new radicals. But the idea of going "beyond good and evil" and questioning the old faith in opposite values has scarcely been examined as yet.

Nobody could have persuaded millions of adults that we are witnessing a vast, possibly worldwide clash of two parties if so many people were not preconditioned to think in terms of two parties. Being used to a two-party system, to the cold war, to believers and unbelievers, good and evil, right and wrong, healthy and sick, just and unjust, "us" and "them," people are quite willing to believe that our social problems are due to, or marked by, the collision between white and black or those over and those under thirty. But these two suggestions are incompatible unless we reinterpret them to mean, for example, that one party consists of all nonwhites as well as all whites under thirty, while the other one is composed of all whites over thirty. That would be logically possible, but it is obviously false.

There are tremendous tensions among nonwhites in Asia, in Africa, and in Latin America. China and Taiwan come to mind, Korea, Vietnam, India and Pakistan, Nigeria and Biafra; and there are immense upheavals in China, enormous conflicts in Pakistan, and anything but serene harmony in India. The American black community is so profoundly split that the very word "community" may be quite inappropriate, and most blacks certainly do not feel any great sense of solidarity with Puerto Ricans, Mexican Americans, and Indians. Nor are the whites under thirty one party: they are scattered over the whole spectrum from George Wallace to Eugene McCarthy, as their fathers at one time ranged all the way from Joe McCarthy to Henry Wallace.

Even the radical students are far from forming a single party: the SDS tends to be shunned by most radical black groups, which in turn are often on bad terms with each other—Malcolm X was shot by the Black Muslims, Eldridge Cleaver and the Panthers are against the Muslims, all these groups are against the movement started by Martin Luther King, Jr., and Roy Wilkins and Whitney Young have different ideas yet. Meanwhile the SDS is deeply divided, too, and the hippies' revolt against the establishment is something else again. More radical in some ways than most of the other groups, the hippies call into question the Manichaean intolerance that most of the rebellious groups share with so many reactionaries. But even they do not go all the way toward tolerance and pluralism: in practice they represent another extreme conformism in hair style, dress, and way of life; and most of them seem to consider themselves the children of light and the nonhippies children of darkness.

It is crucial for any informed and sensitive analysis of the contemporary situation to have some sense of this infinite variety and to think of a multitude of intersecting spectra instead of reducing such colorful multiplicity to black and white. But the courage to face chaos is only a beginning and no substitute for an analysis.

XI

Let us begin with a brief analysis of intolerance. The word has two meanings that must be distinguished sharply. Of course, it has more than two meanings, but the frequent confusion of two senses is calamitous. Intolerance can mean opposition to the free expression of some views. Let us call this *political intolerance* and distinguish it from *emotional intolerance*, which means detestation of some groups of human beings (usually called prejudice). When Marcuse advocates "intolerance against movements from the Right," making it quite clear that he means "censorship, even precensorship" (p. 111), he advocates political intolerance.

Political tolerance is exhibited by one who defends the right of others to express and publish views that he detests, usually with the proviso that he and others have to be allowed to criticize these views in public because the clarification and discovery of truths, as well as political freedom, depend on the free interplay of ideas. But it is common for people to claim that men of this type are intolerant because they sharply criticize the views of others. Marcuse's argument is infected by this confusion: he calls the kind of tolerance he attacks " 'pure' inasmuch as it refrains from taking sides" (p. 85). But it is possible and indeed essential to take sides without having recourse to censorship.

Vigorous criticism of theories and proposals should not be confounded with intolerance, nor need it be Manichaean. Only rigorous exercise of our intellect and examination of the evidence can show us what is tenable and what is not; and the result may well be that more than one view is defensible. It does not follow that *all* views are equally tenable. Those who find no fault with any view do not show tolerance but only that in some ways they resemble vegetables.

Emotional tolerance or what is usually called lack of prejudice consists in not detesting any human beings simply because they belong to a certain group. Whoever sees the Negroes, whites, Catholics, or Jews as sons of the devil or children of darkness, or as pigs, displays emotional intolerance (prejudice).

A humane person distinguishes between the human being who holds and expresses views and the views themselves. But it may be objected that it is by no means inhumane to abhor some views and actions; and if we loathe a man's views and actions and find his habits and behavior arrogant, cowardly, dishonest, and brutal, how can we refrain from the conclusion that *he is* arrogant, cowardly, dishonest, and brutal, and how can we help detesting *him*? To this question we must return later (sec. XIV).

The case for political tolerance depends on pluralism. If all truth were on one side and nothing but error on the other; if there were good criteria for telling which was which but most of mankind were unable to tell truth from error, the case for tolerance would be weak indeed. And if we went one step beyond Marcuse to link error not only with wickedness but also with eternal torment, while associating truth not only, as he does, with goodness but also with endless bliss, the case for intolerance would be won. This is in fact how it was won in the Christian Middle Ages.

Anyone who actually believes that infidels like Spinoza and Voltaire, Marx and Nietzsche, Freud and Sartre, as well as those infected by their views, will probably be punished with eternal torment of some kind, *must* be for the suppression of such views unless he is brutally deficient in charity. But once the traditional beliefs about hell crumbled, the case for intolerance became weaker, and powerful arguments for tolerance can be found in Milton's *Areopagitica* and J. S. Mill's essay *On Liberty*. While it is odd that Marcuse does not come to grips with these arguments, they are familiar enough and there is no need to rehash them here.

XII

Marcuse's basic error is his assumption that all right is on the Left, all wrong on the Right. The moment we cease to see the world in black and white, the instant we see it in color in its inexhaustible variety, we find a multitude of groups and some hate, some aggression, some stupidity, some lack of information, and some errors wherever there are sizable groups of human beings—but fused in ever different proportions with love and humanity, intelligence and information, and even some truth.

There is something highly artificial not only about "the Right" and "the Left" but also about the other pairs of opposites in Marcuse's essay: they all smell of Mani. It is because men think in terms of good and bad that they construct such pairs as love and hate, truth and error.

What is the opposite of love? Is it hate? Or rather lack of love, which could mean ignorance of a person's very existence? Or indifference to a person whom we might be expected to love or whom we did love at one time? Or near-indifference coupled with a little irritation? Or a definite aversion, either faint or strong? Or envy? Or resentment?

Many people would say: Hate, of course. Others: No, hate is really much closer to love than is indifference; and as long as there is hate, love may be kindled. However that may be, hate and love are certainly not opposites; they are not even mutually exclusive, they often coexist and interpenetrate. Love and hate are neither two solid substances nor two liquids that can be mixed. "Love" is a highly abstract term that can be applied to very complex configurations of feelings, thoughts, and actions, and many of these configurations bear very little resemblance to each other.[7]

There are no opposites in nature. What would be the opposite of this rose or that Austrian pine? Of this rock? Of the sun, the sky, this shadow? This human being has no opposite, neither does the hue of his skin, the light on his hair, or the way he speaks.

Only human thought introduces opposites. Neither individual objects nor classes of objects—such as roses, pines, rocks, and human beings—have opposites; nor do colors, sounds, textures, and feelings.

But are not hard and soft opposites? As abstract concepts, they are; but the feel of a rock and the feel of moss are not opposites. It is only by disregarding most of the qualities of both experiences and classifying one as hard and the other as soft that we *think* of them as opposites. Playing with fire and rolling in the snow are not opposites—far from it—but hot and cold are. No specific degree of heat or coldness has any opposite, only the concepts of hot and cold do. The starry heavens and a sunny sky are not opposites, but day and night are. And Mani's minions look everywhere for day concepts and night concepts.

Hot and cold are not like day and night. Temperatures are arranged on a linear scale, like hard and soft, fast and slow. Day and night, like summer and winter, form a cycle and have to be represented by

[7] See my *Critique of Religion and Philosophy* (1958), sec. 29.

a circle, like colors. And colors that are across from each other on a color wheel are not called opposite but complementary colors. Black and white may be opposite, but no two colors are; nor are any two times of day, indeed nothing temporal, nothing living, nothing that is in process.

Hegel grasped this; also that only the understanding introduces opposites. But in the history of ideas what has influence is usually a misunderstanding: either a man's errors and prejudices prevail, or *he* is misunderstood. Hegel was soon taken to have taught that nature and history abound in opposites, and this was believed to be the essence of his dialectic. Marx liked this dialectic better than anything else in Hegel's thought and gave the world dialectical materialism.

Now that Marx's memory is sacred not only to billions of Marxists but also to millions of others, even as Jesus' name is sacred not only to Christians, it is bound to be resented widely if one points to the Manichaean elements in both. Jesus is held to have been love incarnate, and Marx a major social scientist, though both denied the bare integrity and decency of their opponents, substituting gross invective and vituperation for attempts at dialogue. They saw the world in black and white. "Whoever is not for me is against me."

The work of the understanding is of the utmost importance: to understand complex situations that initially strike us as chaotic, we need concepts and abstractions; we disregard what for the moment is irrelevant and focus our attention on a few factors that we idealize, ignoring, as it were, the imperfections of their actual existence. Hegel always associated this power of the understanding, which he hailed repeatedly, with the negative and even with destruction. Let us call it analysis.

Scientists and engineers and analytical philosophers do not need to be told how important it is, but growing numbers of young people see it as the enemy, along with the computer, and extol concrete existence and direct experience, intuition, feeling, confrontation. These neoromantics fall prey to the virus of Mani much more often than do the devotees of analysis. Why?

As Hegel recognized, philosophy requires the understanding as well as intuition, and reason does not do its job as long as either analysis or direct experience are held to be sovereign. Although no other philosopher had made so much of this theme, the partiality of both approaches is felt widely, and the partisans of each feel a need for the other. Thus the analytically minded tend to leave the realms of faith and morals, if not politics, to feeling and intuition, while the prophets of direct experience indulge in a bare minimum of analysis and have a fondness for polarities.

Unimpeded, neither analysis nor experience stops with the recognition of opposites; both lead to pluralism, and so does any thinking that subjects even faith and morals to analysis, without ignoring the concrete experiences of the moral and religious life. Those who see things in black and white limp on both legs: they curtail both the understanding and direct experience, settling for a little of each.

XIII

Are truth and error opposites? Or is *falsehood* the opposite of the truth? Or is the lie? These questions concern words or possibly concepts of the understanding. I say "possibly" because the questions hinge on the meaning of English words. Since "falsehood" cannot always be rendered by *Falschheit*, it is not clear how a German might refer to the concept that in English is designated by "falsehood." The concepts we use to understand our experiences are functions of our language and also of our historical situation and the science and philosophy of our time.

Mani's heirs suppose not only that truth and error are opposites but even that there is a party of truth and a party of error. This seems to mean, and some Manichaeans evidently believe, that the children of light believe only or mainly true statements while the children of darkness believe only or mainly false statements, and that true statements and positions are the opposites of false statements and positions. One is reminded of a true-or-false test. "Abraham Lincoln was born on February 11, 1809: True or false?" False, but hardly the opposite of the truth, seeing that he was born on February 12, 1809. Even a multiple-choice test would allow a little more subtlety: by adding further alternatives to the two dates mentioned, it would allow us to distinguish degrees of falsehood or approximations of the truth.

When we deal with more complex issues that involve philosophy, ideology, or evaluations, it becomes questionable whether the true-false dichotomy is at all applicable. When we are considering an essay, a book, or a position, it stands to reason that some of the propositions in it are true and others false, and that neither epithet should be applied to the whole. And even a single proposition—such as "causality is a category" or "X caused World War I" or "Y is evil"—may require analysis before we can say that on one interpretation it is false and on another perhaps true.

When "true and false" are proclaimed to be the "equivalent" of "progressive and regressive" (Marcuse, p. 104), it is clear that we are no longer concerned with the correctness or incorrectness of propositions. A distinction between mere correctness and Truth is assumed, and this goes back to Hegel's dictum, in the preface to the *Phenomenology*: "The true is the whole."

Hegel went on to explain that propositions depend for their meaning on a wider context of definitions and explanations; that philosophical truth cannot be encapsulated in dogmas (say, "the world is finite," or "the will is free"): it requires a whole system in which crucial terms (e.g., "world" and "finite," "will" and "free") are analyzed in detail and discussed along with other terms to which they are related. What is needed, according to Hegel, is a comprehensive philosophy, and insofar as each philosophy tends to be one-sided and concentrates on a few insights, these insights must be integrated in a more comprehensive philosophy that is in relation to these partial systems—"the whole."

Lacking faith that the future would bring us such an increase in intellectual power, or that he himself was so much more talented than his predecessors, that this integration could be brought off by a stroke of genius, Hegel taught that the search for truth must lead through historical studies. Only by learning from our predecessors could we hope to come closer to the truth than they did. Our successors in turn may use us in the same way, along with the writings of our critics. If we knew how, we could anticipate them; but as long as we cannot, we cannot predict their moves. This insistence that predictions were beyond his powers and beyond the competence of philosophy is one of the striking features of Hegel's decidedly un-Manichaean philosophy.

Marx retained Hegel's interest in history but thought he could predict future developments, although by now it is a commonplace that he could not. In another way, too, he did not share Hegel's resignation: he expected the millennium. One wonders how many of his minions share his grandiose faith in the future. Marcuse is one of the very few who have occasionally exceeded Marx's optimism.

When Marcuse equates the true and the progressive, his point is not that in a free contest of ideas truth may be expected to prevail eventually. Rather he claims that there is no really free contest of ideas and that it is hopeless to work within the present political framework. We cannot pin our hopes on labor, as Marx did, because in advanced industrial societies labor is conservative and mainly concerned with the continued gradual improvement of its standard of living. The party of the future is thus neither labor nor the proletariat, which no longer exists, but those who work for a revolution from "the Left." They are "progressive" because they represent the wave of the future and because their outlook is close to his, while their opposition is "regressive" and false and must be subjected to precensorship.

Granted a few absurd assumptions—or in one word the Manichaeism on which the whole outlook depends—it is all quite plausible. Two great oddities remain. That this black and white analysis should pass for "dialectic" and be widely associated with Hegel's influence is possible only because so few of Marcuse's followers and critics have studied Hegel. And that this Manichaean world picture is acceptable to so many young people who pride themselves on their radicalism is possible only because most of them know so little history.

Even when we bear in mind the reasons we have given for the appeal of this simplistic world view, it remains stunning to hear the Left hailed as the party of humanity, as if Lenin's brutality, Stalin's terror, and Tito's long imprisonment of Djilas were irrelevant. One does not begin to understand history or philosophy until one shakes off the lure of Mani's mythology.

XIV

I am prepared to push my anti-Manichaeism to the point of saying that we should not hate or detest any human being. You should always remain mindful of the other man's humanity and of the ways in which he is "as yourself." Why? I cannot invoke as an authority Moses' "You shall love your neighbor as yourself" (Lev. 19:18) or the extension of the same commandment to the stranger (19:34). If authority is out of the picture, what reasons remain?

Even if a man's views, actions, and behavior are detestable, it might be held that there is more to the man than his views, actions, and behavior and that we therefore ought not to detest or hate *him*. This argument admits of variations, but the refutation is the same in all cases: this reasoning proves too much. By the same token it would be unreasonable to admire a person whose views, actions, and behavior deserved admiration.

This refutation does not depend merely on our desire to go on admiring some people. Rather it shows that the first argument in its desire to protect the other person against negative feelings removes him altogether out of our world to the point where no contact between human beings remains possible at all. The refutation is thus intended as a reduction to the absurd. But those who find such extreme alienation from their fellow men true to their own experience are bound to reject the refutation and insist that we can respond only to behavior, never to another person. They will neither love nor hate, admire or detest other human beings.

Another argument would allow us to admire but not to detest others, to love but not to hate. But it is a pragmatic argument, no strict proof; or, in Kantian language, it is merely a hypothetical imperative and not a categorical one. Within these limits it is a sound argument. There are two good reasons for not hating any man but loving some.

First, it is difficult to discover some of our own faults; they are much plainer in others. If we always make excuses and end up by not accounting them faults at all, we are almost bound to become lax with ourselves. But if we hate and detest as inhuman those in whom we find grievous faults we are more than apt to overlook the same faults or tendencies in ourselves because we do not see the continuity between "us" and "them." Hence it is essential for our own moral health to see those who offend us in their full humanity while judging their faults clearly. Judge your neighbor and remember that he is "as yourself."

Secondly, our ideas and "truths"—especially in faith, morals, and politics—have an inveterate tendency to be one-sided. Even a strong dedication to bold thought experiments cannot wholly remedy this fault. What helps more than anything else is to go out of one's way to consider, with an effort at sympathy, the views of those whom we are tempted to detest. Without suspending our critical faculties, we should ask ourselves how human beings not essentially different from ourselves have come to see things that way. For the sake of truth, insight, and psychological understanding, it is important to cultivate the habit of not hating other men.

There is no parallel argument against love and admiration. On the contrary, the effort to become a better person and the quest for knowledge can be greatly helped by both. What obviously cannot be squared with my position is *blind* admiration or love. Even as we usually do not admire or love those with whom we disagree, we need not agree with those we love or admire. Nor need we deny their faults.

XV

This whole essay is a plea for pluralism but not for indiscriminate relativism. We should not close our minds to the varieties of experience, and we should explore alternatives, asking what might be said for and against each. Many moral codes are muddled, inconsistent, full of ambiguities and hypocrisies, and riddled with false assumptions about facts. It does not follow that either all moral codes or all but one are in this sad condition. There might be several that are equally tenable, even as in science and historiography there sometimes are several theories that are defensible, although most theories can be safely rejected after scrutiny.

Political tolerance has promoted pluralism in religion and philosophy and, within limits, in politics. Actually, limits of tolerance are encountered in religion, too, and social respectability is even more restricted. Robert Paul Wolff's contribution to *A Critique of Pure Tolerance* concludes: "Pluralism answered a genuine social need during a significant period of history," but now we need to go "beyond pluralism and beyond tolerance." Wolff's "Beyond Tolerance" is no more than a prolegomena to a critique of tolerance, and the second of the three essays in the book is staunchly liberal. Only Marcuse offers the critique announced in the title of the book. But Wolff prepares the ground by arguing that pluralism means in practice that only established groups are "in" while new groups or individuals that "fall outside any major social group—the non-religious, say—are . . . relegated in practice to a second-class status" (p. 41). This is clearly true and important: pluralism is indeed "a philosophy of equality and justice whose *concrete application* supports inequality by ignoring the existence of certain legitimate social groups" (p. 43). But at the top of the very next page, Wolff undermines his whole case against pluralism: "With bewildering speed, an interest can move from 'outside' to 'inside' and its partisans, who have been scorned by the solid and established in the community, become presidential advisers and newspaper columnists."

Quite so. Our pluralistic society does allow for these transitions. It does not do so mechanically, automatically, without all human exertion. There is no cause for complacency. But given great exertion or occasionally just good luck, outsiders get on the plateau. To facilitate and speed up changes of this kind is a legitimate goal of reform but does not require us to smash the establishment. On the contrary, the cry that we must first of all destroy the present social order because anything is bound to be better than what we have now, brings back to mind the radical critics of the Weimar Republic who adopted the same stance and got Hitler.

We cannot go beyond pluralism because we have not yet attained pluralism. In at least two ways, our society falls far short of it.

First, too many of our fellow citizens are still Manichaeans under the skin. They are not as extreme as the radicals on the far Right and Left; they are given to compromises and comfort and do not care to go very far in any direction of thought, but they do not see anything wrong in thinking in terms of "us" and "them." To a pluralist it should be obvious that I have much more in common with Marcuse, who happens to be an old friend, than I do with many people to whom I am closer in this respect or that. For a pluralist "we" is a contextual term that refers now to one grouping, now to another. A pluralist can say "we" dozens of times without referring twice to the same group.

Secondly, our present pluralism covers the whole spectrum—from orange to crimson. In any given year, our automobiles tend to look alike; and our colleges, too, come in very few models and are not as different from each other as one might wish. We need a far greater variety of institutions of learning, offering different academic programs as well as divergent styles of life. There is no need for thousands of colleges to do badly what, given our material and human resources, few can do well. To some extent, neighboring institutions can, and have begun to, pool their resources. But it is time to move beyond the melting pot and beyond homogenized education toward more pluralism.

This is not what student radicals demand. On the contrary, they want every college to make the same innovations and introduce, for example, black studies programs, regardless of the quantity and quality of available teachers. The radicals on different campuses are as similar as Fords and Chevrolets.

To offer genuine variety is not enough, we also have to do far more to inform people of the options that are available. Even now students go to Berkeley or the University of Wisconsin and then are surprised at not finding the intimacy and the close contact with professors that actually are available at many smaller schools.

As long as most colleges try to do the same things, it makes at least some sense to try to rank these schools, if only we bear in mind that different departments at the same school are not always close to each other in rank and that there are many less tangible values. But if our schools offered some genuinely different ways of life and sought excellence along divergent lines, freedom would increase.

We must liberate the imagination even of the young. They now seek freedom by asking all schools to abolish the same requirements and to introduce the same options. They all want the same. We should encourage them to think and imagine for themselves instead of copying their peers.

For we need far more imagination than the middle-aged possess, and *we* are no longer likely to come up with bold plans for new institutions and new ways of life. Time is running out on us, and if our children and students show as little imagination as their elders have done, western civilization could well come to an end around the year 2000. If those now young are even more inept than their elders, that is scarcely grounds for gloating.

Time is running out on us. Many of the students have very little patience. Their experience of time differs from ours. Even if we fly far more often than our students, we can also remember taking two weeks to cross the Atlantic in a boat, and longer than that to hitch-hike across the United States. Our sense of time was molded by experiences like that, and we are prone to feel that the condition of the blacks in America has changed a great deal in the last two decades. But our students know that we landed men on the moon less than ten years after Kennedy proclaimed this as a goal, and the speeds reached by the rockets rushing toward the moon have a place in the experience of youth, while we still think in prerocket terms.

Time is running out on us. In a few more decades all who worry about student radicals will be dead, and those now young will run or ruin the world. We might use what little time is left to us to say what most needs saying. And few messages are as urgent as this: It is time to move beyond black and white and to start thinking in color.

8

THE FAITH
OF A HERETIC*

When I was eleven, I asked my father: "What really is the Holy Ghost?" The articles of faith taught us in school—in Berlin, Germany —affirmed belief in God, Christ, and the Holy Ghost, and I explained to my father: "I don't believe that Jesus was God, and if I can't believe in the Holy Ghost either, then I am really not a Christian."

At twelve, I formally left the Protestant church to become a Jew. Having never heard of Unitarianism, I assumed that the religion for people who believed in God, but not in Christ or the Holy Ghost, was Judaism.

A few months after my conversation with my father, but before I left the church, Hitler came to power. Warned of the persecution that my decision might entail, I replied that one certainly could not change one's mind for a reason like that. I did not realize until a little later that all four of my grandparents had been Jewish; and none of us knew that this, and not one's own religion, would be decisive from the Nazis' point of view. My decision had been made independently of my descent and of Nazism, on religious grounds.

I took my new religion very seriously, explored it with enormous curiosity and growing love, and gradually became more and more orthodox. When I arrived in the United States in January 1939, I was planning to become a rabbi. A lot of things happened to me that winter, spring, and summer; and when the war broke out I had what, but for its contents, few would hesitate to call a mystical experience. In the most intense despair I suddenly saw that I had deceived myself for years: I had believed. At last the God of tradition joined the Holy Ghost and Christ.

Of course, I could maintain my old beliefs by merely giving them a new interpretation; but that struck me as dishonest. Ikhnaton, the

* This essay first appeared in *Harper's Magazine*, February 1959. It is discussed at some length in the Introduction above.

monotheistic Pharaoh—as I explained in a letter to my family who were by now in England—could also have reinterpreted the traditional polytheism of Egypt, but was a fanatic for the truth. He taught his court sculptor to make life masks of people to see how they really looked, and in one of the heads which the sculptor had then done of Ikhnaton, his hunger for the truth had become stone. I had loved that head for years. Should I now do what I admired him for not doing?

You may say that Ikhnaton was wrong and that it is the essence of religion to pour new wine into old skins, reading one's current insights into ancient beliefs. But if you do this, disregarding Jesus' counsel not to do it, you should realize that you could do it with almost any religion. And it is less than honest to give one's own religion the benefit of every possible doubt while imposing unsympathetic readings on other religions. Yet this is what practically all religious people do. Witness the attitude of Protestants and Catholics toward each other.

In my remaining two years in college I took all the religion courses offered, while majoring in philosophy; and I continued to study and think about both subjects as a graduate student and in the army. Eventually I got my Ph.D. and a job teaching philosophy. For over ten years now [1958] I have taught, among other things, philosophy of religion.[1] In the process, my ideas developed—into a book: *Critique of Religion and Philosophy*.[2]

The ideas were not all there as a result of the few experiences alluded to here: there were hundreds of others. Profound experiences stimulate thoughts; but such thoughts do not look very adequate on paper. Writing can be a way of rethinking again and again.

In the process of teaching and writing one must constantly consider the thoughts of men with different ideas. And prolonged and

[1] Lest this should create a misleading picture of Princeton, it should be added that in our popular Department of Religion Protestantism is championed vigorously by five full professors and a large staff, and ordained ministers are encountered in other departments, too. Until his recent retirement, Jacques Maritain was a member of the Philosophy Department. Great universities, like this magazine, assume that there is a virtue in confronting students and readers with a variety of responsible approaches.

[2] Harper & Brothers, 1958. Many ideas in this article are more fully developed and backed up in this book which also deals with the positive aspects of various religions and with many topics not even touched on in this article; *e.g.*, existentialism, Freud, mysticism, Bible criticism, the relation of religion to poetry, and Zen. Among the questions that are barely touched in this essay and treated more fully in my book is the inadequacy of such labels as theism and atheism. The contents of the present article, incidentally—which is in no sense a summary of my *Critique*—may greatly surprise many of my students, past and present.

ever-new exposure to a wide variety of outlooks—together with the criticism many professors seek from both their students and their colleagues—is a more profound experience than most people realize. It is a long-drawn-out trial by fire, marked by frequent disillusionment, discoveries, and despair, and by a growing regard for honesty, which is surely one of the most difficult of all the virtues to attain. What one comes up with in the end owes quite as much to this continual encounter as it does to any other experience.

A liberal education, and quite especially a training in philosophy, represents an attempt to introduce young people to this adventure. We have no wish to indoctrinate; we want to teach our students to resist indoctrination and not accept as authoritative the beliefs of other men or even the ideas that come to us as in a flash of illumination. Even if one has experiences that some men would call mystical—and I have no doubt that I have had many—it is a matter of integrity to question such experiences and any thoughts that were associated with them as closely and as honestly as we should question the "revelations" of others. To be sure, it is easier to grant others their "revelations" as "true for them" while insisting on one's own as "true for oneself." Such intellectual sluggishness parades as sophistication. But true tolerance does not consist in saying, "You may be right, but let us not make hard demands on ourselves: if you will put your critical intelligence to sleep, I'll put mine to bed, too." True tolerance remains mindful of the humanity of those who make things easy for themselves and welcomes and even loves honest and thoughtful opposition above less thoughtful agreement.

The autobiographical sketch with which I have begun may do more harm than good. Some amateur psychologists may try to explain "everything" in terms of one or two experiences; some Protestants may say, "If only he had come to *me* about the Holy Ghost!" while some Catholics may feel that it all shows once again how Protestantism is merely a way-station on the road to Hell.

This is the kind of gambit that the shut-ins pull on travelers. As if I had buried the Holy Ghost beyond recall when I was eleven, and God when I was eighteen! I merely started relatively early to concern myself with such questions—and have never stopped since. Let the shut-in explore Judaism and Protestantism, Catholicism and Buddhism, atheism and agnosticism, mysticism, existentialism, and psychology, Thomas and Tillich. Let him consult the lot and not just his own present prejudice; let him subject his thoughts about religion to the candid scrutiny of those who differ with him and to his own ever-new re-examination; let him have a host of deep experiences, religious and otherwise, and think about them. That is the ground on which a genuine conversation can take place: it need not make a show of erudition, if only it has grown out of a series of open-hearted encounters. But as long as one is content to gloat over the silver lining of one's own religion, one bars any serious conversation and merely makes the first move in a game of skill.

To an even moderately sophisticated and well-read person it should come as no surprise that any religion at all has its hidden as well as its obvious beauties and is capable of profound and impressive interpretations. What is deeply objectionable about most of these interpretations is that they allow the believer to say Yes while evading any No. The Hebrew prophets represent a notable exception. When interpreting their own religious heritage, they were emphatically not conformists who discovered subtle ways in which they could agree with the religion of their day. Nor was it their point that the cult was justifiable with just a little ingenuity. On the contrary.

Let those who like inspiring interpretations be no less forthright in telling us precisely where they stand on ritual and immortality, on the sacraments and Hell, on the Virgin Birth and Resurrection, on the Incarnation and the miracles, and on: "Resist not evil." And: "Let him who would sue you in court for your coat have your cloak, too." And: "No one comes to the Father but through Me."

If you must pour new wine into old skins, you should at least follow one of Jesus' other counsels and let your Yes be Yes, and your No, No.

When considering Christianity, it is easy to get lost in the changing fashions of thought that have been read into it or reconciled with it—from Neoplatonism (Augustine) and Aristotelianism (Aquinas) to romanticism (Schleiermacher), liberalism (Harnack), and existentialism (Tillich, Bultmann, and others). There is no room here to cross swords with a dozen apologists; in any case, dozens more would remain.

The central question about Christianity concerns Jesus Christ. If he was God in a sense in which no other man has been God, then Christianity is right in some important sense, however Christendom may have failed. To decide whether Jesus was God in some such unique sense, a philosopher cannot forbear to ask just what this claim might mean. If, for example, it does not mean that Jesus of Nazareth knew everything and was all-powerful, it is perplexing what is meant. But a large part of what most Christians mean is surely that Jesus was the best and wisest man of all time; and many Protestants mean no more than that.

Millions of Christians agree on this claim and back it up by citing Gospel passages they like; but different people pick different passages. To some, Jesus looks like St. Francis, to others like John Calvin, and to many more the way a man named Hoffmann painted him. Pierre van Paassen's Jesus is a Socialist and Fosdick's a liberal, while according to Reinhold Niebuhr Jesus' ethic coincides, not surprisingly, with Niebuhr's. To use a political term: almost everybody gerrymanders, carving an idealized self-portrait from the Gospels and much less attractive straw men from the literatures of other faiths. A great deal of theology is like a jigsaw puzzle: the verses of Scripture are the pieces, and the finished picture is prescribed by each denomination, with a certain latitude allowed. What makes the game so pointless is that not all pieces have to be used, and any piece that does not fit may be reshaped, provided one says first, "this means." That is called exegesis.

In *The Literature of the Christian Movement*, Morton Scott Enslin, one of the outstanding New Testament scholars of our time, remarks that the Jesus of the Fourth Gospel is really not very attractive, and that if it were not for the other three Gospels and the fact that most readers create for themselves "a conflate," the Jesus of St. John would lose most of his charm. Surely, the same consideration applies to all four Gospels.

Those who consider Jesus the best and wisest of men should reread the Gospels and ponder at the very least these five points.

First: Are they prepared to maintain their claim regarding the Jesus of any one of the four Gospels—and, if so, which? Or is it their point that the evidence warrants the assumption that the historical Jesus, however inadequately understood by the Evangelists, was a wiser and better man than Socrates and Jeremiah, Isaiah and the Buddha, Lao-tze and Hillel?

Secondly: Although Jesus is widely considered mankind's greatest moral teacher, the greatest Christians, not to speak of scholars, have never been able to agree what his moral teachings were. Matthew, and he alone, reports that Jesus said: "Let your Yes be Yes, and your No, No." But the four Evangelists agree in ascribing to Jesus evasive and equivocal answers to plain questions, not only those of the high priest and Pilate; and quite generally the Jesus of the New Testament avoids straightforward statements, preferring parables and hyperboles. Some of the parables are so ambiguous that different Evangelists, not to speak of later theologians, offer different interpretations. Nor have Christians ever been able to agree on the import of the hyperboles of the Sermon on the Mount. Luther, for example, taught that Christ's commandments were intended to teach man his utter incapacity for doing good: man must throw himself on the mercy of God, believing that Christ died for our sins. On concrete moral issues, Jesus can be, and has been, cited on almost all sides. The Buddha and the Hebrew prophets were not so equivocal.

Third: One of the few things about Jesus' moral teachings that seems fairly clear is that he was not greatly concerned about social justice. This makes his ethic much less impressive than the prophets'.

Fourth: Albert Schweitzer has argued in considerable detail that this lack of concern was due to the fact that Jesus predicated his entire message on a false belief: namely, that the world was about to come to an end. If Schweitzer is right, as I think he is, Jesus was surely not the wisest of men. And can we call him the greatest moralist unless we accept his radical depreciation of *this* life and his belief in Heaven and Hell?

Finally, the Jesus of the New Testament believed, and was not greatly bothered by his belief, that God would damn and torment the mass of mankind in all eternity. According to all three Synoptic Gospels, he actually reassured his disciples:

"If anyone will not receive you or listen to your words, shake off the dust from your feet as you leave that house or town. Truly, I say to you, it shall be more tolerable on the day of judgment for the land of Sodom and Gomorrha than for that town."

This is no isolated dictum; the Sermon on the Mount, for example, is also punctuated by threats of Hell.

Augustine, Aquinas, and Calvin stressed Hell, but many Christian apologists today simply ignore all such passages. A few insist that in a couple of inter-testamentary apocalypses we find far more detailed visions of Hell. They do not mention that these apocalypses would not be known today if it had not been for the esteem in which the early Christians held them. For the Jews rejected them while accepting the humane teachings of men like Hillel and Akiba. Rabbi Akiba, a contemporary of Paul and the Evangelists, taught that "only those who possess no good deeds at all will descend into the netherworld"; also that "the punishment of the wicked in Gehinnom lasts twelve months."

Of course, Jesus also stressed love, citing—or agreeing with a Pharisee who cited—Moses. But this as well as the fact that he said some lovely things and told some fine parables is hardly sufficient to establish the Christian claims about him: that much he has in common with Moses, Micah, and Hosea, with the Buddha, Confucius, and Lao-tze, to name a mere half-dozen teachers who preceded him by a few centuries.

It might be countered that the story of Jesus is the best possible symbol of love. But is it? Consider the story the way it looks to people not committed to, and prejudiced in favor of, Christianity: God caused a virgin, betrothed to Joseph, to conceive His Own Son, and this Son had to be betrayed, crucified, and resurrected in order that all those—and only those—might be saved who should both believe this story and be baptized and eat and drink on regular occasions what they themselves believe to be the flesh and blood of this Son (or, in some denominations, merely the symbols of His flesh and blood); meanwhile, the rest of mankind suffer eternal torment, and according to many Christian creeds and teachers, they were predestined for damnation by God Himself from the beginning.

One might choose to be a Christian in spite of all this if one could intensely admire the great Christians who came after Jesus. But Peter and Paul, Athanasius and Augustine, Luther and Calvin, seem far less admirable to me, for all their admitted virtues, than Hosea and Micah, Isaiah and Jeremiah, Hillel and Akiba; or the Buddha, Socrates, and Spinoza. Maimonides, unlike Aquinas whom he influenced, did not believe in eternal damnation or that heretics should be executed. Some recent Protestant writers have been wonderfully forthright about Luther's and Calvin's shortcomings; but for candid portraits of the saints one must on the whole turn to non-Catholic writers—with at least one notable exception. In 1950, Malcolm Hay, a Catholic, published one of the most moving books of our time, *The Foot of Pride*, which is admirably frank about some of the most celebrated saints.

In an essay published in Germany in 1939—or rather in a book seized barely before publication by the Gestapo and destroyed except for about half-a-dozen copies—Leo Baeck, probably the greatest rabbi of our time, said something profoundly relevant:

A good deal of church history is the history of all the things which neither hurt nor encroached upon this piety, all the outrages and all the baseness which this piety was able to tolerate with an assured and undisturbed soul and an untroubled faith. And a spirit is characterized not only by what it does but, no less, by what it permits. . . . The Christian religion, very much including Protestantism, has been able to maintain silence about so much that it is difficult to say what has been more pernicious in the course of time: the intolerance which committed the wrongs or the indifference which beheld them unperturbed.[3]

This thought may diminish even one's affection for St. Francis, but not one's admiration for the prophets.

The world's other religions remain. If we apply the same criteria, only two issue a real challenge to us, or at least to me: Judaism and Buddhism. I admire Genesis and Job, the Book of Jonah and the Dhammapada far above any book in the New Testament. But popular Buddhism with its profuse idolatry, its relics, and its superstitions repels me, and I have reservations even about the teachings of the Buddha. I admire much of his profound analysis of man's condition: the world has no purpose; it is up to us to give our lives a purpose; and we cannot rely on any supernatural assistance. Life is full of suffering, suffering is rooted in desire and attachment, and much desire and attachment are rooted in ignorance. By knowledge, especially of the Buddha's teachings, it is possible to develop a pervasive detachment, not incompatible with a mild, comprehensive compassion—and to cease to suffer. But consider the Old Testament and Sophocles, Michelangelo and Rembrandt, Shakespeare and Goethe: the price for the avoidance of all suffering is too high. Suffering and sacrifice can be experienced as worthwhile: one may find beauty in them and greatness through them.

Much of the appeal of Christianity is due to the fact that it contains at least intimations—but really no more than that—of this tragic ethos. But the story of Christ remains uncomfortably similar to the saga of the boss's son who works very briefly in the shop, where he makes a great point of his home and is cruelly beaten by some of his fellow workers, before he joins his father as co-chairman of the board and wreaks horrible revenge. This "happy" end makes

[3] The essay, "Romantic Religion," is included in Baeck's *Judaism and Christianity*, translated with an introductory essay, by Walter Kaufmann, Jewish Publication Society, 1958.

most of the Christian martyrs, too, untragic figures. These observations may strike believers as blasphemous, but they might do well to reflect on the manner in which they pass judgment on other religions, and there may be some point in considering how one's own religion must strike those who don't accept it.

Probably the only great religion in which genuine self-sacrifice and tragedy have occupied a central place is Judaism, especially prior to the introduction of belief in any after life. Moses is the very incarnation of humane devotion, wearing himself out in the service of God and men, expecting, and receiving, no reward whatever, but finding his reward in his work. He asks God to destroy him rather than his people and intercedes for them again and again. In the prophets, from Hosea to the songs of the suffering servant, we find the same outlook.

Why, then, do I not accept Judaism? In view of all the things I do not believe, I have no wish to observe the six-hundred-odd commandments and prohibitions that define the traditional Jewish way of life, or to participate in religious services. With most so-called orthodox Jews I have much less in common than with all kinds of other people, Jews and Gentiles. Reform Judaism seems to me to involve compromise, conformism, and the wish to be innocuous. To that extent, it, too, stands opposed to the ethos of the prophets. And if a succession of great Jews should equal the boldness of the prophets, who repudiated the ritual of their day, and go a step further by also renouncing, and denouncing, all kinds of belief—would not this amount to giving up religion?

What remains if you give up the great religions? Many people think: only Communism, Nazism, and immorality. But the morality of Socrates, Spinoza, and Hume compares favorably with Augustine's, Luther's, and Calvin's. And the evil deeds of Communism and Nazism are not due to their lack of belief but to their false beliefs, even as the evil deeds of the Crusaders, Inquisitors, and witch hunters, and Luther's exhortation to burn synagogues and Calvin's decision to burn Servetus, were due to *their* false beliefs. Christianity, like Islam, has caused more wars than it has prevented; and the Middle Ages, when Europe was Christian, were not a period of peace and good will among men. Does it make sense that those who refuse to let their Yes be Yes and their No, No—those who refuse to reject false beliefs, those who would rather stretch them and equivocate—should have a monopoly on being moral?

Renouncing false beliefs will not usher in the millennium. Few things about the strategy of contemporary apologists are more repellent than their frequent recourse to spurious alternatives. The lesser lights inform us that the alternative to Christianity is materialism, thus showing how little they have read, while the greater lights talk as if the alternative were bound to be a shallow and inane optimism. I don't believe that man will turn this earth into a bed of roses either with the aid of God or without it. Nor does life among the roses strike me as a dream from which one would not care to wake up after a very short time.

Some evils and some kinds of suffering can be abolished, but not all suffering can be eliminated; and the beauty, goodness, and greatness that redeem life on earth are inseparable from suffering. Nietzsche once said: "If you have an enemy, do not requite him evil with good, for that would put him to shame. Rather prove that he did you some good." If life hurts you, the manly thing is neither to whine nor to feel martyred, but to prove that it did you some good.

No one way is the best way of life for all. To me the *Apology* of Socrates, as immortalized by Plato in less than thirty pages, presents a challenge from which I cannot, and have no wish to, get away. Here is part of Socrates' answer to the charges of impiety and corruption of the Athenian youth, on which he was convicted and put to death:

> I am better off than he is—for he knows nothing but thinks he knows, while I neither know nor think I know. . . . If you say to me, . . . you shall be let off, but upon one condition, that you are not to inquire . . . in this way any more, and that if you are caught doing so again you shall die—if this was the condition on which you let me go, I should reply: . . . while I have life and strength I shall never cease from the practice and teaching of philosophy, exhorting anyone whom I meet. . . . Are you not ashamed of heaping up the greatest amount of money and honor and reputation, and caring so little about wisdom and truth? . . . The unexamined life is not worth living. . . . If you suppose that there is no consciousness, but a sleep like the sleep of him that is undisturbed even by dreams, death will be an unspeakable gain. . . . Eternity is then only a single night.

It would be folly to wish to foist this outlook on everybody. Professors of philosophy discourage and fail a large percentage even of their graduate students and are assuredly not eager to turn all men into philosophers. In philosophy, as in religion, teaching usually involves a loss of dimension; and the Socratic fusion of philosophy and life, critical acumen and passion, laughter and tragic stature is almost unique.

One need not believe in Pallas Athena, the virgin goddess, to be overwhelmed by the Parthenon. Similarly, a man who rejects all dogmas, all theologies, and all religious formulations of beliefs may still find Genesis the sublime book *par excellence*. Experiences and aspirations of which intimations may be found in Plato, Nietzsche, and Spinoza have found their most evocative expression in some sacred books. Since the Renaissance, Shakespeare, Rembrandt, Mozart, and a host of others have shown that this religious dimension can be experienced and communicated apart from any religious context. But that is no reason for closing my heart to Job's cry, or to Jeremiah's, or to the Second Isaiah. I do not read them as mere literature; rather, I read Sophocles and Shakespeare with all my being, too.

Moreover, I am so far quite unable to justify one of my central convictions: that, even if it were possible to make all men happy by an operation or a drug that would stultify their development, this would somehow be an impious crime. This conviction is ultimately rooted in the Mosaic challenge: "You shall be holy; for I the Lord your God am holy."

To communicate to others some feeling for man's religious quest, to arouse an aspiration in them which nothing but death can quell, and to develop their critical powers—that is infinitely more important to me than persuading anybody that Shakespeare was right when he wrote these lines:

> The cloud-capp'd towers, the gorgeous palaces,
> The solemn temples, the great globe itself,
> Yea, all which it inherit, shall dissolve;
> And, like this insubstantial pageant faded,
> Leave not a rack behind. We are such stuff
> As dreams are made on, and our little life
> Is rounded with a sleep.

I do not believe in any afterlife any more than the prophets did, but I don't mind living in a world in which people have different beliefs. Diversity helps to prevent stagnation and smugness; and a teacher should acquaint his students with diversity and prize careful criticism far above agreement. His noblest duty is to lead others to think for themselves.

Oddly, millions believe that lack of belief in God, Christ, and Hell leads to inhumanity and cruelty while those who have these beliefs have a monopoly on charity—and that people like myself will pay for their lack of belief by suffering in all eternity. I do not believe that anybody will suffer after death nor do I wish it.

Some scientists tell us that in our own galaxy alone there are probably hundreds of thousands of planets with living beings on them, more or less like those on the earth, and that there are about 100 million galaxies within the range of our telescopes. Man seems to play a very insignificant part in the universe, and my part is surely negligible. The question confronting me is not, except perhaps in idle moments, what part might be more amusing, but what I wish to make of my part. And what I want to do and would advise others to do is to make the most of it: put into it all you have got, and live and, if possible, die with some measure of nobility.

9

THE FUTURE
OF JEWISH IDENTITY*

I

Time was when a convertible, a glamorous girl friend, and member-ship in some fraternities or clubs were status symbols among Ameri-can students. In the late sixties, however, they became symbols of a way of life despised by avant-garde students. No single set of symbols took their place: neither beards, drugs and Yoga, nor civil rights work, demonstrations, and occupying buildings. Trying some of this, like reading Hermann Hesse and talking about existentialism, is part of a search, a quest, a crisis. And this is the new status symbol. It even has a name: the identity crisis.

You can be "with it" without a beard and without taking drugs, and you certainly do not have to occupy a building; but if you are not concerned about your identity you are really "out of it."

This way of putting it may seem not merely nasty but downright wrong. For the identity crisis is not acquired like a car, or member-ship in a club, or a glamorous girl friend; it may involve sleepless nights and despair. So, of course, may a glamorous girl friend. But in the case of the girl, suffering is incidental, while an identity crisis is painful through and through. Still, that does not mean that it cannot be a status symbol. The dueling scars that German fraternity students used to sport were no mere side effect of dueling; often salt was rubbed into the gash to make sure that the scar would become huge and highly visible. The parallel to the identity crisis is palpable. Here, too, it is fashionable to rub salt into the wound.

I find this practice rather distasteful. The irritation of a grain of sand may prompt an oyster to produce a pearl, but men are not oysters, and it is highly questionable whether making so much of

---

* This paper was read at the American-Israeli Dialogue in Haifa in July 1969 and first appeared in print a few days later in *The Jerusalem Post Magazine*. It has been reprinted a number of times. For further details see the Introduction above.

one's worries about one's identity is very often fruitful. Such worries may be a part of growing up and to some extent inevitable; but if an adult has not resolved them we do not expect him to publicize that fact. If he is a good writer, he may deal with his identity crisis in an illuminating manner, not necessarily in the context of adolescence. He may show us, as Tolstoy does in *The Death of Ivan Ilyitch*, how an incurably sick man, about to die, looks back on a futile life, and asks himself what and who he really is.

If the Jewish people were either very young, or incurably sick and about to die after a pointless life, it would be fitting for us to worry about Jewish identity. But our people is much more than three thousand years old, our life has not been futilely frittered away on trivialities, and prophets of our impending death have been proved wrong so often that it seems more fitting for us to continue to do worthwhile things rather than worry a great deal about our identity.

Consideration of the future of Jewish identity poses an additional problem. An active, healthy person does not try to predict his own future. He creates it, knowing that sudden, unforeseen, capricious events are almost certain to make the result quite different from his dreams. He therefore does not dream too much but acts, finding an element of fascination in the never ceasing challenge of the unexpected. The same is true of an active, healthy people.

By these criteria, the men and women of Israel are a paradigm of an active and healthy people. Nobody needs to tell them about the unexpected and the unpredictable. Nobody needs to tell them that it is fruitless to keep talking and worrying about the future. Nobody needs to tell them about the fascination of challenges, about courage, about action.

If the question of Jewish identity is incomparably more acute in the United States than it is in Israel, this is not merely because America is the home of the identity crisis, or because American students and blacks make so much of their concern with their identity. The intellectual climate in the United States accounts for the formulation of the problem in terms of identity, but the basic concern is older. Assimilation calls into question the *future* of Jewish identity, and the decline of religion raises the problem of the *nature* of Jewish identity.

Indeed, a surprising number of Jews in Israel are worried about Jewish identity. They are much less likely to think of the problem in terms of "identity," but large numbers of Israelis wonder about their relationship to the Jews abroad. What is it that they have in common? What constitutes Jewishness? (Meanwhile many Egyptians debate whether they are, above all, Arabs or Egyptians.)

The concerns that lead to such questioning and discussion among Jews both in the Diaspora and in Israel are perfectly understandable. But discourses on "Jewishness" and the frequent use of the term "un-Jewish" bring to mind the House Committee on Un-American Activities. The concept of "un-American activities" became so odious to so many Americans that the committee eventually changed its name; but liberal Jews who for years criticized the notion of "un-American activities" have no qualms at all about branding all sorts of conduct and ideas as "un-Jewish." What would they think of equally prolonged discussions about Polishness and what is un-Polish, Russianism and what is un-Russian, or what is truly German and un-German?

Such terms may seem descriptive, but the discussion is rarely about facts. The terms are evaluative, and what we are offered are persuasive definitions, prescriptions, exhortations, and denunciations. Even as anti-Semites use the word "Jewish" as an opprobrium, many Jews use "Jewish" as an encomium and "un-Jewish" as a term of censure. Therefore most discussions of this sort are quite as sterile as disputes about what is "un-Christian." From a multitude of rich traditions many Jews and Christians distill what they strongly favor and call it "Jewish" or "Christian." What they fervently dislike becomes "un-Jewish" and "un-Christian"—precisely if it is something that is done by many Jews or Christians.

As long as terms are used this way, no dialogue is possible. As long as each discussant feels free to ignore change and development, and to freeze as the norm certain favored elements from the tradition, Orthodox, Conservative, and Reform Jews will disagree as predictably at Calvinists, Catholics, and liberal Protestants.

In sum, we should try to discuss the future of Jewish identity without getting caught in the semantic pitfalls of "Jewishness."

II

In biblical times a Jew was distinguished from other men by his beliefs—and even more by his disbeliefs—his way of life, his language, his traditions. After the emergence of Christianity and the destruction of the Temple, being a Jew became primarily a matter of religion. But it never was *only* that. Ever since the days of Ruth, a person becoming a Jew did not merely embrace another religion but also cast his lot with the Jewish people. *Amech ami, v'elohayich elohai; ba'asher tamuti amut*—your people is my people, your God my God, and where you die I shall die.

For roughly three thousand years the words of Ruth have summed up the meaning of being a Jew or choosing to be a Jew: membership in a people, in a religion, and in a *Schicksalsgemeinschaft*—a community that shares a common fate.

The erosion of religion in the modern world calls the traditional meaning of "Jewishness" into question. Both the beliefs and the disbeliefs that at one time distinguished Jews are widely shared by non-Jews; and many Jews have lost all religious beliefs. The way of life governed by the six-hundred-thirteen do's and don't's of traditional Judaism has been abandoned by millions of Jews, while millions more pick and choose a few of the traditions, giving up others. Many feel that what they keep is genuine "Jewishness," and that what others choose to perpetuate are mere frills. Differences abound even among those who call themselves Orthodox. For centuries, being a Jew meant primarily that one adhered to the Jewish religion. In the twentieth century that is becoming the exception rather than the rule.

Nor is it clear that being a Jew still means membership in a *Schicksalsgemeinschaft*. When I formally left the Lutheran church into which I had been baptized (although my mother and all of my grandparents were Jewish) and chose to become a Jew, in Berlin in 1933, I seemed to choose not only a religion but a common fate. *Amech ami, v'elohayich elohai; ba'asher tamuti amut*. But where *they* died, *we* did not die. We did *not* share their fate.

Still we share the fate of being survivors. For some of us that is a large part of the meaning of our being Jews—an experience at the very core of our existence, with which we keep trying to cope.

Yet it is a small number of Jews with whom we share this bond. Most American Jews and a large number of Israelis did not share this fate either, and the experience of the rapidly growing majority of Jewry—those born since World War II—is different from ours. The fate of the Jews in the United States and in the Soviet Union is not at all the same, and neither of these two large communities has shared the hardships and the hazards of the Jews in Israel, any more than most Israelis have shared the miseries of Soviet Jewry. Being a Jew no longer involves sharing a common fate.

Did it ever? The fate of Judah was not that of Israel, and the Jews who returned to Jerusalem after the Babylonian Exile did not share the fate of those who remained in Mesopotamia. The fate of the Jews in Alexandria was not that of the Jews in Palestine, and later the Sephardim and the Ashkenazim went their separate ways. Even in Germany in 1933, the fate I chose was that of half-a-million German Jews, not that of the vast majority of Jews abroad.

Our common fate exists only in memory and apprehension. Talk of a *Schicksalsgemeinschaft* suggests that, given a long enough span of time, we can always count on persecution and destruction, and that only a remnant will survive. Talk of a community of fate involves a degree of fatalism.

In the mid-thirties we had a newspaper in Berlin that was called *C-V Zeitung*. The full name of the *C-V* was *Centralverein deutscher Staatsbürger jüdischen Glaubens*, Central Association of German Citizens of the Jewish Faith. That organization and its anti-Zionist spirit quickly became dated by events. But many Israelis wonder whether American Jewry does not look upon itself the same way— as American citizens of the Jewish faith. One important difference, however, is that many of us have given up the Jewish faith, the Jewish religion; for us the Jews are a people. And the Americans are not a people in the same sense as the German or Italian people. The United States is a pluralistic country in which many citizens take pride in their Italian, German, Irish or Jewish background. In the American framework one may try to preserve or develop a Jewish sub-culture. But it is far from clear what its distinctive content might be, apart from either religion or such highly dispensable folkways as eating *gefilte* fish. And you don't have to be Jewish to eat Jewish foods, which are now available in supermarkets.

III

For the past two thousand years Jewish identity depended on the twin pillars of religion and persecution. With both of them disappearing, what remains? There is a deep reluctance to face up to this crucial question. Many Israelis take refuge in the fancy that there is a great deal of anti-Semitism and discrimination against Jews in the United States. If there were, American Jews would not have to worry about the future of Jewish identity. In fact, it is extraordinary that the provocations of the S.D.S., among whose widely publicized leaders there have been so many Jews, have not elicited a wave of anti-Semitism in the press, on Capitol Hill, and among grass roots politicians. That American Jewry may nevertheless eventually suffer something like the fate of Spanish or German Jewry is possible. But instead of defining Jewish identity in terms of this possibility, it makes more sense to exert oneself to prevent such a catastrophe.

Many Israelis insist that *all* Jews ought to come to Israel. This would not only turn the whole country into one vast Tel-Aviv; it would also deprive Israel of crucial financial and political support. The United States and England would then cease to sell arms to Israel, and would give their full support to the Arab countries. After the events of 1967, Israel's feeling that she cannot depend on other countries is fully understandable—and yet her survival depends on at least half-hearted support from some countries with large Jewish populations.

Some Jews prefer to doubt the effects of the erosion of religion. Certainly, one can grant that it was, in large measure, the Jewish religion that kept the Jewish people alive after the destruction of the Second Temple; but if the survival of Jewry in the future should depend on religion, only a very small remnant would survive, while those engaged in the most creative and promising work, both in Israel and in the Diaspora, would be lost.

In my *Critique of Religion and Philosophy* (1958), in which I dealt at length with Judaism and Christianity, I expressed a profound sympathy for Orthodox Judaism, although I doubted the future of religion. But the behavior of the Orthodox in Israel toward the un-Orthodox fills me with revulsion, and the idolatry of the Western Wall is an abomination that brings to mind Isaiah's and Jeremiah's protests.

What remains if neither religion nor the community of fate can vouchsafe the future of the Jewish people? Nationalism.

My opposition to nationalism does not entail any hostility toward Israel. In the years before, during, and after World War II, Zion ceased to be an ideological question. The rest of the world did not receive the Jewish refugees with open arms as it later accepted Gentile fugitives from Hungary; even the survivors of the war were sent back to D.P. camps in Germany. One did not have to be a nationalist to feel that this was intolerable. After the state of Israel was proclaimed, I could have wished for it to become a model to the nations in some ways in which it did not; for example, in its treatment of minorities. To say that there were extenuating circumstances would be a gross understatement. Nonetheless, I wish that Israel were less nationalistic —and I know that many Israelis feel the same way, although mine is, as usual, a minority view.

"Nationalism" is not a univocal term. In the course of its history it has been applied to different things, and I do not abhor everything that has ever been called by this name. The kind of nationalism that might be invoked to guarantee the future of the Jewish people—and that I reject—can be sketched rapidly. It consists of the demand for a nation state, with one language, in which minorities are treated as outsiders and in some ways as second-class citizens. Often nationalism of this kind is accompanied by a feeling of superiority to other peoples and by irredentism.

Nationalism of this sort represents one powerful tendency in the modern world; internationalism represents another. Millions of Europeans and North Americans have come to look upon nationalism as a nineteenth-century disease of which humanity might yet perish; the Common Market, the United States, and the relationship between the United States and Canada are harbingers of internationalism.

"Internationalism" can also mean many things. What I mean is the lowering of barriers to travel and trade, the willingness of people who speak different languages to work together on an equal basis, and the habit of seeing others first of all not as Jews, Arabs, blacks, Indians, Mexicans, Germans, or Frenchmen, but as human beings. That the United States still has a long way to go in this direction is obvious, but growing numbers of Americans, including the majority of American Jews, recognize this ideal. I am not alone in my wish to be recognized as a human being and an individual—as me—instead of being stereotyped as an American, a Jew, a professor, one of those over thirty, or whatever other category may serve to dehumanize me.

One can be against nationalism and love Israel. The future of Israel —whether it develops along nationalistic lines or not—is a great issue. Most of my friends in Israel oppose nationalism as I do, and they need the help of their friends in the Diaspora.

It is a disgrace when Jews who are nonobservant at home not only suddenly sprout skull caps when they visit Israel but sentimentally condone religious compulsion. And it is inhuman when Jews who insist that blacks are first of all human beings and must not be reduced to second-class citizenship in the United States do not extend the same consideration to the Arabs in Israel.

As long as the Arab countries refuse to discuss peace with Israel, the treatment of the Arabs in Israel poses special problems, the differences between the Jews in Israel will continue to be dwarfed by an intense feeling of solidarity, and Jews all over the world will go on identifying with Israel. But if peace came and persecution ceased, what might then be the future of Jewish identity? It is a large "if," and the condition may not be fulfilled in our lifetime. But should the whole point of being a Jew be limited to defiance, refusal to bow out in the face of overwhelming odds, the proud determination to survive one's persecutors? Growing numbers of Jews in Israel and abroad feel that this is not enough. But what else is there?

I have argued that it is pointless to define Jewishness. An accurate description of what has been Jewish in the past would have to include much that we have no wish to preserve. But what many reject, others prize. Persuasive definitions of Jewishness make dialogue impossible and get us nowhere. What remains? The question whether a non-religious and non-nationalistic selection from our heritage is viable.

For twenty-five centuries, since the destruction of the First Temple which might well have spelled the end of a brief but glorious history, generations of Jews have endured exile, a persecution, war and martyrdom—for what? Are we content to say that the finest hour of our people lies a few thousand years back? Are we satisfied to be a living anticlimax?

Of course not. Our achievements in the twentieth century need not fear comparison with those of any other people during the same period. We have no reason to be obsessed by the question of who or what we are. The most crucial question that confronts us is what to do next. But in a quiet moment we may also ask if there is any continuity between our accomplishments in modern and in biblical times.

IV

There is, but before we come to that, it is worth noting that a Jew's attitude toward time is apt to be distinctive. More and more Americans are fascinated by "antiques," meaning anything that is a hundred years old and sometimes even a mere fifty or sixty. Englishmen may expect you to feel impressed if they live in an eighteenth-century house or when they mention that New College at Oxford was founded in the fourteenth century. Roman Catholics boast of the antiquity of their church. For me, Moses, David, and the pre-exilic prophets are early, and everything Hellenistic and Roman is late.

If my historical perspective, which is so different from the unhistorical outlook of many English-speaking thinkers, owes something to German philosophy, especially to Hegel, it is nevertheless rooted in the Bible. There we find genuinely historical thinking centuries before Thucydides.

Contrasts between the Greeks and the time-conscious and history-minded Hebrews have been attempted by Leo Baeck, Hans Kohn, and Erich Auerbach. This is not the place to reflect on the significance of either Greek sculpture or Plato's denial of the reality of time. It is undeniable that in the Bible we find a striking concern with time, development, and history, and that this is one of the major distinctions between ancient Judaism on the one hand and the religions of the Greeks, the Chinese and the Indians, on the other. Similarly, what distinguishes Marx from previous economists, and Freud from earlier psychologists, is their preoccupation with time, development, and history. Perhaps one could say something similar of Einstein.

It would be absurd to claim that an interest in development is a Jewish trait, or to speak of "Jewishness" and "un-Jewish" in this connection. But here is an element in the Jewish tradition that is worth preserving and developing.

What Jewish identity comes to in the end is the acceptance of the history of the Jewish people as one's own. And if anyone accepts that, it is inhuman to refuse to consider him a Jew merely because his mother was not Jewish.

Anyone concerned with the future of Jewish identity should above all else see to it that young Jews learn Jewish history, including the Bible and Jewish literature. The feeling that many of us have for the land of Israel and for Jerusalem comes of that; it is not religious faith, but thousands of associations that make our skin creep.

The teaching of Jewish history in America is as disgraceful as the religious instruction in most Christian Sunday schools. If Jewish identity survives in spite of that, it will be a miracle. Jewish survival has always depended to some extent on miracles, but it is not decent to rely on them. Those who speak and write so much about Jewish identity ought to know what they can do to preserve it.

Claims about the essence of Jewishness or Judaism that are not based on the study of Jewish history and literature can hardly be taken seriously. But even intensive research cannot reveal this essence. Leo Baeck wrote a very remarkable book on the essence of Judaism (*Das Wesen des Judentums*), prompted by Adolf von Harnack's influential lectures on the essence of Christianity (*Das Wesen des Christentums*); but neither Judaism nor Christianity has an essence. Both have a rich history and literature—and it is up to us to determine what strands in our traditions we choose to develop. Study has to come first, but eventually a decision is required. As long as we are alive, our character is not fixed.

The choice we have to make is not between life and death, good and evil, or black and white. We are confronted by a wealth of possibilities. There are various versions of Orthodox Judaism, there is a great variety of more recent models, and we can also opt for one of many secular paths. Here is *my* way; and I might add, like Nietzsche's Zarathustra: Where is yours?

V

Jews are heirs to a tradition marked by three fierce concerns that are very far from entailing each other: a concern with *social justice*, with *music and literature*, and with *learning*. This combination is highly unusual. Nowhere else have all *three* been cultivated.

The first concern—with social justice—is the most distinctive. Nothing like it is to be found in the scriptures of the other major religions. Love of learning is found in many religions and cultures—as the province of a small élite; as an almost universal concern of the whole community it remained, until recent times, a distinctive trait of Jewry. Love of music and literature is found in many places, but not in the Upanishads or in the Dhammapada, in the Book of Tao or in the New Testament.

Being used to all three concerns, we are prone to overlook the singularity of their conjunction. In other cultures, concern with social justice is quite apt to lead to some impatience with music and literature, and even with learning. Conversely, those interested in scholarship often have no time for music or for a social conscience. The Jewish tradition is distinguished by the fusion of these three intense concerns. A name may help to focus attention on this unusual combination: Let us call it the *Kaufmann syndrome*.

The persistent concern with social justice from the Law of Moses and the Hebrew prophets down to the twentieth century, the disproportionate presence of Jews in movements of social reform, and the central place of philanthropy in the Jewish tradition are not likely to be questioned. But is there really any continuity between the biblical injunction "You shall be unto Me a people of priests," and the staggering number of Jews among twentieth-century scientists? Surely, the kind of learning cultivated in the ghettos of Eastern Europe and the training required to become a leading physicist or mathematician are utterly different. (Freud's interpretation of dreams and parapraxes is not that different from the traditional approach to Scripture.) The ancient insistence that no Jew should remain illiterate, and the medieval love of learning, bore abundant fruit wherever opportunities arose—in Spain during the age of Maimonides, and then again after the emancipation. In utterly disproportionate numbers, Jews crowded into colleges and universities, obtained professorships and Nobel Prizes, and made their mark in almost every field of learning. Such an explosion was possible only because there was such a pent-up force that had been cultivated for thousands of years.

It is precisely the same with the love of music and literature. There are not so many names of the first rank in these fields—Mendelssohn-Bartholdy, Heine, Kafka—but there are legions of distinguished Jewish writers and musicians who are not quite of that order. The point is not how we should rank this composer or that novelist. Rather consider the world's major violinists and ask yourself why most of them are Jews. And why so many of the better writers in Germany and Austria during the first third of the century, and in the United States during the second third, have been Jews. And why you see so many Jews when you go to a concert; and why in Israel you can scarcely get into a concert hall unless you have held a series subscription for years.

Jews have not been equally outstanding in all fields. They have not produced major composers as the Germans and Austrians have, or painters as the Dutch and Italians have. Painting and sculpture have not been part of the Kaufmann syndrome, no doubt owing to the Mosaic prohibition. It is a delightful surprise that so many beautiful mosaics have been found in the ruins of ancient synagogues under the sands in Israel. Many of them are exceptionally lovely, and to my mind Jacob Epstein was the greatest sculptor of our time; but it is nevertheless plain that painting and sculpture have not been cultivated persistently by Jews since biblical times.

A traveling Van Gogh exhibition in Warsaw, October 1962, found the museum all but empty and the intellectuals of Warsaw largely unaware and unconcerned, while at a similar Van Gogh exhibition held three months later in Tel-Aviv one could hardly see the pictures for the people who thronged in to see them, although the doors were open until midnight. The syndrome is not a static thing that is given once and for all, but is capable of development and expansion.

Being a Jew means having the good fortune to have such a background. One deserves no blame or credit for one's parents, but one can feel grateful or hateful. It is the same with the tradition out of which one comes. What I feel is love and gratitude. If I were about to be born and could choose what people to be born into, I'd say, feeling that the wish was presumptuous and that I could not expect its fulfillment but that after all I had been asked to indicate my first choice: I should like to be a Jew.

To have such a history is marvelous. To have such ancestors is unbelievable. And to have ready access to such a tradition and such a syndrome is a great blessing.

In Poland one is struck by the great effort that has gone into the reconstruction of palaces and other buildings that are a few centuries old. In a country that is far from rich this vast expense of wealth and labor testifies to an intense desire to establish a national past. But to how much high culture does a Pole have first-hand access? . . . To much more than most people do—even if he should only speak Polish.

Not all national heritages are equally rich. Not every nation has a great literature. And if an Israeli spoke only Hebrew and always stayed in Israel . . .

I am glad I am a Jew. But I am also grateful that I grew up in Germany, speak German, and have the kind of easy access to German literature and philosophy that anyone with a different upbringing must work for years to achieve. And it is my good fortune that I can write English, a language that hundreds of millions of men can read; that I can easily read what is written in that language; and that I live in a large country that abounds in interesting men and women, splendid libraries and museums, and magnificent scenery—a country in which I can travel freely and have a sense of space and freedom—and where, if one does not like it in one place it is easy to go to another.

I do not mean to give the impression that life is wonderful. Where they died we did not die; Israel is embattled; and poverty, starvation, misery, injustice, and despair abound—also in the United States. But upon mentioning what one loves in the Jewish tradition one may be suspected, unjustly, of being a chauvinist. Actually, the Kaufmann syndrome should be seen in perspective. The Jews certainly do not have a monopoly on everything good. But the sense of history and the syndrome I have described are worth preserving and developing.

The stones of religion and nationalism that I reject may nevertheless remain the cornerstone of "Jewishness." Still there is the question of what might happen if my wishes came true. My own outlook is never likely to be shared by very large numbers of people; it is very personal though far from unique.

We Jews are a family. We often irritate each other, we dislike some of our relatives, and there are many people outside the family whom we like far better. Being always with each other makes for a great deal of tension, and it is quite possible that some of us are more creative and work better in the Diaspora.

VI

No discussion of the future of Jewish identity should concentrate exclusively on preservation and transmission. From the start of the Zionist movement it was part of the dream that new dimensions might be added to Jewish identity. In the *kibbutzim* the traditional concern with social justice, music and literature, and learning was to be developed into a new life style. High hopes were also centered in the creation of the Hebrew University. We should ask to what extent these hopes have been realized.

It is my impression—but I should love to be convinced that I am wrong—that the younger generation is less fiercely intellectual than were the founders, that the three-pronged tradition of which I have spoken is in danger, and that the scarcely credible linguistic versatility of the older generation is now dying out. If so, the *kibbutzim* will not enrich the meaning of Jewishness as much as they might have, and the universities, though they may be excellent for a tiny country, will not, in time to come, hold their own with the best schools elsewhere. To that end the students would have to be at least effectively bilingual. But there are degrees of perfection, and even now Israel has already added immensely to the meaning of Jewish identity.

There is always the unexpected, and the armed forces of Israel are more unique than her universities. It may be here more than anywhere else that a truly new style has been developed—a style, to be sure, that owes much to the *kibbutzim*. It is doubly impressive that such a highly effective army and air force should have succeeded to such an extent in avoiding both authoritarianism and militarism. This is due partly to the palpable dangers that make such effective armed forces necessary, and partly to the true universality of service which extends to women, too.

The spirit in the top echelons of Israel's government is also striking. There is a directness, an authenticity, and a lack of formality, evasiveness and airs that sharply distinguishes Ben-Gurion, Golda Meir, Moshe Dayan, and Yigal Allon from the leading statesmen or politicians of other countries. They listen and speak man to man, without fancying that their high office makes them different. This is a rare quality among famous men: Einstein possessed it in the highest degree. Its presence at the top level of government may be unique. It certainly has no precedent either among the kings of ancient Israel or among the *tsadikim* of the Hasidim. Ben-Gurion deserves a great deal of credit for having set this tone when he became the first Prime Minister of Israel.

Confronted with so much creativity and so many innovations, we should not look blindly to the past as if our only problem were to guard our precious heirlooms. Giving up orthodoxy is not a negative thing; it liberates us to concentrate on the future.

The Jews gave the world monotheism. Let us now work for pluralism, both in the countries of the Diaspora and in Israel. Let us continue to work for the rights of minorities—not only of Jews but also of blacks, American Indians, and Israeli Arabs. Let us not embody in the state of Israel those features of nationalism which were the bane of our existence when we lived in nation-states. Let us build an exemplary pluralistic society.

If Israel could prove to the world that Jews can excel as farmers and soldiers and pilots, if it could triumph over all odds in 1967, it cannot be content to plead extenuating circumstances for its treatment of the Arabs in Israel and in the occupied territories. Of course, there *are* extenuating circumstances, and it is maddening that most of mankind continues to apply a double standard to Jews and Arabs—for example, by expressing much concern about the treatment of the Arabs by Israel but hardly any, if any, about the treatment of Jews in the Arab countries. But if Israelis had failed as farmers, there would have been extenuating circumstances, too. And had Israel lost in 1967, there would have been extenuating circumstances. And if the Jews had produced no Nobel Prize winners, there would have been extenuating circumstances. And if there had been no more prophets after Micah and Isaiah, there would have been extenuating circumstances. And if no more books worthy of inclusion in the Bible had been written after the return from Babylon, there would have been extenuating circumstances. It was by never settling for the justified excuse of extenuating circumstances that the Jews became a light to the nations.

Nobody has any right to ask the Jews to go on demanding more of themselves than other nations do—nobody, except a Jew.

10

THE FUTURE OF THE JEWS
IN THE DIASPORA*

I

In my teens I learned that the Hebrew prophets had not been prophets who predicted future events. Instead of being like pagan soothsayers, they said in effect: This is what will happen if you continue to act the way you act now; therefore change your ways. Jonah, who had not wanted to prophesy the destruction of Nineveh in the first place but had been made to do it, understandably reproached God when asked to tell the Assyrians that Nineveh would not be destroyed after all because they had repented. It is part of the point of the book that the future is not predictable because it depends on what people do.

While the prophets were not prophets, legions of pundits and journalists fancy that they are prophets, and a large public hangs on their lips and pays them for their forecasts. But prophets who predict the future are false prophets.

I am neither a false prophet nor a true prophet. I neither claim the power to predict, nor do I have the knowledge to say to my people: If you do this, then that will happen. Such qualified, hypothetical predictions may seem safe enough; in fact, they are not. One can still warn people that a certain policy invites disaster, but we can never be sure that a good policy will succeed.

A Victorian poet, William Ernest Henley (1849–1903), expressed the optimism of his age in sixteen eloquent lines:

Invictus

Out of the night that covers me,
Black as the Pit from pole to pole,

---

* This paper was presented to the World Jewish Congress in New York City, November 17, 1974, and has not been published before. The topic was assigned to me.

I thank whatever gods may be
  For my unconquerable soul.

In the fell clutch of circumstance
  I have not winced nor cried aloud.
Under the bludgeonings of chance
  My head is bloody, but unbowed.

Beyond this place of wrath and tears
  Looms but the Horror of the shade,
And yet the menace of the years
  Finds, and shall find me, unafraid.

It matters not how strait the gate,
  How charged with punishments the scroll,
I am the master of my fate:
  I am the captain of my soul.

Coming from a poet who was crippled by tuberculosis of the bone, this was no mere bluster; and there is an important sense in which we *are* the masters of our fate. It is up to us how we bear it, and in extremity we can end our life and decide how. But it is not up to us whether or when worse comes to worst, nor is it up to us how much of a future is left to us. In the late nineteenth century it was widely felt that if one gave up the belief in God one also shed the sense of the contingency of human life. But one does not have to be a theist to be vividly impressed by that.

Friedrich Schleiermacher, the outstanding German theologian of the romantic era, had said, "The essence of religion consists in the feeling of an absolute dependence." Sigmund Freud replied in 1927, in *The Future of an Illusion* (the illusion he meant was religion): "It is not this feeling that constitutes the essence of religiousness, but only the next step, the reaction to it, which seeks a remedy against this feeling." Freud meant the attempt to overcome this absolute dependence and to influence God or the gods by prayer, sacrifices, or whatever else may be thought to please the divine. Freud continued: "He who goes no further, he who humbly resigns himself to the insignificant part man plays in the universe, is, on the contrary, irreligious in the truest sense of the word" (sec. VI).

Twenty years later, the sense of man's radical contingency came to be widely associated with existentialism, and the generation that grew up after World War II made much of Albert Camus and "the absurd." Another twenty years later, Alexander Solzhenitsyn con-

cluded his great novel *Cancer Ward* with a definitive image of <u>this
capricious and unpredictable element in human life and history</u>: "An
evil man threw tobacco in the Macaque Rhesus's eyes. Just like
that . . ." This view of Stalin's terror, which brought death to tens of
millions and immense suffering to many more, was an affront to
Marxist views of history. But it is so deeply disturbing for non-
Marxists, too, that most people are unwilling to face up to it. Great
philosophers before Marx—Spinoza and Hegel, for example—had
argued that the way to peace of mind led through the recognition
that what happens is rational and inevitable. Without the benefit of
intricate philosophies, that is what most people still feel, confronted
with the infamies of Stalin and Hitler.

Those who are middle-aged tend to be Newtonians in the sense
that they like to think of the universe as if it were a clock, predictable. Most of them simply cannot understand the catastrophic
sense of life that we encounter in Greek tragedy and in the Hebrew
Bible. Yet who in the spring of 1914 would have predicted Stalin's
crimes, or Hitler's? Who in the 1920's would have predicted the events
of 1945, including the division of Germany? Certainly, the pundits
and journalists who pose as prophets did not. When the death camps
were suddenly publicized in 1945, nobody I know predicted the
economic and political recovery of West Germany in the sixties and
seventies.

The story is essentially the same when we shift perspectives and
in the seventies read studies of the making of Hitler's mind. It is
deeply unsettling to feel how unnecessary and how unpredictable the
great atrocities of our time have been. It is always tempting to take
refuge in the false faith or, as Jean-Paul Sartre might say, the bad
faith that somehow what happened was, more or less, inevitable and,
granted a little bit of hindsight, predictable. But this a blatant self-
deception.

II

Do not ask: What will happen? But: What do we *want* to happen?
One might add: If you will, it is no dream. The true prophets implied
that what you do makes a difference. I believe that our best may not
be good enough, but it is still reasonable to suppose that our decisions
will at least influence the future.

We should ask:

What do we most want to happen?

What wishes are realistic?

What can we do about it?

Of these three questions, the first is by far the hardest. In fact, it is so hard and frightening that it rarely gets asked. The choice of goals is much harder than the choice of ways and means. People go to great lengths to avoid an open choice of goals. They would much rather treat the goals as given, as agreed on, as not calling for any decision. In my book *Without Guilt and Justice* (1973), I have dealt at length with this fear of fateful decisions, which I call "decido-phobia," and I have described some of the major strategies people use to avoid such decisions. As for the question of the future of the Jews in the diaspora, the obvious dodge is to proceed as if the question called for a prediction and not a decision. But if those who now pose as prophets have been unable to predict the history of our time, why should we suppose that they can tell us much about the future of the Jewish people thirty years hence, not to speak of a hundred or two hundred years?

Individuals do make a difference, more so than ever in an age in which the time required to destroy a people has shrunk to a fraction of one day. The scope for villainy has been increased. We have seen rare goodness, too—Einstein and Pope John—and the unexampled courage of Solzhenitsyn and Sakharov. But the good that men do can so easily be undone, while their crimes are often irrevocable. Hence we simply cannot know what will happen and how much of a future the Jewish people will have, either in Israel or in the diaspora. We should ask instead: What do we most want to happen?

Let me split up this question into three subquestions. The first of these is easy to answer; the second not much harder; and the third one very hard indeed.

1. Do we want the Jews to have a future and to live, if possible, another few thousand years?

As an individual, I certainly should not want to live that long. I hope to die long before I reach a hundred. But the Jewish people show no signs of aging or becoming feeble. Far from living on their memories of ancient glory, they have added to their past achievements in the present century. They are now living through one of their most creative periods. Having survived immense ordeals with undiminished vitality, most Jews naturally want to have a future, and I share that wish.

The second question is not much harder:

2. Do we want *diaspora* Jewry to have a future?

Not long ago, some Jews in Israel might have answered this question negatively, insisting that all Jews ought to come to Israel. For several reasons, that was foolish. To place the strongest reason first: It is foolish to believe that the Jewish people could survive without diaspora Jewry. Those who did not realize this before must surely have realized it in the days following Yom Kippur 1973. Without diaspora Jewry, the Jews in Israel might well be doomed. In no small measure, their survival depends on the survival of diaspora Jewry. But that is not to say that I want diaspora Jewry to survive only for the sake of Israel. Scattered among the nations, the Jews have made overwhelming contributions to humanity in the last hundred years. Why snap the string of these creative triumphs? For our sake and for humanity's I want it to continue.

With that we come to the hard question:

3. What kind of future do we desire for the Jewish people in the diaspora?

Any answer is bound to seem unappealing if not unacceptable to many Jews, but that is no good reason for not giving an answer. To choose goals intelligently and responsibly, we must consider alternatives; and there is no better way to that end than for many of us to think seriously about our goals and then to say: Here are mine; in what way, if any, are yours preferable?

I do not consider protracted survival, or longevity as such, a supreme good either in the case of individuals or in that of nations. When one has nothing to live *for*, it may well be better to die. And even when one does have something to live for, the price for survival may be too steep. The price paid by the Jews for their longevity has been staggering—almost as staggering as the use they have made of a life purchased so dearly. To go on suffering as the Jews have suffered merely in order to survive indefinitely makes no sense. In the past we have been able to wring meaning from our sacrifices. We have turned our firsthand knowledge of human suffering to account, as we were bidden to do by Moses over three thousand years ago. Having been slaves in the land of Egypt, we understood how slaves felt; having been strangers, we knew what it meant to be a stranger;

and we turned to account our experience of human misery, of inhuman misery, by doing more than our share to arouse our fellow men to the voice of their brothers' blood. The work of Moses and the prophets was continued by religious teachers and by social theorists, by political leaders and novelists, physicians and psychologists, scholars and critics. If any people ever was the social conscience of humanity, the Jewish people was.

It may seem presumptuous to make such a claim for any people. It is fashionable nowadays to be unhistorical and to suppose that all decent people everywhere have a social conscience and always have had one. But the ancient Greeks and Romans, to whom Western civilization owes so much, hardly bequeathed to it a sensitive social conscience. Looking back, we are appalled in this respect by Plato and by Aristotle and find comfort in a few marginal figures, like Euripides and the Gracchi. The sacred books of India, from the Vedas to the Upanishads, the Laws of Manu, and the Gita, are impressive in many ways, but the less we say about them in relation to a social conscience, the better. I have argued at length in *The Faith of a Heretic* (1961) that, compared with its Hebrew background, the New Testament, too, is surprisingly lacking in a social conscience. But the most imposing and convincing demonstration of this fact is still that provided by a Christian scholar, Ernst Troeltsch, in *The Social Teachings of the Christian Churches* (1912). The English version of this work (1931) falsifies the title, turning it into *The Social Teaching*, singular, as if his book were of a kind with the popular homilies about the teaching, the morality, the message, or whatever, of Christianity. Troeltsch, however, though he had begun as a professor of theology, had become a first-rate historian and sociologist, and concluded his career as a professor of philosophy.

One may still wonder seriously whether in the modern world the social conscience has not become so widespread, partly owing to the work of Jews in many different fields, that the Jewish people are no longer needed to cultivate it. This I doubt. It is still a feeble growth, much younger in most places than is widely realized, and badly in need of thoughtful cultivation. It would be foolish to predict that, without the efforts of the Jews in years to come, it would wither and die, but its emergence during the past hundred years certainly owes a great deal to Jews.

Similar considerations apply to social criticism generally; to the social sciences, including sociology and anthropology, psychology and economics; to the natural sciences, including physics and mathematics, as well as to the arts, to literature, and the humanities. It would be the height of arrogance to suppose that their continued existence depends on any single people; yet the twentieth-century record suggests forcibly that without the contributions of Jews they would all be in a poorer state.

The most obvious answer, then, to the question of goals is this: *The kind of future I desire for the Jews in the dispersion is that they should continue to be in the forefront of humane endeavors, enriching humanity.*

In the last chapter I pointed out that "The Jewish tradition is distinguished by the fusion of . . . three intense concerns. A name may help us to focus attention on this unusual combination: Let us call it the *Kaufmann syndrome*." These three concerns, which are "far from entailing each other," are a keen social conscience, a deep concern with music and literature, and a fierce devotion to learning. "Nowhere else have all three been cultivated." The Jews have no monopoly on any of these three concerns, and here and there Gentiles have combined all three. But no other people has so consistenly cultivated the whole syndrome. What I *want* to happen is that the Jews should continue to cultivate it and produce worthy successors to an imposing tradition.

III

It would be unrealistic to suppose that the Jews could survive without their ancestral religion, deriving their sense of identity solely from their dedication to the Kaufmann syndrome. Those working for these highly worthwhile goals will often have a sense of kinship with Gentile fellow workers, will often marry Gentiles, and will often fail to instill much of a sense of Jewishness in their children. And even if their children should still have that sense, what of their children's children? What can we do about that?

Most apparently, what is needed is not only a sense of history (though this has become so rare in our time that it alone almost sets one apart) but a sense of *Jewish* history, a *knowledge* of Jewish history—the kind of knowledge that sustains a sense of identity. We are just beginning to develop Jewish studies in some of our colleges and universities. For a generation or more, most Jewish students were as illiterate regarding the history and literature of their religion as were most of their Christian contemporaries. Now the emergence of "Black studies" has triggered a reaction that, to return to my first theme, nobody I know predicted twenty years ago: the development of secular curricula in Jewish studies at a growing number of our best universities. This is the realization of a hope that would have seemed unrealistic a mere ten years ago.

Still, one may wonder whether mere courses and mere study can possibly be enough to preserve the Jews. Surely, it may be objected, the intellect is much too thin for that, and what is needed is emotion and profound determination. True, but the very phrase "mere study" is—to use a word I do not like and hesitate to use—un-Jewish with a vengeance. I mean, it is belied by over two thousand years of Jewish learning. We have reason to know that study need not be something purely intellectual, excluding the emotions, the imagination, and the will. We know that "mere study" can open up to us worlds that engage the emotions at least as much as the everyday realities around us. Nor does this entail a frivolous estimate of the world of scholarship and learning and the subordination of intellectual rigor and excellence to wishful thinking. What it does involve is love, imagination, and loyalty, but no sacrifice whatsoever of the intellectual conscience.

The modern student who identifies with the people whose history he studies, who stands at Mount Sinai with them, who hears Moses and the prophets, who goes into the Babylonian exile and returns, who suffers with Job and cries with the Psalmist, "My God, my God, why have you forsaken me?"—who sees the temple and the holy city laid waste again by the Romans and goes off into the diaspora, suffering endless persecutions and expulsions, torture and calumny— who reads not only the Hebrew and Yiddish classics, as well as Heine, Freud, and Kafka, but also the slanders published by his enemies, the records of German and Soviet persecution in our time, and *The Last of the Just*, *The Painted Bird*, and *Night*—will not emerge unscarred, unscathed, with the shallow confidence that the Jews and he as a Jew are like *kol hagoyim*, like all other people. Even if he should live in a land in which Jews are not persecuted, not resented, and not stigmatized—and although many Israelis are loath to believe this, we are in this happy condition in some Western countries—he will still feel alienated by his past.

Once again, I claim no monopoly for the Jews, and some of the experiences I have in mind have perhaps been formulated best by a Gentile philosopher, Nietzsche: "Only great pain is the ultimate liberator of the spirit . . . Only great pain, the long, slow pain that takes its time—on which we are burned, as it were, with green wood —compels us . . . to descend into our ultimate depths . . . I doubt that such pain makes us 'better'; but I know that it makes us more *profound*. . . . One emerges as a different person, with a few more question marks—above all, with the *will* henceforth to question further, more deeply, severely, harshly, evilly, and quietly . . . What is strangest is this: afterward one has a different taste—a second taste. Out of such abysses . . . one returns . . . more childlike and yet a hundred times more subtle than one has ever been before."

In another passage Nietzsche remarks that "it almost determines the order of rank how profoundly human beings can suffer" and explains that "Profound suffering makes noble; it separates." Both in his late preface (1887) to *The Gay Science*, from which I quoted first, and in *Beyond Good and Evil* (sec. 270), cited afterward, Nietzsche was thinking of himself and a few kindred spirits. In a late note, included in *The Will to Power* (#910), he said: "To those human beings who are of any concern to me I wish suffering, desolation, sickness, ill-treatment, indignities—I wish that they should not remain unfamiliar with profound self-contempt, the torture of self-mistrust, the wretchedness of the vanquished: I have no pity for them, because I wish them the only thing that can prove today whether one is worth anything or not—that one endures."[1]

In my own book, *Without Guilt and Justice*, I have argued in the chapter on "The Need for Alienation" that alienation is the price of self-consciousness, autonomy, and integrity. But how is one to teach this defiant ethos? There are many ways. One can use Nietzsche or Greek tragedy, but most students will never acquire it that way. There are Jews who have argued that there is no substitute for persecution. I suggest and hope that Jewish studies might be a substitute.

Of course, this is not how Jewish studies are taught. The motivation behind the whole enterprise is above all a romantic hankering for community, a nostalgia to belong, to feel at home, *heimish*. But teach-

[1] My English versions of all three books, with commentaries, have been published by Random House. The last two sentences of the first quotation are found only in the slightly revised version that Nietzsche included in *Nietzsche contra Wagner*, Epilogue. My translation of that book is included in *The Portable Nietzsche*, The Viking Press.

ing Jewish history that way is a betrayal of the martyrs' blood. When I go to Yad Vashem or Auschwitz, when I read the historical records or *The Painted Bird* and *Night*, I don't feel *heimish*. I feel alienated from the world, my fellow men, and from my own everyday existence. My conception of study is not "mere study."

Am I calling for a kind of masochism? Can you dispose of my ethos by ascribing it simply to survivor guilt and a pathological need for self-punishment? I have dealt very critically with guilt feelings, including those of survivors, in *Without Guilt and Justice*, and I am strongly opposed to self-punishment. My ethos is goal-directed. In an age in which so many intellectuals succumb to the siren song of community and would like to escape from alienation to be like all the people, I insist that humanity desperately needs the independence of judgment, the integrity, and the autonomy that cannot be had without alienation.

At no point do I mean to suggest that only the Jews have the qualities that I commend. But I do believe that we have cultivated them in a sustained way longer than any other group; and if we ceased to do so, humanity would be much poorer for it. The Jews should continue to cultivate them without the benefit of the clergy.

Many will wonder whether this is possible or desirable. I have refrained from talking about religion, but cannot refrain any longer. I shall conclude with a poem called "Religion," from my *Cain and Other Poems*:[2]

I

> They know how to deal with death
> solemnly doling out dole
> dolled up as for a play
> pray-acting to draw tears
> a few at a time
> like grains of salt
> spice
> on the dry crumbs of life
> something to talk of later
> as one chats of a meal
> the day we buried . . .
> dolled up
> solemn
> know how.

[2] 1962; third ed., enlarged, New American Library, 1975.

II

They still know how to answer Job
and when sedative language fails
there are pills
and cells
to silence scream and vision
starched white to help flowing black
keep up the pretense of peace
lest anyone wake up
in the dark.

III

To know how to sleep in the dark
is religion.
What doth it profit man
to open his eyes in the night
and to see the dark
while most men dream?
Not all that scream
are prophets
but every prophet is mad.
The priests have always known that
and known how
to spice the dry crumbs
stuffing the mouth of Job.

IV

City of almost dry bones
where the not quite dead generation
waits for the trains and the trucks and the lime pits
starving and stinking in filth
patriarchs dying in gutters
and corpses piled high on wheel barrows.
Yisgadal v'yiskadash shmay rabo.
And the bones came together
bone to his bone
an exceeding great army.
Distant voices from buried worlds
grandfathers
and their fathers beyond them
straight backs
and stakes

and stiff necks
and soon
mountains of false teeth
an exceeding great army.
May The Great Name Magnify And Sanctify Itself.

V

Yisgadal v'yiskadash shmay rabo.
Triumph over the dust and filth of reality.
Sedative language
dreams in the dark.
But does anyone know
how to face the void?
What does it profit to scream
when the heart is not eased
and eyes dry as bones
to wake those who sleep
and break up the play
for what?
Why rob the dust of its dignity
sleep of its dreams
and death of
Yisgadal v'yiskadash shmay rabo.

VI

Thou shalt not steal
faith from the filth that remains
and pills from the sick
but neither shalt thou bear false witness
or take in vain The Great Name.
And words that were triumph once
cried from the stake
are false in the face
of those piles of false teeth
and faith cannot whiten
the ovens and lime pits
and no incantation
can silence the scream
of Job.

VII

They know how to deal with deaths
a few at a time
something to talk of later
but not how to speak of this.
What shall we do when their play ends
even between acts
or when their lines are so palpably learned
and their holy tone hollow
and we see through the holes
into emptiness?
After the pray-act and
the spice and the vision
after the filth and the dust and
shantih shantih shantih and Zen
and profanity
no new incantation
or seduction
by ritual
language
or pills
only what some become
and the gift of new eyes
not for dreams and visions and refuge
eyes that see dust as dust
without blinking
and the will to endure and defy and prevail.

11

EXISTENTIALISM
AND DEATH*

Existentialism is not a doctrine but a label widely used to lump together the works of several philosophers and writers who consider a few extreme experiences the best starting point for philosophy. Spearheading the movement, Kierkegaard wrote *Fear and Trembling* (1843), *The Concept of Dread* (1844), and *The Sickness unto Death*, which is despair (1849). Three-quarters of a century later, Jaspers devoted a central section of his *Psychology of Weltanschauungen* (1919) to extreme situations (*Grenzsituationen*), among which he included guilt and death. But if existentialism is widely associated not merely with extreme experiences in general but above all with death, this is due primarily to Heidegger, who discussed death in a crucial 32-page chapter of his influential *Being and Time* (1927). Later, Sartre included a section on death in his *Being and Nothingness* (1943) and criticized Heidegger; and Camus devoted his two would-be philosophic books to suicide (*The Myth of Sisyphus*, 1942) and murder (*The Rebel*, 1951).

It was Heidegger who moved death into the center of discussion. A discussion of existentialism and death should therefore begin with Heidegger, and by first giving some attention to his *approach* it may throw critical light on much of existentialism. At the end of this chapter I shall present my own views in a manner altogether different from that of the two sections on Heidegger.

---

* Through the end of sec. V, this essay appeared in 1959 in *Chicago Review* and in *The Meaning of Death*, ed. Herman Feifel. In 1961 secs. II through V were embodied with minor modifications in *The Faith of a Heretic*, and I added the conclusion that appears below as sec. VI. This chapter has not appeared previously in its present form, and I have used this opportunity to make some minor revisions.

I

Heidegger's major work, *Being and Time*,[1] begins with a 40-page Introduction that ends with "The Outline of the Treatise." We are told that the projected work has two parts, each of which consists of three long sections. The published work, subtitled "First Half," contains only the first two sections of Part One. The "Second Half" has never appeared.

Of the two sections published, the first bears the title, "The preparatory fundamental analysis of human Being." *Dasein* (human Being; literally, being there) is Heidegger's term for human existence as opposed to that of things and animals. Heidegger's central concern is with "the meaning of Being"; but he finds that this concern itself is "a mode of the Being of some beings" (p. 7), namely human beings, and he tries to show in his Introduction that "the meaning of Being" must be explored by way of an analysis of "human Being." This, he argues, is the only way to break the deadlock in the discussion of Being begun by the Greek philosophers—a deadlock due to the fact that philosophers, at least since Aristotle, have always discussed beings rather than Being.[2] To gain an approach to Being, we must study not things but a mode of Being; and the mode of Being most open to us is our own Being. Of this Heidegger proposes to offer a *phenomenological* analysis, and he expressly states his indebtedness to Husserl, the founder of the phenomenological school (especially on p. 38). Indeed, *Being and Time* first appeared in Husserl's *Jahrbuch für Philosophie und phänomenologische Forschung*.

It is entirely typical of Heidegger's essentially unphenomenological procedure that he explains "The phenomenological method of inquiry" (paragraph 7) by devoting one subsection to "the concept of the phenomenon" and another to "the concept of the *logos*," each time offering dubious discussions of the etymologies of the Greek words, before he finally comes to the conclusion that the meaning of phenomenology can be formulated: "to allow to be seen from itself that

---

[1] All references are to *Sein und Zeit* (1927). The page numbers of the original German edition are also given in the translation.

[2] My suggestion that the distinction between *das Sein* and *das Seiende* be rendered in English by using "Being" for the former and "beings" for the latter has Heidegger's enthusiastic approval. His distinction was suggested to him by the Greek philosophers, and he actually found the English "beings" superior to the German *Seiendes* because the English recaptures the Greek plural, *ta onta*. (Cf. my *Existentialism from Dostoevsky to Sartre*, p. 234.)

which shows itself, as it shows itself from itself. (*Das was sich zeigt, so wie es sich von ihm selbst her zeigt, von ihm selbst her sehen lassen*)." And he himself adds: "But this is not saying anything different at all from the maxim cited above: 'To the things themselves!' " This had been Husserl's maxim. Heidegger takes seven pages of dubious arguments, questionable etymologies, and extremely arbitrary and obscure coinages and formulations to say in a bizarre way what not only could be said, but what others before him actually had said, in four words.

In *Being and Time* coinages are the crux of his technique. He calls ". . . the characteristics of human Being *existentials* (Existenzialien). They must be distinguished sharply from the determinations of the Being of those beings whose Being is not human Being, the latter being categories" (p. 44). "Existentials and categories are the two basic possibilities of characteristics of Being. The beings that correspond to them demand different modes of asking primary questions: beings are either *Who* (existence) or *Which* (Being-at-hand in the widest sense)" (p. 45).

It has not been generally noted, if it has been noted at all, that without these quaint locutions the book would not only be much less obscure, and therefore much less fitted for endless discussions in graduate seminars, but also a fraction of its length—considerably under 100 pages instead of 438. For Heidegger does not introduce coinages to say briefly what would otherwise require lengthy repetitions. On the contrary.

While Kierkegaard had derided professorial manners and concentrated on the most extreme experiences, and Nietzsche wrote of guilt, conscience, and death as if he did not even know of academic airs, Heidegger housebreaks Kierkegaard's and Nietzsche's problems by discussing them in such a style that Hegel and Aquinas seem unacademic by comparison. The following footnote is entirely characteristic: "The auth. may remark that he has repeatedly communicated the analysis of the about-world (*Umwelt*) and, altogether, the 'hermeneutics of the facticity' of human Being, in his lectures since the wint. semest. 1919/20" (p. 72). Husserl is always cited as "E. Husserl" and Kant as "I. Kant"—and his own minions dutifully cite the master as "M. Heidegger."

How Kierkegaard would have loved to comment on Heidegger's occasional "The detailed reasons for the following consideration will be given only in . . . Part II, Section 2"—which never saw the light of day (p. 89)! Eleven pages later we read: ". . . only now the here accomplished critique of the Cartesian, and fundamentally still presently accepted, world-ontology can be assured of its philosophic rights. To that end the following must be shown (cf. Part I, Sect. 3)." Alas, this, too, was never published; but after reading the four questions that follow one does not feel any keen regret. Witness the second: "Why is it that in-worldly beings take the place of the leaped-over phenomenon by leaping into the picture as the ontological topic?" (That is, why have beings been discussed instead of Being?) Though Heidegger is hardly a poet, his terminology recalls one of Nietzsche's aphorisms: "The poet presents his thoughts festively, on the carriage of rhythm: usually because they could not walk."[3]

If all the sentences quoted so far are readily translatable into less baroque language, the following italicized explanation of under-standing (p. 144) may serve as an example of the many, more opaque pronouncements. (No other well-known philosophic work contains nearly so many italics—or rather their German equivalent which takes up twice as much space as ordinary type.) "Understanding is the existential Being of the own Being-able-to-be of human Being itself, but such that this Being in itself opens up the Where-at of Being with itself. (*Verstehen ist das existenziale Sein des eigenen Seinkönnens des Daseins selbst, so zwar, dass dieses Sein an ihm selbst das Woran des mit ihm selbst Seins erschliesst.*)" The sentence following this one reads in full: "The structure of this existential must now be grasped and expressed still more sharply." Still more?

Heidegger's discussion of death comes near the beginning of the second of the two sections he published. To understand it, two key concepts of the first section should be mentioned briefly: The first is *Das Man*, one of Heidegger's happier coinages. The German word *man* is the equivalent of the English *one* in such locutions as "one does not do that" or "of course, one must die." However the German *man* does not have any of the other meanings of the English word *one*. It is therefore understandable why *Das Man* has been translated some-times as "the public" or "the anonymous They," but since Heidegger also makes much of the phrase *Man selbst*, which means "oneself," it is preferable to translate *Das Man* as "the One." The One is the despot that rules over the inauthentic human Being of our everyday lives.

---

[3] *Human, All too Human*, sec. 189.

The other notion in the first section of *Being and Time* which requires mention is the concept of *Angst* to which Kierkegaard had already devoted a major work. It is sharply distinguished from fear, which is said to be focused on objects. Kierkegaard's book has been translated as *The Concept of Dread*, but probably the only way to crystallize the crucial contrast in English is to use "anxiety." In anxiety we are said not to be afraid of any thing or object. *"The of-what of anxiety is Being-in-the-world as such."* "The of-what of anxiety is no in-worldly being." "That that which is threatening is *nowhere*, is characteristic of the of-what of anxiety." "In the of-what of anxiety the 'it is nothing and nowhere' stands revealed" (p. 186). And on the next page Heidegger repeats, again in italics: *"The of-what of which anxiety feels anxiety is Being-in-the-world itself."*

This is surely dubious. It is true that human beings occasionally experience anxiety without being able to say of what they are afraid, but Heidegger has not shown at all that either in many or in any of these cases people are afraid of "Being-in-the-world"—either *"itself"* or *"as such."* Nor has he shown or given reasons to believe that investigation might not show a man who feels anxiety without knowing of what he is afraid that he was in fact afraid of this or that. The fact that some of us sometimes feel a desperate sense of loneliness and abandonment does not settle such questions.

There might be different types of anxiety, and one might find that a sense of guilt and intimations of possibilities that we associate with guilt play a crucial role in some types. This was suggested by Kierkegaard, whom Heidegger merely paraphrases when he says: "Anxiety reveals in human Being the *Being* for ownmost Being-able-to-be, i.e., the *Being-free* for the freedom to choose and grasp our selves. Anxiety confronts human Being with its *Being-free* for—(*propensio in*)—the ownmost authenticity of its Being as a possibility, which it always is already. . . . Anxiety makes single and thus opens up human Being as *'solus ipse'* " (p. 188).

"Fear is," according to Heidegger, "inauthentic anxiety which conceals anxiety from itself" (p. 189). "The physiological triggering of anxiety becomes possible only because human Being feels anxiety in the ground of its Being" (p. 190). A footnote on the same page begins with the preposterous assertion that "The phenomena of anxiety and fear . . . have, without exception, never been differentiated" and then ends with the startling understatement: "In the analysis of the phenomena of anxiety S. Kierkegaard has penetrated relatively farthest. . . ."

In fact, Kierkegaard, for better or for worse, anticipated Heidegger's distinction and linked anxiety with the concept of "nothing": "What effect does Nothing produce? It begets anxiety. . . . One almost never sees the concept of anxiety dealt with in psychology, and I must therefore call attention to the fact that it is different from fear and similar concepts which refer to something definite, whereas anxiety is the reality of freedom as possibility anterior to possibility." Kierkegaard reveals that the linking of anxiety with Nothing was suggested to him at least in part by a Danish idiom. Later he mentions that Schelling "often talks about anxiety," and then he offers us the epigram: "Anxiety is the dizziness of freedom."[4]

A distinction between fear and anxiety was also made by Freud in his lecture on "Anxiety" in *General Introduction to Psychoanalysis* (1917): "Anxiety refers to the state and ignores the object, while fear directs attention precisely to the object." Freud's distinction, unlike Heidegger's, leaves open the question whether in the case of anxiety, too, there may not be an object after all, even though not, as it were, in focus. The object, of course, need not be a *thing* any more than in fear. It could be an event, for example, or a situation.

Heidegger's discussion of anxiety ends with the claim that anxiety, by making man feel single or, as we might say, completely alone, tears him out of the everyday world, dominated by the anonymous One, "and reveals to him authenticity and inauthenticity as possibilities of his Being. These basic possibilities of human Being, which is always mine, show themselves in anxiety as in themselves, without being obstructed by any in-worldly beings to which human Being at first and for the most part clings" (p. 191).

II

The second of the six chapters that constitute the second and last section of *Being and Time* bears the title: "The possible Being-whole of human Being and Being-toward-death (*Das mögliche Ganzsein des*

[4] See *Existentialism from Dostoevsky to Sartre* (rev. ed., 1975), pp. 101–05.

Daseins und das Sein zum Tode)." On page 235 where it begins we find a footnote referring to the preceding, introductory discussion in which we are told about Kierkegaard that "from his 'edifying' discourses one can learn more philosophically than from his theoretical works—excepting his treatise on the concept of anxiety."

At great length, Heidegger argues to establish this conclusion (pp. 239 and 253): "Death does reveal itself as a loss, but rather as a loss experienced by the survivors. The suffering of this loss, however, does not furnish an approach to the loss of Being as such which is 'suffered' by the person who died. We do not experience in a genuine sense the dying of the others but are at most always only 'present.' " . . . "The public interpretation of human Being says, 'one dies,' because in this way everybody else as well as oneself can be deceived into thinking: not, to be sure, just I myself; for this One is *Nobody*. . . . In this way the One brings about a *continual putting at ease about death*." A footnote on page 254 adds: "L. N. Tolstoy, in his story, *The Death of Ivan Ilyitch*, has presented the phenomenon of the shattering and the collapse of this 'one dies.' "

No doubt, Tolstoy's story was one of the central inspirations of Heidegger's discussion. *The Death of Ivan Ilyitch* is a superb book—with an emphatic moral. It is a sustained attack on society in the form of a story about a member of society whose life is utterly empty, futile, and pointless—but no more so than the lives of all the other members of society who surround him, notably his colleagues and his wife. They all live to no point and tell themselves and each other "one dies" without ever seriously confronting the certainty that they themselves must die. The only appealing person in the book is a poor muzhik who, realizing that he, too, will have to die one day, patiently and lovingly does all he can to help Ivan. In the final pages of the book Ivan becomes aware of the futility of his own life and overcomes it, realizing that his malady is not merely a matter of a diseased kidney or appendix but of leaving behind a pointless life to die. He ceases pretending, and "From that moment began that shriek that did not cease for three days"; but during these three days he learns to care for others, feels sorry for his wife, and, for the first time, loves. Now, "In place of death was light! . . . 'What joy!' " Death had lost its terror.

Heidegger on death is for the most part an unacknowledged commentary on *The Death of Ivan Ilyitch*. "Even 'thinking of death' is publicly considered cowardly fear . . . *The One does not allow the courage for anxiety of death to rise."* Propriety does not permit Ivan to shriek. He must always pretend that he will soon get better. It would be offensive for him to admit that he is dying. But in the end he has the courage to defy propriety and shriek. "The development of such a 'superior' indifference alienates human Being from its own-most, unrelated Being-able-to-be" (p. 254). It is only when he casts aside his self-deceiving indifference that Ivan returns to himself, to his capacity for love, and leaves behind the self-betrayal of his alienated inauthentic life. "Being-toward-death is essentially anxiety," says Heidegger (p. 266)—and we might add: in Tolstoy's story if not elsewhere.

It is no criticism of Tolstoy to note that not all men are like Ivan Ilyitch. I might suppose that I myself am possibly exceptional in frankly living with the vivid certainty that I must die, were it not for the fact that in a recent World War my whole generation—millions of young men—lived with this thought. Many got married, saying to themselves, "I do not have much time left, but I want to live just once, if only for one week or possibly a few months." And Heidegger's generation (he was born in 1889) had the same experience in the First World War. Tolstoy's indictment of an un-Christian, unloving, hypocritical world cannot simply be read as a fair characterization of humanity. Nor is it true that "Being-toward-death is essentially anxiety," and that all illustrations to the contrary can be explained as instances of self-deception and the lack of "courage for anxiety of death."

At this point one begins to wonder whether, under the influence of the First World War, some other thinker did not possibly consider death a little earlier than Heidegger, without basing himself so largely on a single story. Indeed, in 1915, Freud published two essays under the title, *Timely Thoughts on War and Death*. I shall quote from the first two pages of the second essay, which he called "Our Relation to Death." Heidegger did not refer to Freud and did not even list Freud's later discussions of conscience in his footnote bibliography on conscience (p. 272). But while Heidegger's discussion of conscience is the worse for ignoring Freud's analyses, Heidegger's pages upon pages about death are in large part long-winded repetitions of what Freud had said briefly at the beginning of his paper:

. . . The war has disturbed our previous relation to death. This relation was not sincere. If one listened to us, we were, of course, ready to declare that death is the necessary end of all life, that every one of us owed nature his own death and must be prepared to pay this debt—in short, that death is natural, undeniable, and unavoidable. In reality, however, we used to behave as if it were different. We have shown the unmistakable tendency to push death aside, to eliminate it from life. We have tried to keep a deadly silence about death: after all, we even have a proverb to the effect that one thinks about something as one thinks about death. One's own, of course. After all, one's own death is beyond imagining, and whenever we try to imagine it we can see that we really survive as spectators. Thus the dictum could be dared in the psychoanalytic school: At bottom, nobody believes in his own death. Or, and this is the same: In his unconscious, every one of us is convinced of his immortality. As for the death of others, a cultured man will carefully avoid speaking of this possibility if the person fated to die can hear him. Only children ignore this rule. . . . We regularly emphasize the accidental cause of death, the mishap, the disease, the infection, the advanced age, and thus betray our eagerness to demote death from a necessity to a mere accident. Toward the deceased himself we behave in a special way, almost as if we were full of admiration for someone who has accomplished something very difficult. We suspend criticism of him, forgive him any injustice, pronounce the motto, *de mortuis nil nisi bene,* and consider it justified that in the funeral sermon and on the gravestone the most advantageous things are said about him. Consideration for the dead, who no longer need it, we place higher than truth—and, most of us, certainly also higher than consideration for the living.[5]

The simple, unpretentious clarity of these remarks, their unoracular humanity and humor, and their straight appeal to experience could hardly furnish a more striking contrast to Heidegger's verbiage. It is said sometimes that Heidegger more than anyone else has provoked discussion of phenomena which, in spite of Kierkegaard and Nietzsche, were ignored by the professors and their students. But, in the wake of Heidegger, discussion concentrated not on these phenomena but on his terms and weird locutions. Death, anxiety, conscience, and care became part of the jargon tossed about by thousands, along with *Dasein,* to-hand-ness, thrown-ness, Being-with, and all the rest.

[5] *Gesammelte Werke*, vol. X, p. 341f. My translation. For a critique of one of Freud's central points, see the next essay.

But he did not present definite claims for discussion, not to speak of hypotheses.

His remarks about death culminate in the italicized assertion (p. 266): "The *running-ahead* reveals to human Being the lost-ness into Oneself and brings it before the possibility . . . of Being itself—itself, however, in the passionate *freedom for death* which has rid itself of the illusions of the One, become factual, certain of itself, and full of anxiety." (The words italicized here are printed in boldface type in the original.) Unquestionably, the acceptance of the fact that I must die (my running-ahead to my death in thought) may forcibly remind me of the limited amount of time at my disposal, of the waste involved in spending it in awe of the anonymous One, and thus become a powerful incentive to make the most of my own Being here and now. But Heidegger's habits of gluing his thoughts to words, or of squeezing thoughts out of words, or of piling up such weird locutions that, as he himself insists, not one of his disciples of the days when he wrote, taught, and talked *Being and Time* seems to have got the point, have not encouraged questions like this one: Is it necessary that the resolute acceptance of my own death must still be accompanied by a feeling of anxiety, as Heidegger insists?

At this point Heidegger relies too heavily on the Christian writers who have influenced him most: above all, in this case, Kierkegaard and Tolstoy, and perhaps also Jacob Böhme (*Of the Incarnation of Jesus Christ*, part II, chapter 4, sec. 1, and *Six Theosophic Points*, part I) and Schelling, who claimed in *Die Weltalter* that anxiety is the basic feeling of every living creature." In Heidegger, Schelling's *Grundempfindung* becomes *Grundbefindlichkeit*.

Consider the letter which President Vargas of Brazil wrote to his people before committing suicide. It ends:

> . . . I fought against the looting of Brazil. I fought against the looting of the people. I have fought barebreasted. The hatred, infamy, and calumny did not beat down my spirit. I gave you my life. Now I offer my death. Nothing remains. Serenely I take the first step on the road to eternity and I leave life to enter history.[6]

Or consider this letter, included in *The Divine Wind*,[7] which Isao Matsuo, a Japanese flier trained for a suicide mission, wrote to his parents:

[6] *New York Herald Tribune*, August 25, 1955.
[7] R. Inoguchi and T. Nakajima with R. Pineau, *The Divine Wind* (1958).

. . . Please congratulate me. I have been given a splendid opportunity
to die . . . I shall fall like a blossom from a radiant cherry tree . . .
How I appreciate this chance to die like a man! . . . Thank you, my
parents, for the 23 years during which you have cared for me and
inspired me. I hope that my present deed will in some small way
repay what you have done for me.

Or consider David Hume's complete lack of anxiety which so
annoyed his Christian "friends" who hoped for a deathbed conversion. Or Socrates' calm in the face of death. Or the Stoic sages
who, admiring Socrates, committed tranquil suicide when in their
nineties. Or the ancient Romans.

Heidegger's talk about anxiety should be read as a document of
the German 1920s, when it suddenly became fashionable to admit
one was afraid. In Remarque's *All Quiet on the Western Front* (1929)
it was obvious that this new honesty was aimed against militarism and
of a piece with Arnold Zweig's noting that when ". . . Sergeant
Grischa" at the end of Zweig's great novel (1928) is shot, "his
bowels discharged excrement." But while it took some courage to
disregard propriety and to admit that some men, when confronting
death, are scared and that some, when shot, will fill their pants, it
remained for Heidegger to blow up observations of this sort into
general truths about Being.

He was not quickly refuted with a list of fatal counterinstances
because he put things into such outrageous language that reactions
to his prose have in the main been of one of four types:

1. One did not read him at all and ignored him, as the majority of
mankind did.

2. One read him a little, found him extremely difficult, and took
it for granted that the fault was one's own and that, of course, there
must be more to his assertions than they seemed to say—especially
since he himself says frequently that they are not anthropological
but ontological—truths not about man but about Being.

3. One read him, found him difficult, persevered, spent years study-
ing him, and—what else could one do after years of study of that
sort?—one became a teacher of philosophy, protecting one's invest-
ment by "explaining" Heidegger to students, warding off objections
by some such remark as: "There is much that I, too, don't understand as yet, but I shall give my life to trying to understand a little
more."

4. One has not read Heidegger at all but has heard about him and his influence and assumes that there must be a great deal to him.

A fifth type might be summed up as follows: Not everybody who does not write bare nonsense is original, illuminating, or deep. And Heidegger has obstructed thoughtful discussion of death.

III

Sartre has offered one crucial criticism of Heidegger in his own discussion of death in *Being and Nothingness*.[8] Heidegger argues that only the running-ahead to my own death can lead me to my ownmost, authentic Being because *"Dying is something which nobody can do for another.* . . . Dying shows that death is constituted ontologically by always-mineness and existence." And more in the same vein (p. 240). As Sartre points out rightly (p. 533ff.), this in no way distinguishes dying. Nobody can love for me or sleep for me or breathe for me. Every experience, taken as *my* experience, is "something which nobody can do for" me. I can live a lot of my life in the mode of inauthenticity in which it makes no decisive difference that it is I who am doing this or that; but in that mode it makes no difference either whether the bullet hits me or someone else, whether I die first or another. But if I adopt the attitude that it does matter, that it makes all the difference in the world to me, then I can adopt that attitude toward the experience of my loving this particular woman, toward my writing this particular book, toward my seeing, hearing, feeling, or bearing witness, no less than I can adopt it toward death. As Sartre says (p. 535): "In short there is no personalizing virtue which is peculiar to *my* death. Quite the contrary, it becomes *my* death only if I place myself already in the perspective of subjectivity."

Sartre goes on to criticize Heidegger's whole conception of "Being-toward-death." Although we may anticipate that we ourselves must die, we never know when we shall die; but it is the timing of one's death that makes all the difference when it comes to the meaning of one's life.

. . . We have, in fact, every chance of dying before we have accomplished our task, or, on the other hand, of outliving it. There is

[8] All references are to Hazel Barnes's translation (1956).

therefore a very slim chance that our death will be presented to us as that of Sophocles was, for example, in the manner of a resolved chord. And if it is only *chance* which decides the character of our death and therefore of our life, then even the death which most resembles the end of a melody cannot be waited for as such; luck by determining it for me removes from it any character as a harmonious end. . . . A death like that of Sophocles will therefore *resemble* a resolved chord but will not *be* one, just as the group of letters formed by the falling of alphabet blocks will perhaps resemble a word but will not be one. Thus this perpetual appearance of chance at the heart of my projects cannot be apprehended as *my* possibility but, on the contrary, as the nihilation of all my possibilities, a nihilation which *itself is no longer a part of my possibilities*. (p. 537)

. . . Suppose that Balzac had died before *Les Chouans;* he would remain the author of some execrable novels of intrigue. But suddenly the very expectation which this young man was, this expectation of being a great man, loses any kind of meaning; it is neither an obstinate and egotistical blindness nor the true sense of his own value since nothing shall ever decide it. . . . The final value of this conduct remains forever in suspense; or if you prefer, the ensemble (particular kinds of conduct, expectations, values) falls suddenly into the absurd. Thus death is never that which gives life its meaning; it is, on the contrary, that which on principle removes all meaning from life. (p. 539)

. . . The unique characteristic of a dead life is that it is a life of which the Other makes himself the guardian. (p. 541)

Suicide is no way out, says Sartre. Its meaning depends on the future. "If I 'misfire,' shall I not judge later that my suicide was cowardice? Will the outcome not show me that other solutions were possible? . . . Suicide is an absurdity which causes my life to be submerged in the absurd" (p. 540).

Finally, Sartre asks: "In renouncing Heidegger's Being-toward-death, have we abandoned forever the possibility of freely giving to our being a meaning for which we are responsible? Quite the contrary." Sartre repudiates Heidegger's "strict identification of death and finitude" and says:

. . . Human reality would remain finite even if it were immortal, because it *makes* itself finite by choosing itself as human. To be finite, in fact, is to choose oneself—that is, to make known to oneself what one is by projecting oneself toward one possibility to the exclusion of others. The very act of freedom is therefore the assumption and creation of finitude. If I make myself, I make myself finite and hence my life is unique. (p. 545)

Sartre has also dealt with human attitudes toward death in some of his plays and in his story "The Wall," which is reprinted and discussed in my *Existentialism from Dostoevsky to Sartre*. But in the present chapter we cannot analyze his often admirable plays and stories. And before proceeding to an evaluation of the above ideas, let us first consider Camus.

IV

Although Camus' politics were more acceptable to the Nobel Prize committee and are admittedly more attractive than those of Sartre, and although perhaps no other writer has ever equaled Camus' charming pose of decency and honesty and a determination to be lucid, Henri Peyre is surely right when, in a review of Camus' books and of several books about him, he charges *The Myth of Sisyphus* and *The Rebel* with being "not only contradictory, but confused and probably shallow and immature."[9]

With the utmost portentousness, Camus begins the first of his two philosophic works, *The Myth of Sisyphus*:[10] "There is but one truly serious philosophic problem, and that is suicide." Soon we are told that the world is "absurd." A little later: "I said that the world is absurd, but I was too hasty. This world in itself is not reasonable, that is all that can be said. But what is absurd is the confrontation of this irrational and the wild longing for clarity whose call echoes in the human heart. The absurd depends as much on man as on the world" (p. 21).

This point could be put more idiomatically and accurately by saying that the hunger to gain clarity about and to explain all things is really absurd or, to be more precise, quixotic. But Camus prefers to rhapsodize about absurdity, although he says (p. 40): "I want to know whether I can live with what I know and with that alone." He

[9] H. Peyre, "Comment on Camus," *Virginia Quart. Rev.*, 34 (4): 623–629, Autumn 1958. What Peyre says is, to be precise, that Philip Thody, in *Albert Camus*, "is forced to confess when he comes to those two volumes that they are not only . . ."
[10] Page references are to J. O'Brien's translation (1955).

speaks of "this absurd logic" (p. 31), evidently meaning the special logic of talk about the absurd, as if such talk had any special logic. Then he speaks of the "absurd mind," meaning a believer in the absurdity of the world—or rather of the absurdity, or quixotism, of man's endeavors—as when he says (p. 35): "To Chestov reason is useless but there is something beyond reason. To an absurd mind [i.e., Camus] reason is useless and there is nothing beyond reason." The word "useless," too, is used without precision; what is meant is something like "limited" or "not omnipotent." A little later still (p. 40): "The absurd . . . does not lead to God. Perhaps this notion will become clearer if I risk this shocking statement: the absurd is sin without God." Without being shocked, one may note the looseness of the style and thinking: no attempt is made to explain what is meant by "sin," and Camus is evidently satisfied that his vague statement, even if it does not succeed in shocking us, is at least evocative. But from a writer who quotes Nietzsche as often as Camus does in this book—and in *The Rebel*, too—one might expect that he would at least raise the question whether, by not including God in our picture of the world, we don't restore to being its "innocence," as Nietzsche claimed, and leave sin behind.

As far as Kierkegaard, Jaspers, and Chestov are concerned, Camus is surely right that "The theme of the irrational, as it is conceived by the existentials [sic], is reason becoming confused and escaping by negating itself." But when he adds, "The absurd is lucid reason noting its limits," it becomes apparent that all the oracular discussions of absurdity are quite dispensable and that Camus has not added clarification but only confusion to Freud's two-sentence critique of the suggestion that the essence of religion consists in a feeling of absolute dependence: "It is not this feeling that constitutes the essence of religiousness, but only the next step, the reaction to it, which seeks a remedy against this feeling. He who goes no further, he who humbly resigns himself to the insignificant part man plays in the universe, is, on the contrary, irreligious in the truest sense of the word." (*The Future of an Illusion*, section 6—written in 1927, fifteen years before *The Myth of Sisyphus*.) The same thought permeates the books of Nietzsche.

Nietzsche, however, had gone on to celebrate "Free Death," especially in the penultimate chapter of Part One of *Zarathustra* and in *The Twilight of the Idols*: ". . . usually it is death under the most contemptible conditions, an unfree death, death *not* at the right time, a coward's death. From love of *life,* one should desire a different death: free, conscious, without accident, without ambush."[11] Nietzsche's thought is clear, though he collapsed, but did not die, in his boots, as it were—and his relatives then dragged out his life for another eleven years.

Camus' argument against suicide remains sketchy and unclear: "Suicide, like the leap, is acceptance at its extreme. Everything is over and man returns to his essential history. . . . In its way, suicide settles the absurd. It engulfs the absurd in the same death. . . . It is essential to die unreconciled and not of one's own free will. Suicide is a repudiation" (p. 54ff.). Camus wants "defiance." He is really preaching, no less than in his later work, *The Rebel,* in which "the rebel" replaces the editorial "we," and exhortations are presented in the form of literally false generalizations. "The rebel does *x*" means "I do *x* and wish you would." In *The Myth of Sisyphus,* Camus hides similarly behind "an absurd mind" and "an absurd logic."

Now suicide is "acceptance," now it is "repudiation." Surely, sometimes it is one and sometimes the other, and occasionally both— acceptance of defeat and repudiation of hope. Nietzsche's "free death" was meant as an affirmation of sorts, an acceptance of one's own life and of all the world with it, a festive realization of fulfillment, coupled with the thought that this life, as lived up to this point and now consummated, was so acceptable that it did not stand in need of any further deeds or days but could be gladly relived over and over in the course of an eternal recurrence of the same events at gigantic intervals.

The first part of Camus' *Myth of Sisyphus* is ambiguously and appropriately entitled "An Absurd Reasoning." Portentousness thickens toward the end: "The absurd enlightens me on this point: there is no future" (p. 58). "Knowing whether or not one can live *without appeal* is all that interests me" (p. 60). "Now, the conditions of modern life impose on the majority of men the same quantity of experiences and consequently the same profound experiences. To be sure, there must also be taken into consideration the individual's spontaneous contribution, the 'given' element in him. But I cannot judge of that, and let me repeat that my rule here is to get along with the immediate evidence" (p. 61). In sum: men don't, of course, have the same quantity of experiences, and least of all the

[11] See *The Portable Nietzsche* (1954), pp. 183–86 and 536f.

same profound experiences, but in the name of simple honesty we must pretend they do.

This paraphrase may seem excessively unsympathetic; but consider what Camus himself says on the next page:

> . . . Here we have to be over-simple. To two men living the same number of years, the world always provides the same sum of experiences. It is up to us to be conscious of them. Being aware of one's life, one's revolt, one's freedom, and to the maximum, is living, and to the maximum [12] Where lucidity dominates, the scale of values becomes useless. Let's be even more simple. (p. 62)

Why in heaven's name must we be so "over-simple" and then "even more simple"? Two men who live the same number of years do *not* always have the same number of experiences, with the sole difference that one is more aware of them, while the other is partly blind. Life is not like a film that rolls by while we either watch or sleep. Some suffer sicknesses, have visions, love, despair, work, and experience failures and successes; others toil in the unbroken twilight of mute misery, their minds uneducated, chained to deadening routine. Also, Camus overlooks that a man can to some extent involve himself in experiences, that he can seek security or elect to live dangerously, to use Nietzsche's phrase. And finally Camus writes as if experiences were like drops that fall into the bucket of the mind at a steady rate—say, one per second—and as if the sequence made no difference at all; as if seeing *Lear* at the age of one, ten, or thirty were the same.

Let us resume our quotation where we broke off:

> . . . Let us say that the sole obstacle, the sole deficiency to be made good, is constituted by premature death. Thus it is that no depth, no emotion, no passion, and no sacrifice could render equal in the eyes of the absurd man (even if he wished it so) a conscious life of forty years and a lucidity spread over sixty years. Madness and death are his irreparables. . . . There will never be any substitute for twenty years of life and experience. . . . The present and the succession of presents before a constantly conscious soul is the ideal of the absurd man. (p. 63f.)

---

12 This sentence is not that bad in the original and might be rendered: "The more fully one is aware of one's life, . . . the more fully one lives."

Camus is welcome to his absurd man, who is indeed absurd, wishing to imbibe, collect, and hoard experiences, any experiences, as long as they add up to some huge quantity—the more the better. If only he did not deceive himself so utterly about the quality of his own thinking—as when he concludes the second essay of the book by counting himself among those "who think clearly and have ceased to hope."

Of course, Camus' *The Stranger*, *The Plague*, and *The Fall* are superior to *The Rebel* and the arguments discussed here. Camus is a fine writer, but not a philosopher.

V

Camus' confusions bring to mind a poem by Hölderlin: *"Nur einen Sommer . . ."* Heidegger has devoted essay after essay to this poet and eventually collected the lot in a book, but has not written about this poem, which is both clearer and better than the ones Heidegger likes—to read his own thoughts into.

> A single summer grant me, great powers, and
>   a single autumn for fully ripened song
>   that, sated with the sweetness of my
>   playing, my heart may more willingly die.
>
> The soul that, living, did not attain its divine
>   right cannot repose in the nether world.
>   But once what I am bent on, what is
>   holy, my poetry, is accomplished:
>
> Be welcome then, stillness of the shadows' world!
>   I shall be satisfied though my lyre will not
>   accompany me down there. Once I
>   lived like the gods, and more is not needed.[13]

Of the "absurd man" Camus says, as we have seen: "Madness and death are his irreparables." Hölderlin did become mad soon after writing this poem, but the point of the poem is that still he should not have preferred to be Camus, not to speak of lesser men. There is not only a "substitute" for twenty years of life but something more desirable by far: "Once I lived like the gods, and more is not needed."

---

[13] In *Twenty-five German Poets* the original text faces my translation. The poem is discussed further in the last chapter, below.

This is overlooked by Sartre, too. Rightly, he recognizes that death can cut off a man before he has had a chance to give his life a meaning, that death may be—but he falsely thinks it always is—"the nihilation of all my possibilities." Not only in childhood but long after that one may retain the feeling that one is in this sense still at the mercy of death. "But once what I am bent on, what is holy, my poetry, is accomplished," once I have succeeded in achieving—in the face of death, in a race with death—a project that is truly mine and not something that anybody else might have done as well, if not better, then the picture changes: I have won the race and in a sense have triumphed over death. Death and madness come too late.

We see the poet's later madness in the light of his own poem; nor does it greatly matter that Nietzsche, like Hölderlin, vegetated for a few years before death took him: his work was done. To be sure, others make themselves the guardians of the dead life and interpret it according to their lights; but we have no defense if they begin to do the same while we are still alive. Nor can we say that this is the price of finitude, of finite works no less than finite lives. Men say that God is infinite but can hardly deny that theologians and believers make themselves the guardians of the infinite and offer their interpretations, if not behind his back then in his face.

And Heidegger? Does he not say little indeed? He reminds us of the commonplace—much better, more succinctly and humanely, put to us by Freud and, still earlier at greater length, but much more vividly, by Tolstoy—that most men would rather not face up to the certainty that they themselves must die. Before the end of World War I it may even have taken courage to be openly afraid of death—or of anything else, for that matter; but since the 1920s it has been fashionable to admit to *Angst*. That the man who accepts his death may find in this experience a strong spur to making something of his life and may succeed in some accomplishment that robs him of the fear of death and permits him to say "welcome then" was better said by Hölderlin in sixteen lines than by Heidegger in sixteen books.

Kierkegaard and Nietzsche challenged their age and were, to use two Nietzschean phrases, "untimely" and "born posthumously." Heidegger's reputation, on the contrary, depends on his great timeliness: long before most other philosophers of his generation he took up the concerns of his age. In view of the exceeding difficulty of his prose, the reader who penetrates to the point of recognizing that the author is alluding to a genuine experience—say, the recognition of one's utter loneliness in this world—feels that there is more to Heidegger than those who shrug him off as "all nonsense" admit. But the question remains whether Heidegger has illuminated the phenomena of which he speaks and which others had described better before he did. The answer is that he is invariably less enlightening than the best among his predecessors.

A common fault of Heidegger, Sartre, and Camus is that they overgeneralize instead of taking into account different attitudes toward death. The later part of *The Myth of Sisyphus* represents a somewhat arbitrary and portentous attempt at a study of types: three ways are open to "The Absurd Man"—to become a Don Juan, an actor, or a conqueror. Surely, one learns more from Malraux's novel, *La Condition Humaine* (*Man's Fate*), which offers almost a catalogue of different ways of meeting death. Nor did either these men or Tolstoy initiate the concern with death.

Heinrich von Kleist (1777–1811) was a Prussian officer more than a century before World War I. His *Prinz Friedrich von Homburg* is one of the most celebrated German plays; and here Kleist had the courage to bring to life on the stage the Prince's dread after he, a general who has disobeyed orders, is sentenced to death. Then Kleist went on to depict his hero's conquest of anxiety, to the point where in the final scene he is ready to be shot without the slightest remnant of anxiety. Indeed, he welcomes death, is blindfolded, and—one thinks of Dostoevsky and of Sartre's story "The Wall"—pardoned. Kleist himself committed suicide.

Georg Büchner (1813–37), best known as the author of *Woyzek*, dealt with death in an even more strikingly modern way in another play, *Danton's Death*. But these playwrights do not claim to offer any general theory of death, any more than Shakespeare did. I tried to show in the first chapter of *From Shakespeare to Existentialism* how many supposedly existentialist themes are encountered, and important, in Shakespeare. Surely, he also offers an imposing variety of deaths and suicides.

Among the points understood by Shakespeare but neglected by the existentialists are these. Much dread of death is due to Christian teaching, and pre-Christian Roman attitudes were often very different. So, we might add, was the Buddha's: after his enlightenment experience he transcended all anxiety, and the stories of his death represent an outright antithesis to the Gospels' account of Jesus' dreadful death.

Vitality influences one's reaction to impending death: a soldier in a duel does not die like patients in their beds. And attitudes toward death may be changed, too, by the confidence that there is absolutely nothing one will miss—either because the world will end for all when we die or because life "is a tale told by an idiot, full of sound and fury, signifying nothing," and it is well to be rid of "tomorrow, and tomorrow, and tomorrow."

Finally, not one of the existentialists has grasped the most crucial distinction that makes all the difference in facing death. Nietzsche stated it succinctly in *The Gay Science*, section 290: "For one thing is needful: that a human being attain his satisfaction with himself —whether it be by this or by that poetry and art; only then is a human being at all tolerable to behold. Whoever is dissatisfied with himself is always ready to revenge himself therefor; we others will be his victims, if only by always having to stand his ugly sight. For the sight of the ugly makes men bad and gloomy." Or, as Hölderlin says: "The soul that, living, did not attain its divine Right cannot repose in the nether world." But he that has made something of his life can face death without anxiety: "Once I lived like the gods, and more is not needed."

VI

Our attitude toward death is influenced by hope as much as it is by fear. If fear is the mother of cowardice, hope is the father.

Men accept indignities without end, and a life not worth living, in the hope that their miseries *will* end and that eventually life may be worth living again. They renounce love, courage and honesty, pride and humanity, hoping. Hope is as great an enemy of courage as is fear.

The early Romans and Spartans faced death not only fearlessly but also void of mean hopes. There was nothing for the surviving coward to hope.

In the Israel of Moses and the prophets, religion did not hold out hope for individuals. There was hope for the people as long as men and women lived and died with courage and without hope for themselves.

Paul made of hope one of the three great virtues. Doing this, he did not betray Jesus, whose glad tidings had been a message of hope for the individual. Neither of them abetted cowardice or fear of death as such; for their hope was not of this world. Men who accepted the faith of Paul died fearlessly, hopefully, and joyously when the Romans made martyrs of them.

Indeed, "the desire for martyrdom became at times a form of absolute madness, a kind of epidemic of suicide, and the leading minds of the Church found it necessary to exert all their authority to prevent their followers thrusting themselves into the hands of the persecutors. Tertullian mentions how, in a little Asiatic town, the entire population once flocked to the proconsul, declaring themselves to be Christians, and imploring him to execute the decree of the emperor and grant them the privilege of martyrdom. . . . 'These wretches,' said Lucian, speaking of the Christians, 'persuade themselves that they are going to be altogether immortal, and to live for ever, wherefore they despise death, and many of their own accord give themselves up to be slain.' "

"Believing, with St. Ignatius, that they were 'the wheat of God,' they panted for the day when they should be 'ground by the teeth of wild beasts into the pure bread of Christ!' "[14]

As the otherworldliness of Jesus and Paul gave way to a renewed interest in this world, as Christianity became the state religion, hope reverted from the other world to this. The temporary bond of hope and courage was broken. The age of the martyrs was over. Now Christianity became the great teacher of fear of death, and dread of purgatory and damnation became fused with hope for a few more years in *this* world.

The Greeks had considered hope the final evil in Pandora's box. They also gave us an image of perfect nobility: a human being lovingly doing her duty to another human being despite all threats, and going to her death with pride and courage, not deterred by any hope—Antigone.

Hopelessness is despair. Yet life without hope is worth living. As Sartre's Orestes says: "Life begins on the other side of despair." But is hope perhaps resumed on the other side? It need not be. In honesty, what is there to hope for? Small hopes remain but do not truly matter. I may hope that the sunset will be clear, that the night will be cool and still, that my work will turn out well, and yet know that nine hopes

14 W. E. H. Lecky, *History of European Morals from Augustus to Charlemagne,* Vol. I (1869), p. 415ff.

out of ten are not even remembered a year later. How many are recalled a century hence? A billion years hence?

> The cloud-capp'd towers, the gorgeous palaces,
> The solemn temples, the great globe itself,
> Yea, all which it inherit, shall dissolve;
> And, like this insubstantial pageant faded,
> Leave not a rack behind. We are such stuff
> As dreams are made on, and our little life
> Is rounded with a sleep.
>
> (*Tempest*, IV, i.)

It is possible that this is wrong. There may be surprises in store for us, however improbable it seems and however little evidence suggests it. But I do not hope for that. Let people who do not know what to do with themselves in this life, but fritter away their time reading magazines and watching television, hope for eternal life. If one lives intensely, the time comes when sleep seems bliss. If one loves intensely, the time comes when death seems bliss.

Those who loved with all their heart and mind and might have always thought of death, and those who knew the endless nights of harrowing concern for others have longed for it.

The life I want is a life I could not endure in eternity. It is a life of love and intensity, suffering and creation, that makes life worth while and death welcome. There is no other life I should prefer. Neither should I like not to die.

If I ask myself who in history I might like to have been, I find that all the men I most admire were by most standards deeply unhappy. They knew despair. But their lives were worth while—I only wish mine equaled theirs in this respect—and I have no doubt that they were glad to die.

As one deserves a good night's sleep, one also deserves to die. Why should I hope to wake again? To do what I have not done in the time I've had? All of us have so much more time than we use well. How many hours in a life are spent in a way of which one might be proud, looking back?

For most of us death does not come soon enough. Lives are spoiled and made rotten by the sense that death is distant and irrelevant. One lives better when one expects to die, say, at forty, when one says to oneself long before one is twenty: whatever I may be able to accomplish, I should be able to do by then; and what I have not done by then, I am not likely to do ever. One cannot count on living until one is forty—or thirty—but it makes for a better life if one has a rendezvous with death.

Not only love can be deepened and made more intense and impassioned by the expectation of impending death; all of life is enriched by it. Why deceive myself to the last moment, and hungrily devour sights, sounds, and smells only when it is almost too late? In our treatment of others, too, it is well to remember that they will die: it makes for greater humanity.

There is nothing morbid about thinking and speaking of death. Those who disparage honesty do not know its joys. The apostles of hope do not know the liberation of emergence from hope.

It may seem that a man without hope is inhuman. How can one appeal to him if he does not share our hopes? He has pulled up his stakes in the future—and the future is the common ground of humanity. Such rhetoric may sound persuasive, but Antigone gives it the lie. Nobility holds to a purpose when hope is gone. Purpose and hope are as little identical as humility and meekness, or honesty and sincerity. Hope seeks redemption in time to come and depends on the future. A purposive act may be its own reward and redeem the agent, regardless of what the future may bring. Antigone is not at the mercy of any future. Humanity, love, and courage survive hope.

Occasionally, to be sure, they may not persist in despair; but that does not prove that they depend on hope. Much more often, humanity has been sacrificed to some hope; love has been betrayed for some hope; and courage has been destroyed by some hope.

Humbition,[15] love, courage, and honesty can make life meaningful, and small hopes can embellish it. For a few decades one may be able to love and create enough to make suffering worth while. If that becomes impossible:

> I will despair, and be at enmity
> With cozening hope: he is a flatterer,
> A parasite, a keeper-back of death,
> Who gently would dissolve the bands of life,
> Which false hope lingers in extremity.
> (*Richard II*, II, ii.)

We do not all have the same breaking point; each man has to discover his. When Freud heard of Franz Rosenzweig's unusual exertions

[15] A fusion of humility and ambition, discussed in *The Faith of a Heretic* and *Without Guilt and Justice.*

to work to the end, he said, "What else could he do?" But a man unable to emulate Rosenzweig or Freud need not resign himself to becoming a vegetable. It is better to die with courage than to live as a coward.

Of course, there are deaths that one views with horror: slow, painful deaths; deaths that destroy us by degrees; deaths that, instead of taking us in our prime, demean us first. But, fearing such deaths, I do not fear death, but what precedes it: pointless suffering, disability, and helplessness. Death in a crash might be exhilarating; death in sleep, peace; death by poison, dignified.

When Hannibal, who had humiliated the Romans like no man before him, could not escape from their vengeance and had nothing to look forward to but being led in triumph through the streets of Rome, and then imprisonment, and finally a miserable death, why should he not have taken poison as he did? Suicide can be cowardice; it need not be. In *Antony and Cleopatra*, Shakespeare contrasts suicides: Antony botches his, while Cleopatra's death has enviable dignity and beauty.

The Greeks have often been held up as models of humanity. There are few respects in which their humanity compares more favorably with that of most modern nations than the way in which death sentences were carried out. They did not grab men unawares in the middle of the night to drag them to the guillotine and chop their heads off, as the French did until recently; they did not hang them, British fashion; burn them, Christian fashion; or strap them, the American way, into an electric chair or a gas chamber—depriving a human being of his dignity and humanity as far as possible: Socrates was given hemlock and could raise the cup to his own lips and die a man.

Is it possible that the fear of death and the prohibition of suicide have been as deliberately imposed on men as laws against incest— not owing to any innate horror, but because dying, like incest, is so easy? Culture depends on men's attempting to do what is difficult. We are naturally endowed with aspirations but also with a tendency toward sloth; and when ambition meets obstacles we are always tempted to take the easy way out.

Even if there is a natural instinct of self-preservation and an innate aversion to death, culture depends both on reinforcing this aversion and on teaching men to overcome it under certain circumstances. Culture requires that men should not seek death too easily, but also that they should sometimes consider it the lesser evil. A life worth living depends on an ambivalence toward death.

My own death is no tragedy. But may I deny that the death of others is unjust, unfair, and irremediably tragic? We like to blame death rather than those who died, if we loved them; hence we deceive ourselves as they might have deceived themselves. We do not say, "How many months did they waste!" but, "If only they had had a few more weeks!" Not, "How sad that they did not do more!" but, "How unfair that they died so soon!" Still, not every death allows for this response. There are deaths that reproach us, deaths that are enviable.

Often we mourn the death of others because it leaves us lonely. But we do not hate sleep because we are sometimes lonely when others have gone to sleep and we lie awake. Death, like sleep, can mean separation; it usually does. We rarely have the honesty to remember how alone we are. The death of those we loved reminds us of what dishonesty had concealed from us: our profound solitude and our impending death. In the quest for honesty, death is a cruel but excellent teacher.

Our attitudes toward death are profoundly influenced by religion. From the Old Testament we have learned to think of every single human being as crucially important. Buddhism and other Oriental religions spread a very different view. To men brought up on the idea of the transmigration of souls, the teaching of Darwin could not have come as a shock: they assumed all along that a generation or two ago I, or any man, might well have been an animal, and that after death I might become one again. To men who had read in their scriptures of millions of myriads of ten million cycles, of thousands of worlds and vast numbers of Buddhas who had appeared in these worlds in different ages, the Copernican revolution would not have involved any blow to man's pride. That there are about a hundred million galaxies within range of our telescopes, and that our own galaxy alone contains hundreds of thousands of planets which may well support life and beings like ourselves seems strange to those brought up on the Bible, but not necessarily strange to Oriental believers.

For those not familiar with the sacred books of the East, the contrast may come to life as they compare Renaissance and Chinese paintings: here the human figures dominate the picture, and the landscape serves as a background; there the landscape is the picture, and the human beings in it have to be sought out. Here man seems all-important; there his cosmic insignificance is beautifully represented.

Modern science suggests that in important respects the Oriental religions were probably closer to the facts than the Old Testament or the New. It does not follow that we ought to accept the Buddha's counsel of resignation and detachment, falling out of love with the world. Nor need we emulate Lao-tze's wonderful whimsey and his wise mockery of reason, culture, and human effort. There are many ways of living and dying.

It is astonishing how little existentialist philosophers have illuminated the alternatives. The Manichaean crudity of Heidegger's contrast of authenticity and inauthenticity and his involuted chatter about Being-toward-Death have impeded discussion of the fateful choices facing us. The other existentialists have not equaled his pretensions, but their philosophical writings share a portentous obscurity that hides a lack of thoughtfulness. In a scholastic age, the existentialists have held aloft the banner of Socrates and Plato, Spinoza and Nietzsche, who tried to help humanity to choose responsibly between different ways of life. But existentialism has not kept its promise. Anyone who really wants to illuminate the alternatives we face and defend some above others must go it alone.

12

ON DEATH AND LYING*

Even the most humane studies of death are still permeated by prejudices. Nineteen hundred years of Christian teaching have left their mark on non-Christians, too. Consider two books whose central motivation is altogether admirable: A. Alvarez, *The Savage God: A Study of Suicide* (1971),[1] and Elisabeth Kübler-Ross, *On Death and Dying* (1969).[2]

Both books have won wide attention, and Kübler-Ross continues to be a focal point of discussion. Yet even authors of such caliber make unwarranted assumptions.

Alvarez has shown very fully—writing beautifully—how suicide was at one time regarded without horror and loathing. His chapter on "The Background" goes back far into the past, while the chapters on "Suicide and Literature" quote writers closer to us, like Montaigne, Shakespeare, John Donne, David Hume, and many others, including some twentieth-century writers. And yet we find Alvarez saying: "This is not to say people commit suicide, as the Stoics did, coolly, deliberately, as a rational choice between rational alternatives. The Romans may have disciplined themselves into accepting this frigid logic, but those who have done so in modern history are, in the last analysis, monsters" (pp. 120f.). The evidence that Alvarez himself presents so movingly does not in any way support this emotional outburst; and it is to his credit that he immediately proceeds to give an example that seems to contradict him. But the case against his *obiter dictum* does not rest on one example; witness, as Alvarez himself shows, the pre-Christian world, including the Old Testament and the Greeks as well as the Romans, and Montaigne and Shakespeare,

* This paper was written for a conference of The Foundation of Thanatology in November 1973 and also published in the first volume of *Psychiatry and the Humanities*, ed. Joseph Smith, Yale University Press, 1976.

[1] Weidenfeld & Nicolson (London, 1971); Random House (New York, 1972).
[2] Macmillan (New York, 1969). Citations refer to the paperback ed. (Macmillan, 1970).

Donne and Hume. There are at least two reasons for mentioning Alvarez. First, he cites a wealth of evidence to show how contemporary attitudes toward suicide are culturally conditioned. Secondly, he nevertheless shares some of the prejudices that he undermines.

Much the same is true of Kübler-Ross. Her cast of mind is more dogmatic than Alvarez'. On the opening pages of her book she makes some totally unsupported claims with an air of absolute certainty, insisting, for example, on the "*basic knowledge* that, in our unconscious, death is never possible in regard to ourselves" (p. 2, italics supplied). This article of psychoanalytic faith she brings to her investigation and maintains in spite of the data she herself presents so movingly.

Her first chapter is called "On the Fear of Death," but nothing in that chapter supports her dogmatic claim that "the fear of death is a universal fear even if we think we have mastered it on many levels" (p. 5). This sweeping statement, thrown out at the start, is soon contradicted by her very first case history: ". . . he was not afraid to die, but was afraid to live" (p. 20). Under the circumstances described by her, this seems an eminently rational and plausible attitude. Again, she explains very well how some students project their own feelings "onto the patients. The last has occasionally happened when a patient apparently faced death with calmness and equanimity while the student was highly upset by the encounter. The discussion then revealed that the student thought the patient was unrealistic or even faking, because it was inconceivable to him that anyone could face such a crisis with so much dignity" (p. 27).

A grave error that Kübler-Ross shares with many others is the failure to distinguish between a patient's attitude toward *death* and *dying of cancer*. In a book *On Death and Dying* and a chapter on "Attitudes Toward Death and Dying" few confusions could be more fateful; of course, the prospect of being very slowly tortured to death, of becoming increasingly helpless and a burden to others, is fearful; but it obviously does not follow that the fear of *death* is universal.

Kübler-Ross also fails to note how her data in the chapter on "Attitudes Toward Death and Dying" point to cultural conditioning—and to the inauthenticity of those who minister to the patients. They carry on an elaborate, institutionalized ritual of deception. She mentions "that all the patients knew about their terminal illness anyway, whether they were explicitly told or not" (p. 31), but how they were usually not told the whole truth, and how the doctors rationalized their own deception by claiming "that their patients do not want to know the truth, that they never ask for it, and that they believe all is well" (p. 32). Her evidence is abundant and clear, but does not seem to budge her own dogmatic faith. "I approached him hesitantly and asked him simply, 'How sick are you?' 'I am full of cancer . . .' was his answer. The problem was that nobody ever asked a simple straightforward question. They mistook his grim look as a closed door; in fact, their own anxiety prevented them from finding out . . ." (p. 35). But seven pages later she repeats her dogma: "Since in our unconscious mind we are all immortal, it is almost inconceivable for us to acknowledge that we too have to face death."

The point is not to find fault with an author who has done her best to humanize the care of the dying. She deserves our respect and gratitude. But her data show much more than she realizes and expose forcefully not only the *inhumanity* of legions of people who minister to the dying but also their—*dishonesty.* Kübler-Ross, like many other authors, makes much of the self-deception of the dying, of their inauthentic faith that they are *not* dying. But she also shows, without seeming to notice it, that the whole project of prolonging the lives of the terminally ill reeks of the inauthentic faith that the patient is not about to die. Not only is the patient systematically deceived with words, but all the tremendous effort and expense make sense only on the assumption that the patient is *not* about to die. If he occasionally comes to believe that he is not about to die, it is scarcely reasonable to blame him or to seek an explanation in terms of Kübler-Ross's psychoanalytic dogma. After all, one is generally said to show the seriousness of one's beliefs by one's actions and by how much money one is willing to put up for them. If people spend thousands of dollars on one's hospital care, it stands to reason that one is led to think at least sometimes that one is *not* about to die.

It has become fashionable to play with the idea that the "insane" are really sane while our society is insane. My point is not so Manichaean. From the obvious fact that our society is insane in some ways it hardly follows than the "insane" are really sane. In our society some dogmas about death and suicide that are part of the legacy of Christianity, and as unsupported by empirical evidence as most other Christian dogmas, are still very widely accepted. There are other dogmas that come from other sources, including Freud. The point is not to blame either Christianity or Freud. We have seen (on page 213) how eager many early Christians were to die a martyr's death. Not long after, Christian attitudes changed. But our concern here is not with the *origin* of dogmas but rather with the ways in which to this day unsupported articles of faith lead to irrational behavior, large-scale deception, and inhumanity.

Kübler-Ross is exceptionally humane, but even she shares this irrationality. She is superb when she derides the nurses who are reluctant to ease the intolerable pain of the dying with an injection because they are afraid that the patient, on the threshold of death, might become an addict. But take, as a final example, the twenty-page interview she prints in her fourth chapter. It is far from clear why she should include all those pages; they certainly do not prove any point she might wish to make. But they allow us once again to look behind the scenes and see how an author who wants to be non-judgmental keeps passing highly irrational judgments on a patient who is far more rational than the doctor and the chaplain, who come across as feeling superior and rather in a hurry.

In the end, I remain quite unconvinced that the fear of death is universal. I have stated my own very different views in the chapter on "Death" in *The Faith of a Heretic* (1961).[3] But being a philosopher who lacks the wealth of concrete experience that so many doctors and nurses have, I naturally wonder sometimes whether there is evidence that proves me wrong. The two books considered here provide a great deal of evidence to show that it is quite possible to face one's own death without fear, although the widespread disbelief in this possibility makes it harder than it need be. Moreover, our hospital system seems to be predicated on the irrational and vicious notion that death is unnatural and must be fought and postponed as long as at all possible, no matter how much dishonesty and inhumanity this may involve. Frederick the Great is said to have sent his soldiers into battle, saying sardonically: *Kerls, wollt ihr denn ewig leben?* "What is the matter with you guys? Do you want to live forever?" Our attitudes toward war have changed, but our modern attitude toward death is not necessarily more humane. It is insane to try to make the terminally ill live forever, and to try to make them believe, by word and deed, that they will. It would be far better to discuss with them rationally what the options are and to give those

[3] See "Existentialism and Death" above and "Dead without Dread" below.

who have the wish to do so the means to live well as long as that is possible and then to make a dignified end of it all. Women have won the right to have an abortion. It is high time to win everyone's right to end his own life without futile humiliation, torture, and indignity. Here, as so often, humanity depends on honesty.

13

DEATH WITHOUT DREAD*

I

Death has come to be associated with old age. That is a recent development. In many parts of the world more people are still dying as infants than in old age, and death has generally been distributed over the whole life span. One never felt immune from it.

Death has always been a staple of religion and literature. Those writing about death should not forgo research about different attitudes toward death in different religions. To a large extent, the fear of death, or the anxiety associated with death, is a product of Christianity, and we encounter very different attitudes at the burning ghats in Varanasi in India and in Buddhist lands.

Fascinating and important as this question is, one cannot deal with it well in a brief space because the great religions are not monolithic. Unquestionably, Christianity has spread the horror of death through its threats of hell and its perennial attempts to frighten people into repentance on the threshold of eternity. Yet in the early days of Christianity so many Christians coveted martyrdom with its assurance of heaven that a Roman proconsul felt unable to oblige such multitudes, although the Romans were not squeamish about dying and even less so about killing.[1] Not only have there been vast changes in the great religions over the centuries, but there are also countless sects and geographical variations in Christianity as well as Islam, Hinduism, and Buddhism.

The variety of religious attitudes is vast, but it is really crucial to realize that our attitudes are not due to the timeless constitution of

---

* Prepared for a conference on "Human Values and Aging: New Challenges for Research in the Humanities," November 1975.

[1] A. Alvarez, *The Savage God: A Study of Suicide* (1971), p. 67; Kaufmann, *The Faith of a Heretic* (1961), sec. 98. See p. 213 above.

the human mind but to historical and cultural conditioning. Immanuel Kant, writing in the last two decades of the eighteenth century, bequeathed to us the notion that our certainties are due to the structure of the human mind and not subject to change. Almost 150 years later, Martin Heidegger still played essentially the same game, but played it worse. Kant had looked for a firm foundation for Euclidean geometry, Newtonian science, and the categorical imperative, and we can still see how a wise man in his time and place might have supposed that history and psychology or, in one word, conditioning, would be irrelevant here. But Heidegger came after the rapid growth of the historical consciousness in Germany and after Freud and the explosion of interest in anthropology and sociology, and there is no longer any excuse for supposing that the attitudes toward death and original sin on which Heidegger was brought up as a Roman Catholic are immutable features of human existence, or *Dasein*. Yet many people who have never read Heidegger are still influenced by his claims. For it is comforting to be assured that one's own attitudes are the only ones, and that one need not choose between alternatives —or at least only between two, of which one is authentic and the other inauthentic. Such simplistic Manichaean schemes have always had appeal, and if one is full of anxiety it is pleasant to be told that it takes courage to be scared and that all those who are unafraid are inauthentic.

What Nietzsche said of Kant is no less true of Heidegger and, alas, a great many philosophers: He "tried to prove in a way that would dumfound the common man that the common man was right."[2] And F.H. Bradley's definition of metaphysics applies to other branches of philosophy as well: "the finding of bad reasons for what we believe on instinct."[3] Only the word "instinct" suggests once again something immutable, and it would be more precise to say that a great deal of philosophy is a way of rationalizing what the philosophers have been brought up or conditioned to believe—the common sense of their set. "If, as Bradley added, 'the finding of these reasons is no less an instinct,' it ought to be the aim of philosophy to teach men to master this instinct and become housebroken."[4]

To that end, a good course in comparative religion should be required of all undergraduates. Courses in literature and art history

---

[2] *The Gay Science* (1882), sec. 193.
[3] *Appearance and Reality* (1893), Preface.
[4] Kaufmann, *Critique of Religion and Philosophy* (1958), sec. 1.

should also be designed to produce multiple culture shock, exposing students to impressive alternatives. As far as written materials go, short poems have one immense advantage over all other forms: they sometimes manage to express an experience or attitude in a highly condensed way. History and religion are in a sense infinite. If you quote from some sacred scripture or relate historical incidents, scholars are bound to counter with a big But. A work of art requires some interpretation, and when you have given yours those you are trying to refute may once again say But. Short poems sometimes have a kind of finality.

Again the amount of material is too vast to survey here. Even if each poem is brief, there are simply too many of them. The following selection is no more than a small sample. In 1962 I published *Twenty German Poets*, which was reprinted in The Modern Library the following year. The poets ranged from Goethe to Hermann Hesse, who at that time was not widely known in the English-speaking world. A few were represented by a single poem, Goethe and Rilke by over a dozen poems each. I tried to select the best poets and some of the best poems by each, printing the original texts and my own verse translations on facing pages, and offered an introduction as well as separate prefaces for every poet. It was only in 1974, when I prepared an enlarged version of the book, *Twenty-five German Poets*,[5] adding three poets before Goethe, two at the end, and a few additional poems by the twenty original poets, that I realized how many of the poems dealt with death. Most of these poets have expressed an attitude toward death in one or more brief poems, and what is striking is that for all their variety not one voiced anxiety, nor is there a single poem that associates death with old age.

These poems were chosen initially for their high quality and not to round out an anthology on death or to prove a point. It so happens that many of the best short German poems deal with death. And it seems worthwhile to see how very different they are from the platitudes mouthed by so many recent writers whose claims are based, as dogmas generally are, on a studied disregard for experience. I shall begin in 1779 and end in 1923, spanning a period of 144 years, which is considerably less than twice the life span of an old person. So far from claiming that this tiny sample of German poetry is

5 W.W. Norton & Company (New York, 1975). All of the following poems are from this book. The publisher's permission is acknowledged gratefully.

representative of all of world literature, I should like to issue an invitation to others to broaden the range in at least two ways.

First, it would be interesting to have similar samples from Greek and Latin authors, French and English, Indian and Chinese, as well as other literatures. Secondly, one might proceed, perhaps at a later stage, to arrange the materials according to themes, such as suicide, death in battle, dying of tuberculosis, cancer, or some other disease, dying of old age, dying very young. But for a start I shall deal with my small sample, which was not chosen to begin with to prove any thesis. Of course, these are all poems that appealed to me, and one might therefore wonder whether attitudes I find congenial may be represented disproportionately. While this would not be surprising, I doubt that anyone could find a sizable number of short German poems of comparable quality that voice anxiety in the face of death or that associate death with old age.

II

Friedrich Gottlieb Klopstock (1724–1803) was the most renowned poet in Germany before the young Goethe eclipsed him, and the following poem is quite possibly his best.

Separation

You turned so serious when the corpse
was carried past us;
are you afraid of death? "Oh, not of that!"
Of what are you afraid? "Of dying."

I not even of that. "Then you're afraid of nothing?"
Alas, I am afraid, afraid . . . "Heavens, of what?"
Of parting from my friends.
And not mine only, of their parting, too.

That's why I turned more serious even
than you did, deeper in the soul,
when the corpse
was carried past us.

Klopstock disliked rhyme, and this unpretentious little poem is an early example of free verse. Of course, the poet admits to being afraid but insists that he is not afraid of death or dying. Those who assume that all men are afraid of death may charge him with transparent self-deception and inauthenticity. I should argue on the contrary that he makes needful and illuminating distinctions. He is right in distinguishing being afraid of death and being afraid of dying, and he is also right in suggesting that there are still further possibilities, of which he mentions two: parting from our friends as well as their parting from us. For many of us it makes perfectly good sense to wonder how our children, our old parents, or our wife or husband will fare after our death, and anxiety of that kinds needs to be distinguished from the fear of death and the dread of dying slowly in great pain.

Matthias Claudius (1740–1815) wrote two fine short poems about death. The first, "Death and the Maiden," was set to music by Franz Schubert and sung unforgettably by Marian Anderson.

Death and the Maiden

The Maiden:

Oh, go away, please go,
Wild monster, made of bone!
I am still young; Oh, no!
Oh, please leave me alone!

Death:

Give me your hand, my fair and lovely child!
A friend I am and bring no harm.
Be of good cheer, I am not wild,
You shall sleep gently in my arm.

Again the fear of death is not simply ignored, but the whole point of the poem is to suggest an alternative. We are made to feel that the anxiety is irrational even when one is still young and might feel cheated of a long and happy life, for death is like a gentle sleep.

Another poem by the same poet suggests that it is irrational to lament the death of a woman, or a girl, we loved. But the counterimage is different this time, not sleep but more nearly an awakening. Death spells liberation from the earth. The poem gets off the ground and takes wing only in the last few lines; but given the text, that makes excellent sense, and the final image is very strong. There is a suggestion, going back at least to Plato and the Orphics before him, that, as they put it, the body (*soma*) is the tomb (*sema*) of the soul, and that life is a period of exile.

The Sower

The sower sows the seed,
The earth receives it, and before long
The flower comes out of the soil—

You loved her. Whatever else
Life may offer you, seemed small to you,
And eternal sleep took her hence.

Why do you weep at her grave
And raise your hands to the cloud of death
And decomposition?

Like grass in the field are men,
Gone like leaves. Only a few days
We walk here, disguised.

The eagle visits the earth,
Tarries not, shakes from his wings the dust and
Returns to the sun.

Goethe (1749–1832) did not dwell much on death. Even in his old age he still wrote poems about love, not death. Nor did he associate love with death—except in one great poem that appeared in his *West-Eastern Divan* in 1819, when he was seventy. Here we have a love night and death, but the hero seems to be, quite literally, a butterfly.

Blessed Yearning

Tell it none except the wise,
for the common crowd defames:
of the living I shall praise
that which longs for death in flames.

In the love night which created
you where you create, a yearning
wakes: you see, intoxicated,
far away a candle burning.

> Darkness now no longer snares you,
> shadows lose their ancient force,
> as a new desire tears you
> up to higher intercourse.
>
> Now no distance checks your flight,
> charmed you come and you draw nigh
> till, with longing for the light,
> you are burnt, O butterfly.
>
> And until you have possessed
> dying and rebirth,
> you are but a sullen guest
> on the gloomy earth.

To most readers, the "butterfly" at the end of the penultimate stanza comes as a surprise that explains everything that went before, and being pleased to understand, few indeed go on to wonder why it is a butterfly rather than a moth. After all, it is moths and not butterflies that are attracted to burning candles at night. But Goethe knew that the Greek word for the human soul, *psyche*, also meant butterfly. And what attracted Goethe to this image was that there is no more striking example of a metamorphosis than the transformation of a caterpillar into a butterfly. The final stanza alludes to that— the caterpillar is "a sullen guest on the gloomy earth." But the suggestion is not mainly that our death, too, may be the beginning of another existence; it is above all that the richest life is a series of deaths and transformations. Any existence lacking that is drab and dull.

This theme, powerfully voiced in the last stanza of this poem, was developed by Nietzsche, who, perhaps alone among philosophers, could say even of his prose: ". . . it is my ambition to say in ten sentences what everyone else says in a book—what everyone else does *not* say in a book."[6] While Kant had set a vastly influential example of unprecedented verbosity, Nietzsche managed again and again to write sentences as pregnant as the best short poems; for example, "One pays dearly for immortality; one has to die several times while still alive."[7] Or: "Some are born posthumously."[8] And another somewhat different passage is relevant to this theme, too:

---

[6] *Twilight of the Idols* (1889), sec. 51.

[7] *Ecce Homo*, in sec. 5 of the discussion of *Zarathustra*.

[8] *Antichrist*, Preface, and *Ecce Homo*, third chapter, sec. 1; see also *The Gay Science*, sec. 365.

"The secret for harvesting from existence the greatest fruitfulness and the greatest enjoyment is—to *live dangerously*."[9] The context makes it clear that Nietzsche is not thinking of big-game hunting but of not clinging to the life, the views, the world that are familiar to us and spell security. This is a central theme in his philosophy and was later taken up by Rilke, who celebrated it in his late poetry.[10] It belongs here both because it was inspired by Goethe's great example and because it makes for a different attitude also toward death. It is those who are most afraid of having missed something who are also most afraid of missing out on something when they die. This as well as the converse has never been said more beautifully than by Hölderlin (1770–1843). Though twenty-one years younger than Goethe, he ceased writing long before "Blessed Yearning" appeared; but shortly before insanity reduced him to imbecility he wrote this poem.

To the Parcae

A single summer grant me, great powers, and
  a single autumn for fully ripened song
    that, sated with the sweetness of my
      playing, my heart may more willingly die.

The soul that, living, did not attain its divine
  right cannot repose in the nether world.
    But once what I am bent on, what is
      holy, my poetry, is accomplished:

Be welcome then, stillness of the shadows' world!
  I shall be satisfied though my lyre will not
    accompany me down there. Once I
      lived like the gods, and more is not needed.

Friedrich Schiller (1759–1805), whom Hölderlin vastly admired, had tried to say something similar even more briefly, if somewhat more prosaically. He lived with the knowledge of a relatively early death as he had consumption, but lived intensely and left a large and magnificent body of work.

[9] *The Gay Science*, sec. 283.
[10] See Kaufmann, *From Shakespeare to Existentialism* (1959), the final section of the chapter "Nietzsche and Rilke."

Immortality

> You are frightened of death? You wish you could live
>   forever?
> Make your life whole? When death takes you that will
>   remain.

Much has been done since the early nineteenth century to prolong life as if that were an end in itself. Many people have so little imagination and are so unthoughtful that they think they would enjoy living forever. With death not very likely before old age, they have got into the bad habit of living without any sense of having only so much time and without asking themselves how to make good use of it. They assume that everybody is like them and swallow the dogma that, deep down, *nobody* believes in his own death and *everybody* thinks that he will live forever and is pleased with this prospect, while the thought of one's own death is too painful to face honestly. What I find astonishing is how unwilling even deeply humane scholars are to examine such dogmas in the light of evidence. Some have actually written up the evidence that disproves their own dogmas, but go on professing them with the thoughtlessness of ritual.[11] It would seem more reasonable to assume at the outset that there are many different attitudes, and then to ask later if all of them are really reducible to one.

Friedrich von Hardenberg (1772–1801) died of consumption before he was thirty, a few years before Schiller did. He belonged to the small circle of the original German romantics who, however much they owed to Schiller, liked to denigrate him. His reaction to his fate, like his personality and his work, was rather different from Schiller's. At the age of twenty-two he had met a girl of twelve; they fell in love and were engaged; but in 1797 she died at the age of fifteen. "That he sang himself to death with his 'Hymns to the Night'—aided by consumption—is better known than the fact that within a year of his fiancée's death he became engaged to another girl whom he desired to keep him company in this world until he succeeded in becoming reunited with his true love after death."[12] The "Hymns" appeared in 1800, two years before the poet's death, and introduced the romantic glorification of death that reached its apotheosis in Richard Wagner's "Liebestod" in *Tristan und Isolde*.

[11] See "On Death and Lying" above.
[12] Kaufmann (1975), p. 78.

It will be noted that I am put off by what strikes me as a certain affectation in the "Hymns." The tone is not wholly authentic. But it does not follow that the poet really would like to live until old age. Far from it. The basic feeling strikes me as wholly believable. I shall quote only the rhymed portion of the "Fourth Hymn to the Night."

> Beyond I wander,
> all pain will be
> ere long a spur
> of ecstasy.
> A short span of time,
> I'm free and above,
> and drunken I lie
> in the lap of love.
> Infinite life
> surges in me with might;
> and down toward you
> I incline my sight.
> Your splendor is dying
> on yonder hill.
> A shadow brings
> the wreath of chill.
> Suck me toward you, beloved,
> with all your force
> that I may slumber
> and love at last.
> I am touched by death's
> youth-giving flood,
> to balsam and ether
> is turned my blood.
> I live by day
> full of courage and trust,
> and die every night
> in holy lust.

This is an extreme expression of a voluptuous feeling about death that is not fashionable nowadays. It may help to remind us that there are fashions in such matters, too, and that attitudes some people nowadays take for granted and believe to be part of human nature are in fact also fashions. Certainly, Novalis—to give the poet his pen name under which he is remembered—was far from unique in feeling as he did; he merely voiced with rare intensity the fascination of death and dying.

Instead of sampling other romantic poems about death, I shall proceed straight to Heinrich Heine (1797–1856), who was twenty-five years younger than Novalis and only four years old when Novalis died. Heine, like Goethe, mastered the accents of romanticism, but just as Goethe enjoyed puncturing Faust's effusions with Mephistopheles' sardonic wit, Heine frequently did the same sort of thing even in short poems. The next poem does not illustrate this point but shows restraint throughout. It was written during the years in Paris when Heine was lying, without any hope of recovery, in what he called his *Matratzengruft*, his mattress vault or tomb. Is there any reason to doubt that death often seemed desirable to him?

Morphine

Great is the similarity of these two
Youthful figures, although one of them
Looks so much paler than the other one,
Much more severe—I almost said, much nobler—
Than does that other one who, all affection,
Enclosed me in his arms: How sweetly tender
His smile was then, what bliss was in his eyes!
Then it could happen that the poppy wreath
He wore upon his head touched my brow, too,
And the strange perfume drove away all pain
Out of my soul. But such relief endures
So short a time; complete recovery
Can be mine only when the serious looking
Brother who is so pale lowers his torch—
Good is sleep, but death is better—yet
What would be best is not to have been born.

The last line is virtually a quotation from a chorus in Sophocles' last tragedy, *Oedipus at Colonus* (line 1225ff.):

Nothing surpasses not being born;
but if born, to return where we came from
is next best, the sooner the better.

The poet who wrote these lines shortly before his death was ninety and could look back on a life's work that included one hundred and twenty plays of which ninety-six had won first prize (that is, twenty-four tetralogies) and the rest second prize. He had never placed third, was beloved by the people of Athens, and had reaped many other honors. But his tragedies give unsurpassed expression to despair, and although the lines are spoken by a chorus in a play, a study of the seven extant tragedies shows plainly how at ninety Sophocles felt no dread in the face of death.[13]

Close to two hundred years earlier, Jeremiah had exclaimed (20:14):

> Cursed be the day
> on which I was born!

And in the Book of Job we find almost the same outcry (3.3). Not all have always loved their lives so well or shut their eyes to the miseries of others to the point of feeling that no fate could be worse than death. The claim, popularized by Heidegger, that those not afraid of death are inauthentically shutting their eyes to their own anxiety may apply to some. But many who are afraid of death have closed their eyes to their own wretched condition and the sufferings of humanity.

Our poems here include no war poems. The one that comes closest to that genre is "Hagen's Dying Song" by Felix Dahn (1834–1912), a professor who achieved a great success with his four-volume historical novel, *Ein Kampf um Rom* (A Fight for Rome), which dealt with the defeat and destruction of the Ostrogoths and appeared in 1876, the year when Wagner's *Ring* was first performed in Bayreuth. Dahn also dealt with the Nibelungen story, writing a play on Kriemhild's revenge and the destruction of the Burgundians under King Gunter, but the play was forgotten while his poem about Hagen survived in anthologies to influence the attitudes toward death of generations of German boys throughout two world wars.

Hagen's Dying Song

Now I am growing lonely. The princes are all dead,
and in the moonshine glimmers the hearth in bloody red.

[13] For a detailed discussion of Sophocles, see Kaufmann, *Tragedy and Philosophy* (1968).

The once so gay Burgundians are still, their revels stop.
   I hear how from their bodies the blood runs drop on
      drop.
Out of the house arises a heavy smell of blood,
   and screeching vultures circle, impatient for their food.
King Gunter is still sleeping his fever-maddened sleep,
   since a well sharpened arrow struck from the tower
      steep.
And Volker fell with laughter, and thus bade me adieu:
   "Take all I leave, dear Hagen, my strings I leave
      to you."
Secure from Hunnish cunning, he carried without awe
   the fiddle on his safe back that no foe ever saw.
Like nightingales it sounded, strummed by the fearless
      bard;
   no doubt, it will sound different in my hand, which
      is hard.
Three strings remain to play on, the other four are gone;
   I am not used to singing, I am no fiddle man.
And yet I feel like trying how Hagen's tune might go:
   I think some good sound cursing is a good prayer, too.
Above all, cursed be women; woman is falsity:
   here, for two soft white bodies, perishes Burgundy!
And cursed be the illusion of morals, love, and law:
   love is a lying fiction, and only hate is true.
Repentance is for idiots. Nothing has worth beside
   enduring still when dying with wrath and sword and
      pride.
If I must reconsider my deeds now, one by one,
   I should not leave a single act that I did undone.
And if, the world's enchantment, another Siegfried
      came,
   I'd stab him in the back, too, with the same deadly
      aim.
You tear, strings? Are you cowards, afraid of such a
      song?
   Hah, who comes down the courtyard, with strides
      that are so long?
That is no Hunnish lookout, those are the steps of fate—
   and nearer, ever nearer—I recognize his gait.
Up, Gunter, now awaken, this is the final turn:
   Up, up! Death, the avenger, and Dietrich comes from
      Bern!

Dahn was not a great poet, but this is, at least in the original, a strong poem. It represents a defiant readiness for death that has been anything but exceptional in times of war; and unfortunately times of war have rarely been exceptional.

Although Nietzsche (1844–1900) exerted a profound influence on existentialism, he did not make much of death, and in *The Gay Science* he said in a section (278) entitled "The thought of death":

> How strange it is that this sole certainty and common element makes almost no impression on people, and that nothing is further from their minds than the feeling that they form a brotherhood of death. It makes me happy that men do not want at all to think the thought of death! I should like very much to do something that would make the thought of life even a hundred times more appealing to them.

Six years later, Nietzsche included in *Twilight of the Idols* a section called "Morality for physicians." All of it is interesting, but I shall here quote only a small part of it.

> To die proudly when it is no longer possible to live proudly. Death freely chosen, death at the right time, brightly and cheerfully accomplished amid children and witnesses: then a real farewell is still possible, as the one who is taking leave is still there; also a real estimate of what one has achieved and what one has wished, drawing the sum of one's life—all in opposition to the wretched and revolting comedy that Christianity has made of the hour of death. One should never forget that Christianity has exploited the weakness of the dying for a rape of the conscience . . .

Nietzsche failed to shoot himself as Van Gogh did, and when he collapsed, insane, in January 1889, his mother and later on his sister managed to keep him alive for another eleven and a half years. But he wrote a poem shortly before his breakdown and also managed to finish four superb books during his last few months. The poem is one of his so-called Dionysus Dithyrambs, which influenced Rilke's Elegies, but is not Dionysian in any crude sense. It is the voice of a man who has found peace and leaves life without regrets.

The Sun Sinks

I

Not long will you thirst,
    burnt out heart!
A promise is in the air,
from unknown lips it blows at me
    —the great chill comes.

My sun stood hot over me at noon—
be welcome that you come,
    you sudden winds,
you chilly spirits of afternoon!

The air moves strange and pure.
Does not with warped
    seductive eyes
night leer at me?
Stay strong, courageous heart!
Do not ask: why?

II

Day of my life!
The sun sinks.
Already the smooth
    flood stands golden.
Warm breathes the rock:
    whether at noon
joy slept its noonday sleep upon it?
    In greenish lights
Joy is still playing over the brown abyss.

Day of my life!
Toward evening it goes.
Already your eye
    glows half-broken,
already your dew's
    tear drops are welling,
already runs still over white seas
your love's purple,
your last hesitant blessedness.

III

Cheerfulness, golden one, come!
   you of death
the most secret and sweetest foretaste!
Did I run too rash on my way?
Only now that my foot has grown weary,
   your eye catches up with me,
   your *joy* catches up with me.

Round me but wave and play.
   Whatever was hard
sank into blue oblivion—
idle stands now my boat.
Storm and drive—how it forgot that!
   Wish and hope have drowned,
   smooth lie soul and sea.

Seventh loneliness!
   Never felt I
nearer me sweet security,
warmer the sun's eye.
Does not the ice of my peaks still glow?
   Silver, light, a fish,
   my bark now swims out.

The last two poets I wish to consider belong to my parents'
generation and thus in a sense to our time. Let us begin with Rilke,
who wrote more superb short poems than any other German poet
after Goethe and who remains one of the world's greatest masters
in this genre. A lovely poem in his *Neue Gedichte* (1907) deals with
Orpheus' descent into the underworld to bring back from death his
wife, Eurydice. He goes down accompanied by the god Hermes, it
being understood that if he looks back even once to see if his wife
follows him, she has to remain dead. Although this poem is longer
than any of the others I am using, I shall quote the whole of it. For
the wish to bring back the dead is an important part of our subject
and among the most ubiquitous attitudes toward death.

Orpheus. Eurydice. Hermes

That was the souls' weird mine.
Like silent silver ores they penetrated

as veins its dark expanses. Between roots
welled up the blood that flows on to mankind,
and in the dark looked hard as porphyry.
Else nothing red.

But rock was there
and woods that had no nature. Bridges spanned the void
and that great gray blind pond
suspended over its far distant depth
as rainy skies above a landscape.
And between meadows, soft and full of patience,
appeared the ashen streak of the one way
as a long pallor that has been stretched out.

And it was on this one way that they came.

In front, the slender man in the blue mantle
who looked ahead in silence and impatience.
His paces, without chewing, gulped the way
in outsized swallows; and his hands were hanging
heavy and sullen from the fall of folds,
knowing no longer of the weightless lyre
grown deep into his left as rambler roses
into the branches of an olive tree.
His senses were as if they had been parted:
and while his glances, doglike, ran ahead,
turned back, and came, and always stood again
as waiting at the next turn of the way—
his hearing stayed behind him as a smell.
Sometimes it seemed to him as if it reached
back to the walking of those other two
who were to follow him this whole ascent.
Then it was but the echo of his climbing
and his own mantle's wind that was behind him.
Yet he said to himself that they would come;
said it out loud and heard it fade away.
They would come yet, only were two
walking most silently. And if he might
turn only once (and if his looking back
were not destruction of this whole endeavor
still to be ended), he would surely see them,
the quiet two who followed him in silence:

the god of going and of the wide message,
the travel hood shading his brilliant eyes,

bearing the slender staff before his body,
the beat of wings around his ankle bones;
and given over to his left hand: *she.*

The one so loved that from a single lyre
wails came surpassing any wailing women;
that out of wails a world arose in which
all things were there again: the wood and valley
and way and village, field and brook and beast;
and that around this wailing-world, just as
around the other earth, a sun revolved
and a vast sky, containing stars and stillness,
a wailing-sky full of disfigured stars—
this one so loved.

But she walked at the hand of this great god,
her striding straightened by the grave's long wraps,
uncertain, soft, and void of all impatience.
She was in herself as one high in hope,
not thinking of the man who went ahead,
nor of the way ascending into life.
She was in herself. And her having died
filled her as fullness.
And as a fruit is full of dark and sweetness,
the greatness of her death was filling her
and was so new, she comprehended nothing.

She was wrapped up in a new maidenhood
and one not touchable; her sex was closed
as a young flower is toward evening,
and her hands had become so unaccustomed
to matrimony, even the light god's
immeasurably lightly leading touch
offended her as something intimate.

She was not any longer this blond woman
who in the poet's songs would sometimes echo,
not any more the broad bed's scent and island,
and the possession of this man no more.

She was already loosed as flowing hair
and long relinquished as the fallen rain
and meted out as hundredfold provisions.

She was become a root.

And when with sudden force
the god stopped her and with pain in his cry
pronounced the words: He has turned back—
she comprehended nothing and said softly: Who?

But far off, dark beyond the clear egress,
stood someone, any one, whose countenance
could not be recognized. He stood and saw
how on the pale streak of a meadow path,
with sorrow in his eyes, the god of message
turned silently to follow back the form
that even then returned this very way,
her striding straitened by the grave's long wraps,
uncertain, soft, and void of all impatience.

This poem succeeds in transporting us into a different world, and
it is easy to forget all about our world and death and dying. And yet
no poem could be more relevant to our theme. What is realized in
these lines is the peace of death and the contrast with the lack of
peace that pervades our lives. All else is implications, and to spell
them out seems as obtrusive as Orpheus' intrusion into regions in
which his impatience has no place. We are made to feel that he is
doing her no favor, that the desire to bring back the dead is selfish,
like waking up a sick person in great pain who has finally fallen asleep
—waking her up because we are feeling lonely and want company.

I feel reminded of the great scene in First Samuel where Saul,
about to go into his last battle, asks the woman of Endor to bring
back the dead Samuel, whom Saul wants to consult. Samuel's first
words are: "Why have you disturbed me to bring me up here?"
(28.15). We are led to ask whether men do not project the torments
of life and survival beyond death, where, in the words Marian Anderson used to sing so movingly, all is peace. Would it not make more
sense for Orpheus to join Eurydice than for him to wish her to join
him?

Yet Rilke's poetry as a whole does not glorify death and is not a
curse on life. Rilke, like Nietzsche, celebrates this world and this life.
"There is nothing that gives our lives meaning and, viewed from the
outside, life, which ends in death, is senseless. There is no meaning
outside, but Rilke and Nietzsche proclaim that a certain kind of
life is its own reward" and "that a certain mode of experience makes

life infinitely worth while."[14] In his ninth Elegy, Rilke, in effect, answers the question whether Orpheus should not wish to join Eurydice and seek death. "Why," he begins by asking, "have to be human . . . ?" Not, he replies, for happiness or "for curiosity's sake . . ." But—and I shall cite only some few passages from this poem—

> But because being here is much, and because apparently
> all that is here needs us, all the fleeting that
> strangely concerns us. Us, the most fleeting. *Once*
> everything, only *once*. *Once* and no more. And we, too,
> *once*. Never again. But having
> been this *once*, even though only *once:*
> having been on earth does not seem revokable.
>
> And so we strain and want to accomplish it,
> want to contain it in our simple hands,
> in still more overcrowded eyes and a speechless heart.
> Want to become it. Give it to whom? Would love to
> hold on to all forever. Oh, to that other relation,
> alas, what can one take across? Not the art of seeing, slowly
> learned here, and no event from here. None.
> Only our suffering. Only, that is, what was hard;
> only the long experience of love—only
> what is unsayable. But later,
> under the stars, what matter? *They* are rightly unsayable. . . .
>
> *Here* is the time for what is *sayable, here* is its home.
> Speak and confess. . . .
> Between the hammers endures
> our heart, like the tongue
> between our teeth that yet
> continues to praise.
>
> Praise the world. . . .
>
> And these things that live
> on destruction understand that you praise them; evanescent,
> they trust that we, the most evanescent, can save them.
> Wish that we might transform them entirely in our invisible hearts
> into—oh, infinite!—into ourselves, whoever we may be.

[14] Kaufmann (1959), final paragraph of the chapter "Nietzsche and Rilke." For their similarity see also chap. 13.

Earth, is not this what you want: to arise in us
invisible?—Is it not your dream
to be invisible once?—Earth! invisible!
What if not transformation is your urgent command?
Earth, my beloved, I will. Oh, believe me, it requires
your springs no longer to win me for you; one,
alas, even one is already too much for my blood.
Nameless, I am resolved to you from afar.
Always you have been right, and your holy idea
is intimate death.

Behold, I am living. From where? Neither childhood nor future
grow less.—Superabundant existence
leaps up in my heart.

In this ecstatic affirmation of life, death is included, not only in
the end, almost as an afterthought, but from the beginning: "*Once
/ everything, only once. Once* and no more. And we, too, / *once.*
Never again." This implicit denial of reincarnation leads to the
opposite of that worldweariness which is the starting point of
Buddhism and the lethargy and resignation that pervade so much of
life in India. The most intense love of life takes the sting out of
death and destruction. As Hölderlin had put it more than a hundred
years earlier:

Once I
lived like the gods, and more is not needed.

More is not *wanted*; more would be less. Perfection is finite; infinite
duration, hell. What is most beautiful would not gain from lasting
forever; it would soon turn into torment.

In life, as in art, it is not quantity that counts but quality. To
associate happiness with a long life is a colossal stupidity, led to the
absurd by the miseries of extreme old age. Our culture has long
made the mistake of going in for a mindless cult of quantity, counting
the ever-growing life expectancy as a self-evident success, as if death
were the only enemy of man. This folly depends on the withering of
intensity and meaning. It is only when life has lost its sense that no
standards remain to evaluate it except length. But a superb short
poem would not gain by being made longer and longer, and still longer
and, if possible, endless. A Rembrandt self-portrait would not
become better by being made larger and ever larger. Perfection lies
in intensity, and what is most intense cannot be endured long.

If it should seem that I have fallen into an extreme aestheticism, our last poet strikes a very different note. Gottfried Benn (1886–1956) was nine years younger than Rilke but outlived him by thirty years. His *late* poems seem to me to be too similar to some of Rilke's very late verse to be first-rate. Some of his very early poems are much more original and have an unmistakably distinctive voice. He was a doctor, and his first collection of verse, *Morgue*, appeared in 1912, a few days before his mother died of cancer. Later the same year he published his poem on cancer in a periodical. A greater contrast to Rilke and, for that matter, the other poems cited here would be hard to imagine.[15] The first three poems come from *Morgue*.

Beautiful Childhood

The mouth of a girl who had lain long in the reeds
looked so gnawed at.
When one broke open the breast, the esophagus was so full of holes.
Finally in a bower under the diaphragm
one found a nest of young rats.
One little sister lay dead.
The others were living on liver and kidney,
drank the cold blood and had
spent a beautiful childhood here.
And beautiful and fast their death, too, came:
One threw the lot of them into the water.
Oh, how the little snouts squeaked!

Cycle

The lonely molar of a whore
who had died unknown
had a filling of gold.
The others, as if they had a silent understanding,
had gone out.
That one the morgue attendant knocked out,
marketed, and went dancing.
For, he said,
only earth shall return to earth.

---

15 It would be particularly interesting to compare Benn's poem on the cancer ward, which follows, with Rilke's last poem, in which the poet, dying of leukemia, addresses his own death. In "Rilke: Nirvana or Creation" I have placed this poem—the original and a verse translation—in another context (in *The Times Literary Supplement*, London, December 5, 1975).

Negro Bride

Then, bedded upon pillows of dark blood,
the blond neck lay of a white woman.
The sun was raging in her hair
and licked the length of her light thighs
and kneeled around the slightly browner breasts,
that neither vice nor birth had yet disfigured.
A nigger next to her: by a horse's hoof
his eyes and forehead shredded. He dug
two toes of his dirty left foot
into the inside of her small white ear.
Yet she lay sleeping like a bride:
on the edge of the joys of her first love,
as on the eve of many an Ascension
of the warm youthful blood.
                    Until one plunged
the knife into her white throat, throwing
a crimson apron of dead blood
around her hips.

Man and Woman
Walk Through the Cancer Ward

The man:
Here this row is disintegrated wombs,
and this row is disintegrated breast.
Bed stinks by bed. Nurses change hourly.

Come, do not hesitate to lift this blanket.
Look here, this lump of fat and putrid juices,
this once was great for some man somewhere
and was called ecstasy and home.

Come, look here at this scar on that breast.
You feel that rosary of softened knots?
Don't hesitate. The flesh is soft and hurts not.

Here this one bleeds as if from thirty bodies.
No human has such quantities of blood.
From this a child
had to be cut first from her cancerous womb.

One lets them sleep. Both day and night.—The new ones
are told: here one sleeps oneself healthy.—Only Sundays,
for visitors, they're left a little more awake.

They do not take much nourishment. Their backs
are sore. You see the flies. Sometimes
the nurses wash them. As one washes benches.

Here the field swells already round each bed.
Flesh becomes almost soil. Ardor is spent.
Juices prepare to flow. The earth is calling.

These poems do not spell peace; they arouse anger. One way of
dealing with this anger is to vent it on those who believe that it was
Brecht who first found a new anti-romantic tone—fifteen years later,
well after the horrors of World War I. Hemingway, too, seems a boy
compared to the young Benn. We can no longer deal with death as
if it were mainly a literary phenomenon, an event in poetry. We must
take note of the ugly realities that are not dreamed of in most poems.
But these last poems may help to show that even if we approach
death and dying by way of poetry, as I have done here, we need not
ignore these realities. We must only beware of restricting our sample
too much.

In the end, however, these poems by Benn do not invalidate what
I said earlier. On the contrary. I have maintained all along that we
should not shut our eyes to human misery and the realities of sickness and old age. We should not strive to live as long as possible,
least of all when we become a burden to ourselves and others. Nor
should we instill in children and young people the pernicious notion
that life is necessarily a boon and death a curse, and suicide a sin.
We should awaken them to a variety of attitudes and try to immunize
them against stupid fashions.

If possible, I know even less about old age than about death, but
nobody seems to know much about death while there are many who
know old age intimately. I believe Sophocles when at ninety he suggested that it is far better to die before one becomes old. It makes
sense to carry on the fight against crippling or very painful diseases;
it makes no sense to keep trying to prolong life more and more. We
should teach those we can reach to live well rather than long, and not
to dread death. But for those who reach old age the best insurance
against hopelessness is surely to have lived rich lives, to have lived
intensely, to have used our time so well that it would make little
sense to feel cheated or to feel that we still need a little more time. We
should impress on ourselves how young so many great composers,
painters, poets, writers died, and in our youth we ought to make a

rendezvous with death, pledging to be ready for it at the age of thirty, and then, if we live that long, make another date at forty. Granted that much life, one might well feel that anything beyond that is a present and that henceforth one ought to be ready any time. At the very least one ought to feel that way before one reaches fifty. We should also give up the unseemly Christian teachings about suicide and accept it as a dignified and decent way of ending our lives.

In its heart of hearts our culture still believes in hell and is afraid of what may lie beyond death and of dire punishments for suicide. It is high time that we realize that the belief in hell has made a hell on earth; that those who thought God was so cruel did not shrink from dire punishments and tortures and the Inquisition; and that those who keep prolonging life often visit hell on helpless patients. Freedom from fear is a pipe dream as long as one fears death.

About the Author

Walter Kaufmann is Professor of Philosophy at Princeton University, where he has been teaching since he received his Ph.D. from Harvard in 1947. He has held visiting appointments at many American and foreign universities, including Columbia, Cornell, Heidelberg, Jerusalem, and the Australian National University; and his books have been translated into Dutch, German, Italian, Japanese, and Spanish.

Kaufmann's *Religions in Four Dimensions: Existential and Aesthetic, Historical and Comparative* (1976) includes over 250 of his photographs, 185 of them in color. His *Cain and Other Poems: Enlarged Edition* and *Existentialism from Dostoevsky to Sartre: Revised and Expanded* are Meridian Books.